Design Patterns for High-Quality Automated Tests

Java Edition

Clean Code for Bulletproof Tests

Anton Angelov
Automate The Planet

Table of Contents

Credits

First published: March 2021

1.1 update: July 2021

Production reference: Published by Automate The Planet Ltd.

Address: https://www.automatetheplanet.com/
Book cover design and formatting by Martin Kolev

About the Author

Anton Angelov is CTO and Co-founder of Automate The Planet Ltd, inventor of BELLATRIX Test Automation Framework. Nowadays, he directs a team of passionate engineers helping companies succeed with their test automation. Additionally, he consults companies, leads automated testing training series in C# and Java, writes books, and gives conference talks.

– 280+ Published Articles Automate The Planet
– 120+ Published Articles Code Project
– 60+ Published Articles DZone as Most Valuable Blogger
– 6+ Articles Published in Quality Magazines
– 20+ Given International Conferences Talks
– 3 books published
– 5,000,000+ article views
– 1000 000+ amazing readers for 2020
– Read in 180+ countries

About the Reviewers

Nikolay Avramov is a Senior Developer in Test and Team Lead at Automate The Planet. For the past eight years, he worked as a Quality Assurance Engineer in Telerik (later acquired by Progress software). He started his career in the field from ground zero- from taking part in the Telerik Academy to becoming a Principal QA Engineer/Ninja that is at the heart of any innovation or automation initiative. Through his work, he has developed and integrated multiple custom frameworks and tools used across the entire company. To name a few- a custom Load and Performance Testing Framework; System Testing Framework; Web Service Testing Framework; Visual Verification Framework; and many other productivity tools that assured the highest quality of all web and business assets of the company. He found his true passion in Automation while looking for a 'weapon' to fight the boring, non-productive daily tasks that a QA faces. By reducing the repeatable manual jobs, he believes that we can make the world a better place, full of happy and productive people ready to tackle the next challenging task, instead of the next pile of test scenarios to cover by hand. He is a passionate technology geek and automation specialist that strives to implement optimizations and achieve high-quality standards in any aspect of life.

A few words for the book:

The book will give you the building blocks you need and will take you through the natural process of building a fully fletched test automation framework within a few hour's read.

The beginning and the end of the book show the difference between the rookie QA enthusiast and the automation ninja. This knowledge will give you the power to make educated decisions for common problems in test automation and will give you the right arguments to defend them in front of any manager or developer.

Acknowledgements

The content of the book results from the accumulated knowledge of many great engineers and IT professionals. Many good programmers are very egocentric, believing they are always right and know everything. Often, they forget how they got their knowledge. It is a result not only of our efforts but a mixture of personal effort/work, luck, living, and working environment. I believe that in this phase of my life, I know enough "tips and tricks" so I can write a book. However, this wouldn't be possible without the help of all the people that took some of my life: the example and hard work of my parents, high school, and university teachers. Later, the many mentors and colleagues I had in the past companies I worked for. I am a person who is a natural learner and regularly reads new books and watches video courses/lectures. I wouldn't be as good as I am now without the valuable information in these materials.

As some of you know, for the past several years, I am regularly writing articles on my website- Automate The Planet. The book accumulates a big part of the knowledge I tried to share during the years. But the site wouldn't be what it is without your support! So, I would like to say, "Thank You!" to all fans and readers. The same is valid for all the talks I gave to many international DEV and QA conferences. Thank you for being there, hearing, and trying to apply the ideas I talk about.

Most important, I want to say BIG THANK YOU to my colleague Nikolay Avramov for agreeing to help me with the technical and editorial tasks.

Without his help and support, the quality of the book wouldn't be the same!

My partner in crime at Automate The Planet, Martin Kolev, is responsible for all visual enhancements, marketing, and many other tedious tasks around the project.

Thanks to all my friends that were there for me and hearing me talking geek stuff about the book.

I am trying to be a responsible member of society, organizing various donation campaigns, giving blood for hospitals, planting trees, separating waste, etc. I believe that it is essential to look after future generations. The greener future is the only way. I am organizing book donation campaigns here in Bulgaria 1-2 per year, and all the money is donated to plant trees. For you, friends around the world, there is a way to participate in this effort. You already did! Part of the money that I receive from the book orders I donate for the initiative. At the moment of writing, these efforts generated cash for plating over 5000 trees. Once, twice per year, I participate myself in such planting campaigns over the country. I encourage you to search for such efforts in your country. The only way our children will have a better future on this planet is if more people start being responsible.

Foreword

Since I usually skip the Foreword chapters of other books, I will try to be short. My core belief is that to achieve high-quality test automation that brings value- you need to understand core programming concepts such as SOLID and the usage of design patterns. After you master them, the usual career transition is into more architecture roles, such as choosing the best approaches for solving particular test automation challenges. This is the essence of the book. **No more "Hello world" examples but some serious literature about test automation practices!**

P.S. After the first book's success, Design Patterns for High-Quality Automated Tests C# Edition, many people asked me when there will be a version for Java. This is why I refreshed my Java knowledge and started writing. One year later, the book is here. More or less, the book explains the same concepts, but all code examples and specifics target the Java world. If you have read the C# edition, you can skip some of the more theoretical chapters or recheck them for a refresher.

You may notice I have changed the sub-title for those of you who have purchased the C# version. The new sub-title communicates much better the ideas of the book. I won't bother you with lengthy introductions and discussions about what clean code means. There are whole books about the subject. But if I had to summarize what clean code means in one sentence, I would say: "*Clean code is code that is easy to understand and easy to change*."

Easy to understand means the code is easy to read, whether that reader is the original author of the code or somebody else. Its meaning is clear, so it minimizes the need for guesswork and the possibility of misunderstandings. It is easy to understand on every level. Easy to change means the code is easy to extend and refactor, and it's easy to fix bugs in the codebase. This can be achieved if the person making the changes understands the code and feels confident that the code changes do not break any existing functionality. I will end the intro with two quotes by two famous authors Robert C. Martin and Michael Feathers. [Wcc 14]

"If you want your code to be easy to write, make it easy to read."

"Clean code always looks like it was written by someone who cares. There is nothing obvious you can do to make it better."

Preface

Design Patterns for High-Quality Automated Tests will help you write better tests!

What this book covers

Chapter 1. Defining High-Quality Test Attributes

Many terms are misunderstood, and engineers are using them without understanding them, such as a library, framework, test framework. This is the basic knowledge that all test engineers should have. The reader will learn about the top-quality attributes each test library should strive to have, which we will discuss in much more detail in the next chapters. Since we want to treat the test code as production one, we will talk about SOLID principles and how we can incorporate them into developing the tests.

Chapter 2. Optimizing and Refactoring Legacy Flaky Tests

We will discuss the Hermetic test pattern where each test should be isolated from others. Will learn about the Adapter design pattern where some of the unstable behaviours of WebDriver will be wrapped in a class and fixed. The same pattern will be used to improve the WebDriver API for locating elements and making it easier to use. Finally, we will talk about the random run order principle, where the tests should be able to run no matter their order.

Chapter 3. Strategies for Speeding-up the Tests

After the tests are stabilized and always passing, the next step is to improve their speed. One approach will be to login to a website through cookies instead of using the UI. Next, the readers will see how to reuse the WebDriver browser instead of restarting it all the time earning over a 40% decrease in test execution time. We will talk about how to handle asynchronous requests and make test code parallelizable. Finally, we will mention the "Black Hole Proxy" approach isolating 3rd party services' requests while further improving the speed of the automated tests.

Chapter 4. Test Readability

Learn how to hide nitty-gritty low-level WebDriver API details in the so-called page objects, making the tests much more readable. Also, the readers will see how to create two types of page objects depending on their needs. In the second part of the chapter, we will talk about coding standards - naming the variables and methods right and placing the correct comments. At the end of the section, we will discuss various tools that can help us to enforce all these standards.

Chapter 5. Enhancing the Test Maintainability and Reusability

We will talk about how to reuse more code across page objects by using the Template Method design pattern. Also, we will see the 3rd type of page object model where the assertions and elements will be used as properties instead of coming from base classes, which will introduce the benefits of the composition over the inheritance principle. In the second part of the chapter, we will discuss how to reuse common test workflows through the Facade design pattern. At the end of the section, we will talk about an enhanced version of the pattern where we can test different versions of the same web page (new and old).

Chapter 6. API Usability

In this chapter, we will learn how to make the test library API easy to use, learn, and understand. First, we will talk about different approaches on how to use already developed page object models through the Singleton design pattern or Factory design pattern. After that, we will look at another approach called Fluent API or Chaining Methods. At the end of the section, we will discuss whether to expose the page objects elements to the users of your test library.

Chapter 7. Building Extensibility in Your Test Library

If you create a well-designed library, most probably other teams can use it too, so you need to be sure that your library is easily extensible. It should allow everyone to modify it and add new features to it without causing you to spend tons of time rewriting existing logic or making already written tests fail. In this chapter, the reader will learn how to improve extensibility for finding elements by creating custom selectors through the Strategy design pattern. After that, we will investigate ways on how we can add additional behaviors to existing WebDriver actions via Observer design pattern or built-in EventFiringWebDriver.

Chapter 8. Assessment System for Tests' Architecture Design

In this chapter, we will look into an assessment system that can help you decide which design solution is better- for example, to choose one between 5 versions of page objects. We will talk about the criteria of the system and why they are essential. In the second part of the section, we will use the system to evaluate some of the design patterns we used previously and assign them ratings.

Chapter 9. Benchmarking for Assessing Automated Test Components Performance

The evaluation of core quality attributes is not enough to finally decide which implementation is better or not. The test execution time should be a key component too. In this chapter, we will examine a library that can help us measure the performance of our automated tests' components.

Chapter 10. Test Data Preparation and Configuring Test Environments

One of the essential parts of each automated test is the test data which we use in it. It is important that the data is relevant and accessible. In the chapter, we will discuss how we can create such data through fixtures, APIs, DB layers, or custom tools. Also, we will review how to set up the right way the environment in which the tests run.

Appendix 1. Defining the Primary Problems that Test Automation Frameworks Solve

In the first appendix chapter, we will define the problems that the automation framework is trying to solve. To determine what is needed to deliver high-quality software, we need to understand what the issues are.

Appendix 2. Most Exhaustive CSS Selectors Cheat Sheet

A big part of the job of writing maintainable and stable web automation is related to finding the proper element's selectors. Here will look into a comprehensive list of CSS selectors.

Appendix 3. Most Exhaustive XPath Selectors Cheat Sheet

The other very useful locators are the XPath ones. Knowing them can help you significantly improve the stability and the readability of your tests.

Who Is This Book For?

The book is not a getting started guide. If you have no prior programming experience in writing automated tests through WebDriver, this book won't be very useful to you. I believe it might be invaluable for readers with a couple of years of experience and whose job is to create/maintain test automation frameworks or to write high-quality reliable automated

tests.
The book is written in Java. However, I believe that you can use the approaches and practices in every OOP language. If you have a Python background, you will get everything you need, don't worry. However, if you are a C# developer, I would suggest checking the book's C# version.
Even if you don't get all the concepts from the first read, try to use and incorporate some. Later you can return and reread them. I believe with the accumulation of experience using high-quality practices- you will become a hard-core test automation ninja!

Before You Get Started

You need to have experience in OOP programming languages such as C#, Java, etc. I believe that you can get the book's ideas just from reading the presented code. However, it is recommended to download and run all of the solutions on your machine. To do so, clone the book GitHub repository- https://bit.ly/3rRLpbM

As a bonus to the book, you can find video recordings with explanations for each chapter. To get them, you can join for free the book's LinkedIn group. There you can find even more info about design patterns in automated testing and best practices or use it as an easy way to reach me. Before joining, you need to provide proof you purchased the book. Just go to https://bit.ly/3eGTAUl

To build and execute the code, you will need a Java IDE, such as IntelliJ, Eclipse, or NetBeans. My preferred choice is IntelliJ. Also, it is recommended to install the latest version of the Java SDK. I show examples of new Java versions' features through the book, so I encourage you to install the latest possible version. For software project management, I used Maven, and for unit testing framework TestNG, so depending on the IDE you picked, you must install the required plugins.

Conventions

In this book, you will find several styles of text that distinguish between different kinds of information. Here are examples of these styles, and an explanation of their meaning.
Code words in text are shown as follows: `CartPage`
A block of code is set as follows:

```
public void clickProceedToCheckout() {
    proceedToCheckout().click();
    _driver.waitUntilPageLoadsCompletely();
}
```

Important words or code snippets are shown in **bold**.
Remember that to make the example t and more comfortable to read, I haven't included the 'throws exception' part of the methods' signature.

NOTE

Important notes appear in a box like this

Definition

Definition: Example

Definition description

Reader feedback

Feedback from the readers is always welcome. Let me know what you think about the book, what you liked or disliked. To do so, write me at LinkedIn - https://bit.ly/2NjWJ19

Errata

Although I have taken every care to ensure the accuracy of the content mistakes do happen. If you find a mistake in the book, whatever in the text or in the code- I would be grateful if you would report it. If you find any errors, please send them via LinkedIn - https://bit.ly/2NjWJ19

Piracy

Piracy of copyright material on the Internet is an ongoing problem across all media. If you come across any illegal copies of the work, in any form, on the Internet, please provide me with the location address or website name immediately so I can pursue a remedy.
I appreciate your help in protecting the ability to bring you valuable content!

Questions

You can contact me at LinkedIn - https://bit.ly/2NjWJ19 if you have any problems with any aspect of the book, and I will do my best to address it.

Chapter 1. Defining High-Quality Test Attributes

This book is not only about teaching you how to use some design patterns or practices but furthermore to solve particular test automation problems. Some are flaky tests that are hard to maintain, read, or learn to write new tests, and the list goes on. The book tries to help you write more stable and faster tests. With the many practices and design patterns in the book, you can write automated tests that need less time to figure out what went wrong, to be easier to support new requirements, ease the new team members to learn to use your code and much more.

At the beginning of the chapter, we will go through a short list of the tests. Then, I will define what is a test automation framework and some other related terms. More knowledge is needed to write high-quality automated tests than just knowing how to program in a certain language or use a specific framework. To solve these problems, our automated tests should have some core high-quality test attributes. Also, we will talk about related programming principles abbreviated SOLID.

These topics will be covered in this chapter:

- Different Types of Tests
- What Is a Test Automation Framework? Definitions
- SOLID Principles
- High-Quality Test Attributes

Different Types of Tests

I will define the different tests. This will help us understand where the WebDriver automated tests belong in the development cycle.

Unit Tests

These are, by definition, the smallest test units. This test is written to test an individual object and even individual methods of an object. Unit testing is highly necessary because it prevents bugs from creeping in at the lowest level. These tests rarely use any real test data and often solely rely on generated data.

Integration Tests

They consist of several modules of code put together, allowing them to pass data between each other. The purpose of these types of tests is to make sure that all modules integrate and work with each other. They are also known as **component integration tests** or **integration tests in the small**. Usually, we still isolate third-party services such as network, file system, and OS in this testing. Another related term is **integration tests in the large**, which usually engineers use to mention integration tests that don't isolate 3rd party dependencies.

System Tests

System Testing is testing a complete and fully integrated software product. It is the highest level of testing. It executes against production (PROD) or production-like environments, such as staging (STA). Like integration tests, the system test also tries to verify that all the components, including third-party services, can communicate well with each other.
These tests can verify our software's functional or non-functional requirements. Some engineers refer to these tests as End-to-end tests, UI tests, User Scenario tests. However, there is a slight difference between the terms.
Our WebDriver automated tests fall into the system testing category. If all actions and assertions are performed against the user interface (UI), they should be called **UI tests**. **End-to-end (user scenario) test** would be called a test verifying a real User scenario, from the beginning to the end of the User interaction with the system under test. No shortcuts or mocks are used - the test mimics human interaction entirely. With system tests, we are speaking of highly optimized tests focusing on verifying a particular functionality of the system. For example- instead of logging in each time through the UI or registering new users, we can use internal APIs or DB directly to do so. The same is valid for the performed assertions. If you use these low levels, it is inappropriate to call these tests- UI tests.

NOTE

Sometimes the term system of systems test is used. These tests verify the integration between a couple of systems. For example, our website may use a different internal system to register and authenticate users and another for performing online purchases. The system of system tests would go through them all to verify that the functionality works as expected.

What Is a Test Automation Framework?

During many conversations at conferences, I realized that many developers have a wrong conception of a test automation framework. Here, I will try to give you a definition, but before that, we need to go through some related terms such as what is a software library, a framework, API, test framework, and others. You need to understand the latter to get what the test automation framework is.

What Is a Software Library?

Before we can define what, a software library is, we need to go over what an application is.

Definition: Application

An application is software created to benefit its users by executing specific functions, tasks or other activities. In information technologies, we refer to an application as a computer program developed to aid people to complete specific tasks.

The first conclusion we can make after this definition is that our automated tests are also applications. Over the years, there have been many discussions over the internet and at conferences whether test engineers should be able to program rather than using UI tools for automated testing. The new age test automation QA should be a good programmer, treating his/her code as production code - following high-quality code standards.

Definition: Software Library

The software library contains pre-written code, classes, methods, interfaces, constants, configuration data and such. Other programs can use its methods without defining them

Definition: API

The group of methods that give us access to features of the OS, application or other services is called application programming interface or API. If the API is well designed, it should ease the creation of programs by giving us suitable methods as building blocks.

Many engineers believe that in their companies, they have built custom test frameworks. But they have libraries or groups of methods and classes that can help them to write automated tests. The API of the library defines how the users will access its methods, what arguments they need to pass, and so on. It is a convention of how the library is accessed and used, while the actual implementation is handled in the library itself. The API specifies what we can use, whereas the software library is the actual implementation of this specification. It should follow the prescribed rules. We can have multiple implementations of the same API. For example, Java and Scala implement the Java API. Both are later compiled to bytecode, which enables Java developers to use the same methods. The same is valid for the .NET world where C# and VB.NET are different languages, but both implement the .NET API and compile to MSIL.

What Is a Framework?

Software frameworks have these distinctive features that separate them from libraries:

Definition: Framework

A software framework is a software library by its core, but at the same time, it is different. We use the software libraries to build our application without a way to change or modify them. On the contrary, the software framework is usually developed in a more generic/abstract way and gives us the possibility to override some of its functionalities and modify or customize their behavior. Thus, it gives us a more reusable code written more abstractly so it can be reused in more users' scenarios.

Inversion of control - the framework controls the flow, and it cannot be modified as in standard software libraries.

Default behavior - the software framework provides useful default actions.

Extensibility - as a user, you can customize and modify some of its actions to fit your needs which usually cannot be done for software libraries.

Non-modifiable framework code - you can customize or tweak some actions of the framework, but you cannot change its code.

Examples include ASP.NET and .NET for Windows development, Cocoa for Mac OS X, Cocoa Touch for iOS, and the Android Application Framework for Android.

Definition: Unit Testing Framework

Unit testing frameworks are software libraries consisting of various helper classes, methods, interfaces, and a set of other tools that aid developers in creating unit tests for their code.

In the definition, unit testing frameworks help us write tests more quickly to verify the functionality of our methods and classes. We can execute these tests in an automated way, so we need not repeat them manually repeatedly. They are usually well integrated into the most popular programming IDEs. We can run our tests from there, plus quickly review the results.

Examples of unit testing frameworks are JUnit, TestNG, NUnit, MSTest.

Test Automation Framework

Now, let's finally understand what the test automation framework is.

Definition: Test Automation Framework

The test automation framework consists of various guidelines, coding standards, concepts, processes, practices, project hierarchies, modularity, etc. to support automated testing. The user can follow these guidelines while automating applications and take advantage of the productive results we obtain.

Is Selenium WebDriver a Test Framework?

Many QAs call Selenium WebDriver a test automation framework, but they cannot be more wrong. Here is the official definition on their website.

"Selenium automates browsers. That's it! What you do with that power is entirely up to you."

Primarily, it is for automating web applications for testing, but it is not limited to just that. Boring web-based administration tasks can (and should!) be automated as well."

Based on the definition, we can conclude that **Selenium WebDriver** is mostly known as the standard for web automation testing, but actually, it is a tool for controlling browsers we later use in our software libraries and frameworks to write automated tests.

SOLID Principles

Before we can define the high-quality test attributes, we should mention some of the well-known object-oriented programming principles. Throughout the book, I will mention some. SOLID is a mnemonic acronym for five design principles. These principles aim to help us write more understandable, flexible, and maintainable software. SOLID stands for:

SRP – Single Responsibility Principle
OCP – Open/Closed Principle
LSP – Liskov Substitution Principle
ISP – Interface Segregation Principle
DIP – Dependency Inversion Principle
SRP – Single Responsibility Principle

NOTE

The principles are a subset of many principles promoted by Robert C. Martin (colloquially known as "Uncle Bob"). He is best known for being one of the authors of the Agile Manifesto. Martin's theory of SOLID principles was introduced in his 2000th paper "Design Principles and Design Patterns", although the SOLID acronym itself was introduced later by Michael Feathers.

The principles states- "*Every software module should have only one reason to change*" so every class, method, etc., can do many things, but they should serve a single purpose.

All the methods and variables in the class should support this purpose. Everything else should be removed. It shouldn't be like a Swiss knife providing 20 utility actions since if one of them is changed, all others need to be updated too.

But if we can have each item separated, it would be simple, easy to maintain, and one change will not affect the others. The same principle also applies to classes and objects in the software architecture- you can have them as separate, simpler classes.

Let me give you an example.

```
public void create() {
    try  {
        // Database code goes here
    }
    catch (Exception ex) {
        Path path = Paths.get("C:\\exception.txt");
        BufferedWriter writer = Files.newBufferedWriter(path);
        writer.write(ex.getLocalizedMessage());
    }
}
```

The `CustomerOrder` class is doing something which it is not supposed to do. It should create purchases and save them in the database, but if you look at the catch block closely, you will see it also does log activity. It has too many responsibilities.

If we want to follow the **Single Responsibility principle SRP**, we should divide the class into two separate simple classes. We can move the logging to a separate class.

```
public class FileLogger {
    public void createLogEntry(String error) {
        Path path = Paths.get("C:\\errors.txt");
        BufferedWriter writer = Files.newBufferedWriter(path);
        writer.write(error);
    }
}
```

After that the `CustomerOrder` class can delegate the logging to the `FileLogger` class and be more focused on the creating purchases.

```
public class CustomerOrder {
    private final FileLogger _fileLogger = new FileLogger();

    public void create() {
        try  {
            // Database code goes here
        }
        catch (Exception ex) {
            _fileLogger.createLogEntry(ex.getLocalizedMessage());
```

```
        }
    }
}
```

OCP – Open/Closed Principle

The principle says that "*software entities (classes, modules, functions, etc.) should be open for extension but closed for modification*". It means that if new requirements are written for the already implemented functionality, these can be added in a way, so we don't need to change the whole structure of the existing code that has already been unit tested. If we change it and add it directly, we can trigger new regression problems.

How about looking at an example?

```
public enum OrderType
{
    Normal,
    Silver,
}

public class DiscountCalculator {
    public double calculateDiscount(OrderType orderType, double totalPrice) {
        if (orderType == OrderType.Silver) {
            return totalPrice - 20;
        }
        else {
            return totalPrice;
        }
    }
}
```

Look at the IF condition in the `calculateDiscount` method. The problem is that if we add new order types, we must add one more IF condition, meaning we will have to change the implementation inside the `DiscountCalculator` class, because of a change that has happened outside of it. If we need to change the class every second week, we need to ensure that the previous requirements are still satisfied, and the new ones integrate well with the old ones. Instead of modifying the existing code for every new condition, we strive to develop a solution that can be extensible.

We can easily refactor this code to follow the **Open/Closed principle OCP**, so every time a new order type is added, we create a new class, as shown in the example. The existing code stays untouched, and we need to test and check only the new cases.

```
public abstract class DiscountCalculator {
    public double calculateDiscount(double totalPrice) {
        return totalPrice;
    }
```

```
}

public class SilverDiscountCalculator extends DiscountCalculator {
    @Override
    public double calculateDiscount(double totalPrice) {
        return super.calculateDiscount(totalPrice) - 20;
    }
}

public class GoldDiscountCalculator  extends DiscountCalculator {
    @Override
    public double calculateDiscount(double totalPrice) {
        return super.calculateDiscount(totalPrice) - 50;
    }
}
```

LSP – Liskov Substitution Principle

The principle says that "*you should be able to use any derived class instead of a parent class and have it behaved in the same manner without modification*". It means that the child class shouldn't modify or change how the base class behaves. The child classes can be used as if they are their parent themselves, but unexpected issues could occur if you change behavior in a child class.
Shall we continue with the same `DiscountCalculator` example? We want to introduce a new type of discount for bonus points. To calculate it, we will add a new method to our base class.

```
public abstract class DiscountCalculator {
    public double calculateRegularDiscount(double totalPrice) {
        return totalPrice;
    }

    public double calculateBonusPointsDiscount(double totalPrice, int points) {
        return totalPrice - points * 0.1;
    }
}
```

As you can see, we have renamed the `calculateDiscount` method to `calculateRegularDiscount` and we added a new method for calculating the discounted total price based on the bonus points.

```
public class SilverDiscountCalculator extends DiscountCalculator {
    @Override
    public double calculateRegularDiscount(double totalPrice) {
        return super.calculateRegularDiscount(totalPrice) - 20;
    }

    @Override
    public double calculateBonusPointsDiscount(double totalPrice, int points) {
        return totalPrice - points * 0.5;
    }
```

```
}
public class GoldDiscountCalculator  extends DiscountCalculator {
    @Override
    public double calculateRegularDiscount(double totalPrice) {
        return super.calculateRegularDiscount(totalPrice) - 50;
    }

    @Override
    public double calculateBonusPointsDiscount(double totalPrice, int points) {
        return totalPrice - points * 1;
    }
}
public class PlatinumDiscountCalculator extends DiscountCalculator {
    @Override
    public double calculateRegularDiscount(double totalPrice) {
        return super.calculateRegularDiscount(totalPrice) - 100;
    }

    @Override
    public double calculateBonusPointsDiscount(double totalPrice, int points) {
        throw new NoSuchMethodException("Not applicable for Platinum orders.");
    }
}
```

What we did here is to add a new type of order- Platinum. We have applied the maximum allowed discount, so the bonus points discount is not applicable for Platinum orders. Here, we decide to throw `NoSuchMethodException` to let the calling methods know this operation is not supported for the Platinum type. As the Polymorphism from the OOP Principles states, we can use the child classes calculators derived from the `DiscountCalculator`, as if they are the actual `DiscountCalculator` class.
Thanks to this principle, as you can see in the code below, I have created a collection of `DiscountCalculator` objects where I can add Silver, Gold, and Platinum Discount Calculators as if they are instances of the same type - `DiscountCalculator`. After that, I can go through the list using the parent customer object and invoke the calculation methods.

```
List<DiscountCalculator> discountCalculators = new ArrayList<>();
discountCalculators.add(new SilverDiscountCalculator());
discountCalculators.add(new GoldDiscountCalculator());
discountCalculators.add(new PlatinumDiscountCalculator());
for (var discountCalculator : discountCalculators) {
    double bonusPointsDiscount = discountCalculator.calculateBonusPointsDiscount(1250, 10);
}
```

So far, so good, but when the `calculateBonusPointsDiscount` of the `PlatinumDiscountCalculator` is invoked, it leads to `NoSuchMethodException`. The problem is that the `PlatinumDiscountCalculator` object looks like a `DiscountCalculator`, but implementing the child object has changed the expected behavior of the parent method. So, to follow the **Liskov principle**, we need to create two interfaces, one for the regular and the other for the bonus points discount.

```
public interface RegularDiscountCalculator {
    double calculateRegularDiscount(double totalPrice);
}

public interface BonusPointsDiscountCalculator {
    double calculateBonusPointsDiscount(double totalPrice, int points);
}
```

I will spare you all the refactoring that we need to do. Let's see how we will use the code to fix the problem we faced.

```
List<BonusPointsDiscountCalculator> discountCalculators = new ArrayList<>();
discountCalculators.add(new SilverDiscountCalculator());
discountCalculators.add(new GoldDiscountCalculator());
// discountCalculators.add(new PlatinumDiscountCalculator()); // we cannot add it
for (var discountCalculator : discountCalculators) {
    double bonusPointsDiscount = discountCalculator.calculateBonusPointsDiscount(1250, 10);
}
```

Instead of using the base class, we use the `BonusPointsDiscountCalculator` interface. This means that all added objects to the collection will have this method implemented. Otherwise, we won't be able to add them to the list.

ISP – Interface Segregation Principle

The principle states that "*clients should not be forced to implement interfaces they don't use. Instead of one fat interface, many small interfaces are preferred based on groups of methods, each one serving one sub-module*". The **Single Responsibility principle** can be applied not only for classes but for the interfaces. Each interface should provide methods that serve a single purpose. Here, the interface gives us functions for more than one goal. This could lead our implementation code to include methods not needed in the class.
Why not see an example of why we shouldn't use one fat interface? We can use our previous example for discount calculators. Instead of creating two separate interfaces, we could easily create a single one. To simplify the code, let's remove the inheritance.

```
public interface DiscountCalculator {
    double calculateRegularDiscount(double totalPrice);
    double calculateBonusPointsDiscount(double totalPrice, int points);
}

public class GoldDiscountCalculator implements DiscountCalculator {
    public double calculateRegularDiscount(double totalPrice) {
        return totalPrice - 50;
    }

    public double calculateBonusPointsDiscount(double totalPrice, int points) {
        return totalPrice - points * 1;
    }
}
```

```
public class PlatinumDiscountCalculator implements DiscountCalculator {
    public double calculateRegularDiscount(double totalPrice) {
        return totalPrice - 100;
    }

    public double calculateBonusPointsDiscount(double totalPrice, int points) {
        throw new NoSuchMethodException("Not applicable for Platinum orders.");
    }
}
```

As you can see, we have a similar problem. Since we have one fat interface, we are forced to implement all methods- even when we may not need them. In the future, this could become even worse. Imagine that we need to add another type of discount, but this time it is not applicable to the Silver orders. This would mean that in the `SilverDiscountCalculator` we will have a new method that throws `NoSuchMethodException`. A better solution would be creating a new interface rather than updating the current interface.

DIP – Dependency Inversion Principle

The principle states that *"high-level classes should not depend on low-level classes. Both types should be created based on abstractions. These abstractions shouldn't depend on any low-level details. All details should use the abstractions instead"*. The high-level classes usually contain the business logic, and the low-level ones consist of actions such as CRUD DB operations, reading files or calling web APIs. When we say that a class is tightly coupled, it has access to low-level details (that it shouldn't have) instead of using abstractions.
How about extending our `CustomerOrder` example a bit? The requirements have changed, and we have different orders to process- silver, gold and platinum. Also, new requirements state that we need to add two more ways of notifications if something happens. For example, emailing and SMS with updates. To do so:
We will create a common interface for all loggers called `Logger`.

```
public interface Logger {
    void createLogEntry(String errorMessage);
}
```

After that we will create three loggers- one for file logging, one for email and one more for SMS.

```
public class FileLogger implements Logger {
    public void createLogEntry(String error) {
        Path path = Paths.get("C:\\errors.txt");
        BufferedWriter writer = Files.newBufferedWriter(path);
        writer.write(error);
    }
}
```

```
public class EmailLogger implements Logger {
    public void createLogEntry(string errorMessage) {
        EmailFactory.sendEmail(errorMessage);
    }
}

public class SmsLogger implements Logger {
    public void createLogEntry(String errorMessage) {
        SmsFactory.sendSms(errorMessage);
    }
}
```

The business logic behind the new requirements is we need to send an email for gold orders and an SMS for platinum orders since they bring our company more money.

```
public class CustomerOrder {
    public void create(OrderType orderType) {
        try {
            // Database code goes here
        } catch (Exception ex) {
            switch (orderType)  {
                case NORMAL:
                    new SmsLogger().createLogEntry(ex.getMessage());
                    break;
                case SILVER:
                case GOLD:
                    new EmailLogger().createLogEntry(ex.getMessage());
                    break;
                case PLATINUM:
                    new FileLogger().createLogEntry(ex.getMessage());
                    break;
            }

            fileLogger.createLogEntry(ex.getLocalizedMessage());
        }
    }
}
```

The code violates the **Single Responsibility principle** again. It should be focused on creating purchases and deciding which object to be made, while it is not the job of the `CustomerOrder` class to determine which instances of the `Logger` should be used. The biggest problem here is related to the `new` keyword. This is an extra responsibility of deciding which objects to be created, so if we delegate this responsibility to someone other than the `CustomerOrder` class, that will solve the problem.
We can have different child classes of `CustomerOrder` for the different orders. Also, the logger can be passed as a dependency rather than creating it in the method itself.

```
public class CustomerOrder {
    private final Logger logger;

    public CustomerOrder(Logger logger)  {
```

```
        this.logger = logger;
    }

    public void create() {
        try {
            // Database code goes here
        } catch (Exception ex) {
            logger.createLogEntry(ex.getLocalizedMessage());
        }
    }
}

public class GoldCustomerOrder extends CustomerOrder {
    public GoldCustomerOrder() {
        super(new EmailLogger());
    }
}

public class PlatinumCustomerOrder extends CustomerOrder {
    public PlatinumCustomerOrder() {
        super(new SmsLogger());
    }
}
```

NOTE

Remember, the example was oversimplified. In production code, we usually use special frameworks for the job called inversion of control containers. The container uses the declared injection interfaces to figure out the dependencies and, based on them to inject the correct dependencies, instead of passing them as parameters to the methods.

High-Quality Test Attributes

The time has come to define the automated test's high-quality attributes. You will find that some of these attributes are connected to the SOLID principles, and throughout the book, we will continue to talk about these connections. Since the book is also about design patterns, and we haven't discussed them yet, we will first go through these definitions, and then we will go briefly through each of the high-quality attributes. We will not go into many details now since there will be a dedicated chapter for each attribute.

What Is a Design Pattern?

We can define the design patterns as prescribed solutions to everyday software challenges. They don't consist of code or any specified algorithm, but instead, they describe how to group your logic smartly, reuse it, or make it easier to maintain. It is a template for solving design problems that we can use while creating our software solutions.

Test Maintainability and Reusability

Definition: Maintainability

The ease with which we can customize or change our software solution to accommodate new requirements, fix problems, improve performance.

Imagine there is a problem with your tests. How much time do you need to figure out where the problem is? Is it an automation bug or an issue in the system under test? In the next chapters, we will discuss how to create maintainable tests using various practices and design patterns. But if at the beginning, you haven't designed your code in such a way, the changes may need to be applied to multiple places, which can lead to missing some and thus resulting in more bugs. The better the maintainability is, the easier it is for us to support our existing code, accommodate new requirements, or just fix bugs.

A closely related principle to this definition is the so-called **DRY principle- Don't Repeat Yourself**. The most basic idea behind the **DRY principle** is to reduce long-term maintenance costs by removing all unnecessary duplication.

NOTE

As Donald Knuth so eloquently said, "*Premature optimization is the root of all evil (or at least most of it) in programming.*" We should not remove only the duplicate code and duplicate test implementations, but we also should remove duplicate test goals. David Thomas and Andrew Hunt formulated the DRY principle in their book, The Pragmatic Programmer, by Andrew Hunt and David Thomas, published by Addison-Wesley Professional. The DRY principle is sometimes called **Single Source of Truth (SSOT)** or **Single Point of Truth (SPOT)** because it attempts to store every single piece of unique information in a single place only. [Sdp14]

Test Readability

By reading the code, you should be able to discover what the code does easily. A code that is not readable usually requires more time to read, maintain, understand, and increase the chance to introduce bugs. Some programmers use huge comments instead of writing simpler readable code. It is much easier to name your variables, methods, classes correctly, instead of relying on these comments. Also, as time goes by, the comments are rarely updated, and they can mislead the readers.

API Usability

As we mentioned above, the API is the specification of what you can do with a software library. When we use the term usability with the term API, it means "How easy it is for you, as a user, to find out what the methods do and how to use them?”. In the case of a Test Library - "How much time a new user needs to create a new test?"

In the programming community, we sometimes use another term for the same thing called **syntactic sugar**. It describes how easy it is to use or read expressions. It sweetens the programming languages for humans. The programming statements become more concise and clearer.

NOTE

The term syntactic sugar was invented by Peter J. Landin in 1964. It described the syntax of a programming language similar to ALGOL, which was defined semantically in terms of the applicative expressions of lambda calculus, centered on lexically replacing λ with "where".

Extensibility

One of the hardest things to develop is to allow these **generic frameworks to be extensible and customizable**. The whole point of creating a shared library is to be used by multiple teams across the company. However, the different teams work in different contexts. So, the library code may not be working out of the box for them. To use your library in all these various scenarios that you cannot (and shouldn't) consider while developing it, the engineers should be able to customize parts of it to fit their needs.

With automated tests, imagine that you have a test suite testing a shopping cart. The test workflow consists of multiple steps- choosing the product, changing the quantity, adding more products, applying discount coupons, filling billing info, providing payment info and so on. If a new requirement comes - "The billing info should be prefilled for logged users.", how easy would it be to change the existing tests? Did you write your tests in a way that, if you add this new functionality, it will not affect the majority of your existing tests?

You need not answer these questions yet. We will discuss them in much more detail in the next chapters, explaining how to build such solutions.

As you can see, this high-quality automated test attribute is closely related to the SOLID principles we already discussed.

Learning Curve

I also like to call this attribute "Easy Knowledge Transfer". The attribute answers the question, "How easy is it for someone to learn how to add new or maintain the existing tests by himself?".

The learning curve is tightly coupled to the API usability, but it means something different. If a new member joins your team, is he able to learn by himself how to use your test automation framework, or he needs to read the documentation if it exists? Or you have a mentoring program where you need to teach these new members yourself every time how to use your code? Hopefully, by the time you reach the end of the book, you will know how to develop your test automation code so the new members can learn how to use your solution by themselves.

Summary

This more theoretical first chapter went through some essential terms in automated testing and high-quality programming. We discussed what is a library, API and how they differ from frameworks. After that, we listed the different tests and defined where our automated tests are in this categorization. Next, I explained with a few examples the different SOLID principles. At the end of the chapter, you learned what the design patterns are and the five high-quality test attributes.

In the next chapter, we will create our first automated tests and discuss the most common reasons for failure. After that, I will present a couple of best practices and design patterns to make them more stable.

Questions

1. Why is WebDriver not a test framework?
2. What is the difference between integration and system tests?
3. Can we use the term end-to-end test for a test that does not execute exactly a user scenario?
4. Which principle is not followed if you have copy-pasted multiple times the same code snippet?

Chapter 2. Optimizing and Refactoring Legacy Flaky Tests

In this chapter, we will create our first automated tests for validating an e-commerce website. These tests will simulate how similar tests look as if they were written by someone just starting to use Selenium WebDriver. I will use them to illustrate common problems. One by one, we will address those problems in the chapter and will continue to improve them to the end of the book with various design patterns and best practices.

These topics will be covered in this chapter:

- Writing the First Real-World Automated Test
- Reasons for Failures
- Refactoring Tests
- Decorator Design Pattern for Fixing WebDriver Unstable Actions
- The Test Independence-Isolation Principle

Writing the First Real-World Automated Test

We will start by checking the requirements of what we need to automate. Imagine that you work for a startup called "EU Space Rockets". Our company makes the world a better place by allowing people to buy rockets through our website. How cool is that! Your job is to create automated tests and make sure that everything is working as expected.

Our website uses modern web technologies, and all actions are loading asynchronously instead of reloading the whole page.

First Automated Test Case Explanation

Let us have a look at a step-by-step approach on how to create your first automated test case:

1. We navigate to the home page of our website and then click on the '**Add to cart**' button that adds a '**Falcon 9**' rocket to the cart.

2. Next, we need to click on the '**View cart**' button, leading us to the cart page.

3. If it's our birthday, we can apply the company's special discount coupon.

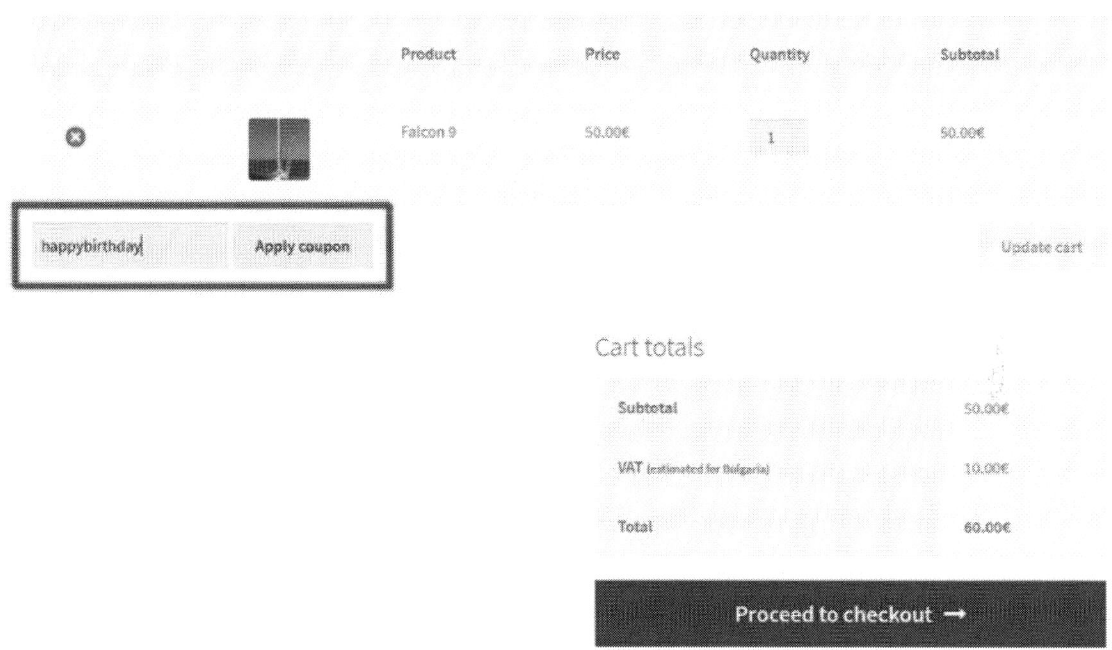

4. Before proceeding with any operations, we need to ensure that the loading indicator is not displayed.

5. Next, since we got a discount, we have additional funding to buy additional rockets. So, we increase the quantity to **2** and click on the '**Update cart**' button.

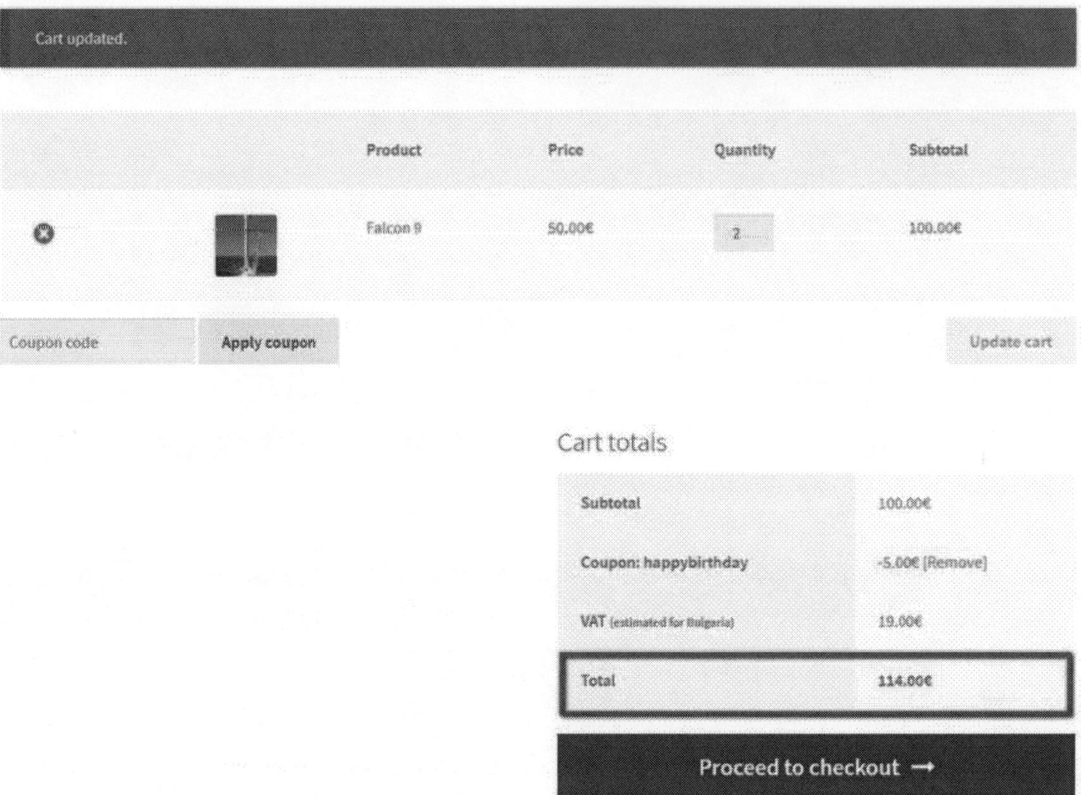

6. After the cart is updated, our test needs to check whether the total price has been changed correctly. If everything is OK, we click on the '**Proceed to checkout**' button.
7. We fill in all required information and click on the '**Place order**' button. When the next page is loaded, we need to verify that the order was placed successfully.

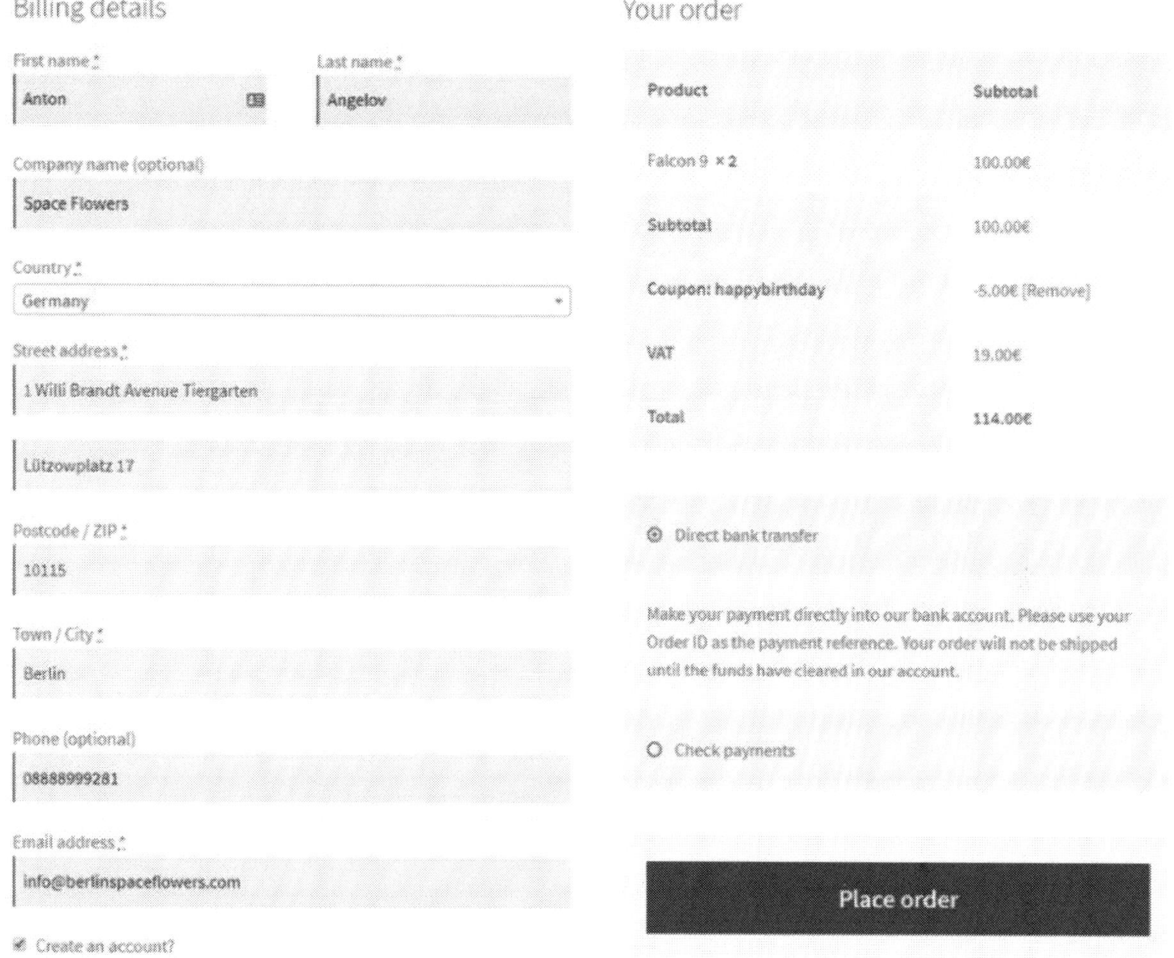

Second Automated Test Case Explanation

After the first automated test executes, the system creates an account for us. If we want to make subsequent purchases with the same email, we should first log in to the website. Once we are authenticated, all our data should be prefilled. So, when we are on the billing page (step 7), instead of filling in the information we click on the '**Click here to login**' link. Then the login form is shown.

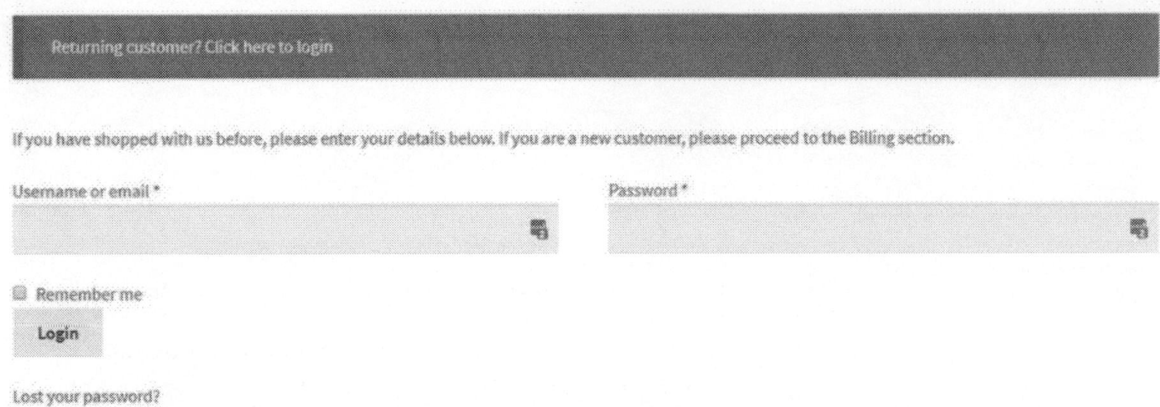

After we are authenticated successfully, we complete the purchase as we did in the first test case.

Third Automated Test Case Explanation

Our third and last automated test has the job to check whether the lastly created order is displayed in the **My Account** section of our website. To do so:

1. We click on the **My account** link in the navigation and log in.

Shop

2. Next, we open the **Orders** tab, and using the order number we saved on completing the last order, we click on this particular row's '**View**' button.

Orders

3. When the next page is open, we verify that the correct data is displayed.

First Automated Test Code

Why not now have a look at the code for our first automated test case?

```
private WebDriver driver;
private static String purchaseEmail;
private static String purchaseOrderNumber;

@BeforeMethod
public void testInit() {
    WebDriverManager.chromedriver().setup();
    driver = new ChromeDriver();
    driver.manage().timeouts().implicitlyWait(10, TimeUnit.SECONDS);
}

@AfterMethod
public void testCleanup() {
    driver.quit();
}

@Test(priority=1)
public void completePurchaseSuccessfully_whenNewClient() {
    driver.navigate().to("http://demos.bellatrix.solutions/");
    var addToCartFalcon9 = driver.findElement(By.cssSelector("[data-product_id*='28']"));
    addToCartFalcon9.click();
    Thread.sleep(5000);
```

```
    var viewCartButton = driver.findElement(By.cssSelector("[class*='added_to_cart wc-
forward']"));
    viewCartButton.click();

    var couponCodeTextField = driver.findElement(By.id("coupon_code"));
    couponCodeTextField.clear();
    couponCodeTextField.sendKeys("happybirthday");
    var applyCouponButton = driver.findElement(By.cssSelector("[value*='Apply coupon']"));
    applyCouponButton.click();
    Thread.sleep(5000);
    var messageAlert = driver.findElement(By.cssSelector("[class*='woocommerce-message']"));
    Assert.assertEquals(messageAlert.getText(), "Coupon code applied successfully.");

    var quantityBox = driver.findElement(By.cssSelector("[class*='input-text qty text']"));
    quantityBox.clear();
    Thread.sleep(500);
    quantityBox.sendKeys("2");

    Thread.sleep(5000);
    var updateCart = driver.findElement(By.cssSelector("[value*='Update cart']"));
    updateCart.click();
    Thread.sleep(5000);
    var totalSpan = driver.findElement(By.xpath("//*[@class='order-total']//span"));
    Assert.assertEquals("114.00€", totalSpan.getText());

    var proceedToCheckout = driver.findElement(By.cssSelector("[class*='checkout-button
button alt wc-forward']"));
    proceedToCheckout.click();

    var billingFirstName = driver.findElement(By.id("billing_first_name"));
    billingFirstName.sendKeys("Anton");
    var billingLastName = driver.findElement(By.id("billing_last_name"));
    billingLastName.sendKeys("Angelov");
    var billingCompany = driver.findElement(By.id("billing_company"));
    billingCompany.sendKeys("Space Flowers");
    var billingCountryWrapper = driver.findElement(By.id("select2-billing_country-
container"));
    billingCountryWrapper.click();
    var billingCountryFilter = driver.findElement(By.className("select2-search__field"));
    billingCountryFilter.sendKeys("Germany");
    var germanyOption = driver.findElement(By.xpath("//*[contains(text(),'Germany')]"));
    germanyOption.click();
    var billingAddress1 = driver.findElement(By.id("billing_address_1"));
    billingAddress1.sendKeys("1 Willi Brandt Avenue Tiergarten");
    var billingAddress2 = driver.findElement(By.id("billing_address_2"));
    billingAddress2.sendKeys("Lotzowplatz 17");
    var billingCity = driver.findElement(By.id("billing_city"));
    billingCity.sendKeys("Berlin");
    var billingZip = driver.findElement(By.id("billing_postcode"));
    billingZip.clear();
    billingZip.sendKeys("10115");
    var billingPhone = driver.findElement(By.id("billing_phone"));
    billingPhone.sendKeys("+00498888999281");
    var billingEmail = driver.findElement(By.id("billing_email"));
```

```
    billingEmail.sendKeys("info@berlinspaceflowers.com");
    purchaseEmail = "info@berlinspaceflowers.com";
    Thread.sleep(5000);
    var placeOrderButton = driver.findElement(By.id("place_order"));
    placeOrderButton.click();

    Thread.sleep(10000);
    var receivedMessage =
driver.findElement(By.xpath("/html/body/div[1]/div/div/div/main/div/header/h1"));
    Assert.assertEquals(receivedMessage.getText(), "Order received");
}
```

Why not see what we did here? We start the Chrome browser in the `testInit` method so that it will be started for every test and closed after its completion.

NOTE

To download the correct version of the selected browser's driver, we use a library called **WebDriverManager**. I installed it through the Maven artifact/dependency **webdrivermanager**. You can find all installed packages in the project's or modules' **pom.xml** files.

NOTE

Maven is a build automation tool used primarily for Java projects. Maven, created by Jason van Zyl, began as a sub-project of Apache Turbine in 2002. It is hosted by the Apache Software Foundation, where it was formerly part of the Jakarta Project. Maven addresses two aspects of building software: how software is built and its dependencies. An XML file describes the software project being built, its dependencies on other external modules and components, the build order, directories, and required plug-ins. It comes with pre-defined targets for performing specific, well-defined tasks such as compilation of code and its packaging. Maven dynamically downloads Java libraries and Maven plug-ins from one or more repositories, such as the Maven 2 Central Repository, and stores them in a local cache.

NOTE

I will not go into much detail about element selectors and WebDriver syntax since I expect that you already know the basics. You can check *Appendix 2* and *Appendix 3* for a better understanding of XPath and CSS selectors.

I mentioned that our website is using modern JavaScript technologies and most operations are asynchronous. To handle them in the first version of our tests, we use hard-coded pauses like `Thread.sleep(5000)`. Since our second test needs to authenticate using the account created in the first one, we save the email in the static variable `purchaseEmail`.

Second Automated Test Code

Our second test is almost identical, except instead of filling out the billing details, we use the saved email to authenticate to the website. After that, all fields are prefilled, and we can complete the purchase.

```
@Test(priority=2)
public void completePurchaseSuccessfully_whenExistingClient() {
    driver.navigate().to("http://demos.bellatrix.solutions/");

    var addToCartFalcon9 = driver.findElement(By.cssSelector("[data-product_id*='28']"));
    addToCartFalcon9.click();
    Thread.sleep(5000);
    var viewCartButton = driver.findElement(By.cssSelector("[class*='added_to_cart wc-
forward']"));
    viewCartButton.click();

    var couponCodeTextField = driver.findElement(By.id("coupon_code"));
    couponCodeTextField.clear();
    couponCodeTextField.sendKeys("happybirthday");
    var applyCouponButton = driver.findElement(By.cssSelector("[value*='Apply coupon']"));
    applyCouponButton.click();
    Thread.sleep(5000);
    var messageAlert = driver.findElement(By.cssSelector("[class*='woocommerce-message']"));
    Assert.assertEquals(messageAlert.getText(), "Coupon code applied successfully.");

    var quantityBox = driver.findElement(By.cssSelector("[class*='input-text qty text']"));
    quantityBox.clear();
    Thread.sleep(500);
    quantityBox.sendKeys("2");
    Thread.sleep(5000);
    var updateCart = driver.findElement(By.cssSelector("[value*='Update cart']"));
    updateCart.click();
    Thread.sleep(5000);
    var totalSpan = driver.findElement(By.xpath("//*[@class='order-total']//span"));
    Assert.assertEquals(totalSpan.getText(), "114.00€");

    var proceedToCheckout = driver.findElement(By.cssSelector("[class*='checkout-button
button alt wc-forward']"));
    proceedToCheckout.click();

    var loginHereLink = driver.findElement(By.linkText("Click here to login"));
    loginHereLink.click();
    Thread.sleep(5000);
    var userName = driver.findElement(By.id("username"));
    userName.sendKeys(purchaseEmail);
```

```
    var password = driver.findElement(By.id("password"));
    password.sendKeys(GetUserPasswordFromDb(purchaseEmail));
    var loginButton = driver.findElement(By.xpath("//button[@name='login']"));
    loginButton.click();

    Thread.sleep(5000);
    var placeOrderButton = driver.findElement(By.id("place_order"));
    placeOrderButton.click();

    Thread.sleep(5000);
    var receivedMessage = driver.findElement(By.xpath("//h1[text() = 'Order received']"));
    Assert.assertEquals(receivedMessage.getText(), "Order received");

    var orderNumber = driver.findElement(By.xpath("//*[@id='post-7']//li[1]/strong"));
    purchaseOrderNumber = orderNumber.getText();
}
```

We extract the generated order number displayed on the success order page at the end of the test. We will use it in our third test to verify that the information is displayed correctly in the **My Account** section.

> **NOTE**
>
> One of the most visible enhancements in JDK 10 is the type inference of local variables with initializers. Until Java 9, we had to mention the local variable explicitly and ensure it was compatible with the initializer used to initialize it. We don't provide the data type of the variable. Instead, we mark it as a `var`. Afterward, the compiler infers the type from the type of initializer present on the right-hand side. Note that this feature is available only for local variables with the initializer.
>
> **NOTE**
>
> Originally, Java defined its major releases around introducing a large feature, which created delays, like those we all experienced with Java 8 and 9. It also slowed language innovation while other languages with tighter feedback cycles evolved. Java now has a release every six months. Each third-year release is called an LTS (long-term support) release.

Third Automated Test Code

In this test, we use some hard-coded pauses to make sure that the test will pass. Also, we use the saved email to log in, and after that, the saved order number to open the correct purchase order view page.

```
@Test(priority=3)
public void correctOrderDataDisplayed_whenNavigateToMyAccountOrderSection() {
    driver.navigate().to("http://demos.bellatrix.solutions/");

    var myAccountLink = driver.findElement(By.linkText("My account"));
    myAccountLink.click();
    var userName = driver.findElement(By.id("username"));
    userName.sendKeys(purchaseEmail);
    var password = driver.findElement(By.id("password"));
    password.sendKeys(GetUserPasswordFromDb(GetUserPasswordFromDb(purchaseEmail)));
    var loginButton = driver.findElement(By.xpath("//button[@name='login']"));
    loginButton.click();

    Thread.sleep(5000);
    var orders = driver.findElement(By.linkText("Orders"));
    orders.click();

    Thread.sleep(5000);
    var viewButtons = driver.findElements(By.linkText("View"));
    viewButtons.get(0).click();
    Thread.sleep(5000);

    var orderName = driver.findElement(By.xpath("//h1"));
    String expectedMessage = String.format("Order #%s", purchaseOrderNumber);
    Assert.assertEquals(expectedMessage, orderName.getText());
}
```

Reasons for Failures

The writing of the automated tests is only the first step in testing your app automatically. The journey doesn't stop there. The more tests you have, the more time you will need to spare to analyse the test results. Why is that? Some tests will fail, and there are a couple of reasons for this.

- Real problem in the system under test
- A problem in the test environment (the application(s) were being re-deployed or not available at the moment, networking issues and such)
- There is a problem with the test itself. The test sometimes passes and sometimes fails. For these tests, we use the term- **flaky tests**.

Usually, we check the test failures and rerun the failed tests to see what will happen and whether the problem will reproduce. If the test passes this time, you probably found a temp problem in the test environment or a fragile test. In both cases, we may need to dig into the test execution logs to see whether we will find any useful information to distinguish whether there is a problem with the test and find a way to fix it.

We finished our three tests, and we should now examine just how fragile they are. Even though the design of our tests made sense at the time of writing them, they will fail at the slightest provocation. Let's review the mistakes we have made:

- **Test on test dependency**: This is the most obvious mistake. If the first test we execute does not complete, the second test won't authenticate and the third one to verify the order.
- **Hard-coded test data**: Every test has the website implementation details hard-coded. The URL of the product page and the title of the product being tested are written in the test itself. If these details ever change even minutely, we must update every test with product data hardcoded. If the product data is different between test environments, these tests cannot be reused.
- **Code duplication**: Many actions, such as clicking on the links and filling out form data, are duplicated between the tests. We will fix this problem in a minute.

We wanted to test the website's features, and not all the decisions we made were obviously inadequate. However, the result is a completely unstable test suite.

NOTE

If you are feeling adventurous and want to destabilize our test suite in a couple of other ways, you can experiment with these changes:

1. Delete the first test altogether, and only run the second test.
2. Run the third test alone without running the first two.
3. Decrease the milliseconds of the hard-coded pauses.

NOTE

If you download the source code and run the tests, you should know a couple of things. The order of test execution is important. The tests should be executed in the following order:

- `completePurchaseSuccessfully_whenNewClient`
- `completePurchaseSuccessfully_whenExistingClient`
- `correctOrderDataDisplayed_whenNavigateToMyAccountOrderSection`

The tests may fail because the hard-coded pauses were not enough. This is the expected behavior showing this is not the best practice.

Refactoring Tests

After we reviewed why the design of our initial tests is not so good, how about seeing how we can improve our existing three tests. Here, we will start with small refactoring- removing some pauses. We will use a WebDriver built-in functionality called "**explicit wait**" exposed through the class `WebDriverWait`. Also, we can create reusable methods for some actions occurring more than once in our code. We used pauses in our tests because WebDriver throws `NoSuchElementException`, e.g., telling us it could not find a particular element.

Implicit VS Explicit Waits

One way to handle the synchronization issues is through a **global implicit wait timeout**.

```
WebDriver driver = new ChromeDriver();
driver.manage().timeouts().implicitlyWait(30, TimeUnit.SECONDS);
```

However, sometimes, you may need a larger wait interval. What do you do if this happens? One option is to increase the global timeout, but this will affect all existing tests. Another option is to mix implicit and explicit wait. But this is not recommended.

Here is a quote from **Jim Evans** (one of the Core Selenium contributors) on why this is not recommended.
"When you try to mix implicit and explicit waits, you've strayed into "undefined behavior". You might be able to figure out what the rules of that behavior are, but they'll be subject to change as the implementation details of the drivers change.
So don't do it. Don't mix implicit and explicit waits.
Part of the problem is that implicit waits are often (but may not always be!) implemented on the "remote" side of the WebDriver system. That means they're "baked in" to IEDriverServer.exe, chromedriver.exe, the WebDriver Firefox extension that gets installed into the anonymous Firefox profile, and the Java remote WebDriver server (selenium-server-standalone.jar). Explicit waits are implemented exclusively in the "local" language bindings. Things get much more complicated when using Remote-WebDriver, because you could be using both the local and remote sides of the system multiple times."

NOTE

To use `ExpectedConditions` in your Java tests, you need to install a Maven dependency called **selenium-support**.

Implementing Explicit Waits in Tests

We can add the following two helper methods to our test class. If we use them, WebDriver will first wait for the element to show up and then it will return it.

```
private WebElement waitAndFindElement(By by) {
    var webDriverWait = new WebDriverWait(driver, 30);
    return webDriverWait.until(ExpectedConditions.presenceOfElementLocated(by));
}

private List<WebElement> waitAndFindElements(By by)  {
    var webDriverWait = new WebDriverWait(driver, 30);
    return webDriverWait.until(ExpectedConditions.presenceOfAllElementsLocatedBy(by));
}
```

NOTE

The method's name `waitAndFindElement` is not the best since it suggests that we perform two operations, which breaks the **Single Responsibility principle**. Later, we will rename it and move it to another more appropriate class.

Our next step is to go to our tests and change all calls from `driver.findElement` to `driver.waitAndFindElement`.
Here is a short example of how the elements are found after the changes are applied.

```
var billingFirstName = waitAndFindElement(By.id("billing_first_name"));
billingFirstName.sendKeys("Anton");
var billingLastName = waitAndFindElement(By.id("billing_last_name"));
billingLastName.sendKeys("Angelov");
var billingCompany = waitAndFindElement(By.id("billing_company"));
billingCompany.sendKeys("Space Flowers");
var billingCountryWrapper = waitAndFindElement(By.id("select2-billing_country-container"));
billingCountryWrapper.click();
var billingCountryFilter = waitAndFindElement(By.className("select2-search__field"));
billingCountryFilter.sendKeys("Germany");
```

Another part of the code we can improve is the following.

```
var quantityBox = driver.findElement(By.cssSelector("[class*='input-text qty text']"));
quantityBox.clear();
Thread.sleep(500);
quantityBox.sendKeys("2");
```

```
Thread.sleep(5000);
var updateCart = driver.findElement(By.cssSelector("[value*='Update cart']"));
updateCart.click();
Thread.sleep(5000);
var totalSpan = driver.findElement(By.xpath("//*[@class='order-total']//span"));
Assert.assertEquals(totalSpan.getText(), "114.00€");
```

Do you see the hard-coded pause over the `updateCart` element? If you remove it, the explicit wait we have just implemented won't help. The test will fail with an exception stating that the web element was not clickable at this moment. We can use `WebDriverWait` class again to wait until the element is clickable. Here, we will use a delegate helper function called `ExpectedConditions.elementToBeClickable`.

```
private void waitToBeClickable(By by) {
    var webDriverWait = new WebDriverWait(driver, 30);
    webDriverWait.until(ExpectedConditions.elementToBeClickable(by));
}
```

We can add the above method just before the interaction with our update button, and everything will work like a charm. Now we can safely remove the hard-coded pause.

DRY- Do Not Repeat Yourself Principle

Treating our framework as a product and more over- treating our tests' code as production code is the key to long-term success. Adopting common software development principles and design patterns will prevent some costly maintenance. One principle is the **Don't Repeat Yourself (DRY) principle**, in which the most basic idea is to reduce long-term maintenance costs by removing all unnecessary duplication.
Shall we start DRY-ing out our tests?

```
private void login(string userName) {
    Thread.sleep(5000);
    var userNameTextField = waitAndFindElement(By.id("username"));
    userNameTextField.sendKeys(userName);
    var passwordField = waitAndFindElement(By.id("password"));
    passwordField.sendKeys(getUserPasswordFromDb(userName));
    var loginButton = waitAndFindElement(By.xpath("//button[@name='login']"));
    loginButton.click();
}

private void increaseProductQuantity() {
    var quantityBox = waitAndFindElement(By.cssSelector("[class*='input-text qty text']"));
    quantityBox.clear();
    quantityBox.sendKeys("2");
    waitToBeClickable(By.cssSelector("[value*='Update cart']"));
    var updateCart = waitAndFindElement(By.cssSelector("[value*='Update cart']"));
    updateCart.click();
```

```java
    Thread.sleep(4000);

    var totalSpan = waitAndFindElement(By.xpath("//*[@class='order-total']//span"));
    Assert.assertEquals(totalSpan.getText(), "114.00€");
}

private void applyCoupon() {
    var couponCodeTextField = waitAndFindElement(By.id("coupon_code"));
    couponCodeTextField.clear();
    couponCodeTextField.sendKeys("happybirthday");
    var applyCouponButton = waitAndFindElement(By.cssSelector("[value*='Apply coupon']"));
    applyCouponButton.click();
    Thread.sleep(5000);
    var messageAlert = waitAndFindElement(By.cssSelector("[class*='woocommerce-message']"));
    Assert.assertEquals(messageAlert.getText() , "Coupon code applied successfully.");
}

private void addRocketToShoppingCart() {
    var addToCartFalcon9 = waitAndFindElement(By.cssSelector("[data-product_id*='28']"));
    addToCartFalcon9.click();
    var viewCartButton = waitAndFindElement(By.cssSelector("[class*='added_to_cart wc-
forward']"));
    viewCartButton.click();
}
```

I have created separate methods for some actions that appeared more than once in our three tests, such as adding the rocket to the cart, applying the discount coupon, increasing product quantity and logging-in. Here is how our second test looks like after the changes:

```java
@Test(priority=2)
public void completePurchaseSuccessfully_whenExistingClient() {
  driver.goToUrl("http://demos.bellatrix.solutions/");
  addRocketToShoppingCart();
  applyCoupon();
  increaseProductQuantity();
  var proceedToCheckout = waitAndFindElement(By.cssSelector("[class*='checkout-button button
alt wc-forward']"));
  proceedToCheckout.click();
  var loginHereLink = waitAndFindElement(By.linkText("Click here to login"));
  loginHereLink.click();
  login(_purchaseEmail);
  var placeOrderButton = waitAndFindElement(By.id("place_order"));
  placeOrderButton.click();
  Thread.sleep(10000);

  var receivedMessage = waitAndFindElement(By.xpath("//h1"));
  Assert.assertEquals(receivedMessage.getText(), "Order received");

  var orderNumber = waitAndFindElement(By.xpath("//*[@id='post-7']//li[1]/strong"));
  purchaseOrderNumber = orderNumber.getText();
}
```

As you can see, we have removed all copy-pasted segments and most hard-coded pauses. We have left a few so we can handle the asynchronous requests on the web page. We will review later how to manage them more appropriately and delete the pauses.

Decorator Design Pattern for Fixing WebDriver Unstable Actions

The next logical step in stabilizing our tests is to make sure that all our improvements will be used in all future tests. We can do that by wrapping the WebDriver enhancements in new classes. We will use the **Decorator design pattern**. It allows us to attach additional responsibilities to an object dynamically easily.

Definition:

It attaches additional responsibilities to an object dynamically. Decorators provide a flexible alternative to subclassing for extending functionality.

- You can wrap a component with several decorators.
- You can change the behavior of its component by adding new functionality before and/or after the component method is called.
- The decorator class mirrors the type of component it decorates.
- Provides an alternative to subclassing for extending behavior.

Decorator Design Pattern

Abstract UML Class Diagram

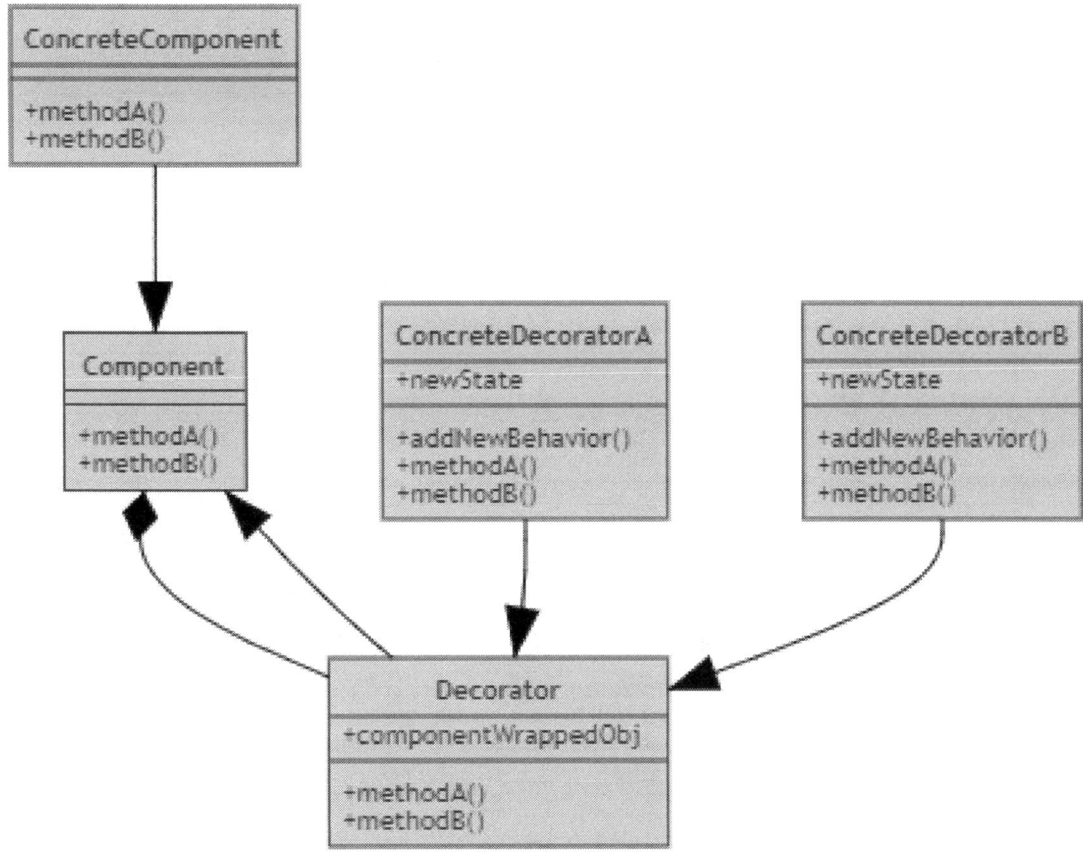

Participants

The classes and objects participating in this pattern are:

- **Component** – Defines the interface for objects that can have responsibilities added to them dynamically.
- **Decorator** – Implements the same interface (abstract class) as the component they will decorate. It has a HAS-A relationship with the object it is extending, so the **Component** has an instance variable that holds a reference to the latter.
- **ConcreteComponent** – The object that is going to be enhanced dynamically. It inherits the Component.

- **ConcreteDecorator** – Decorators can enhance the state of the component. They can add new methods. The new behavior is typically added before and/or after an existing method in the component.

Decorator Design Pattern Implementation for IWebElement

The first thing we need to do is to implement the pattern for the `IWebElement`, so we can optimize the web element's actions, such as typing or clicking. To do so:
Create the **Component** - the interface for all element objects.

```
public abstract class Element {
    public abstract By getBy();
    public abstract String getText();
    public abstract Boolean isEnabled();
    public abstract Boolean isDisplayed();
    public abstract void typeText(String text);
    public abstract void click();
    public abstract String getAttribute(String attributeName);
}
```

The next part is to create the **ConcreteComponent** from the diagram- in our case, a class called `WebCoreElement`. It derives from the abstract `Element` class.

```
public class WebCoreElement extends Element {
    private final WebDriver webDriver;
    private final WebElement webElement;
    private final By by;

    public WebCoreElement(WebDriver webDriver, WebElement webElement, By by)
    {
        this.webDriver = webDriver;
        this.webElement = webElement;
        this.by = by;
    }

    @Override
    public By getBy() {
        return by;
    }

    @Override
    public String getText() {
        return webElement.getText();
    }

    @Override
    public Boolean isEnabled() {
        return webElement.isEnabled();
    }
```

```
    @Override
    public Boolean isDisplayed() {
        return webElement.isDisplayed();
    }

    @Override
    public void typeText(String text) {
        Thread.sleep(500);
        webElement.clear();
        webElement.sendKeys(text);
    }

    @Override
    public void click() {
        waitToBeClickable(by);
        webElement.click();
    }

    @Override
    public String getAttribute(String attributeName) {
        return webElement.getAttribute(attributeName);
    }

    private void waitToBeClickable(By by)  {
        var webDriverWait = new WebDriverWait(webDriver, 30);
        webDriverWait.until(ExpectedConditions.elementToBeClickable(by));
    }
}
```

We will now emphasize a few lines of code. Look closely at the constructor of the class:

```
private final WebDriver webDriver;
private final WebElement webElement;
private final By by;

public WebCoreElement(WebDriver webDriver, WebElement webElement, By by)  {
    this.webDriver = webDriver;
    this.webElement = webElement;
    this.by = by;
}
```

One parameter it accepts is the `WebElement`, which is the component.
We use composition to have an instance of the native `WebElement`, and we keep a reference to the `By` locator.

We use it later in implementing the `Click` method, where we wait for the element to be clickable via the `WebDriverWait` class.

NOTE

Composition over inheritance (or composite reuse principle) in object-oriented programming (OOP) is the principle where classes should achieve polymorphic behavior and code reuse by their composition (by containing instances of other classes that implement the desired functionality) rather than inheritance from a base or parent class. This is especially important in programming languages like Java, where multiple class inheritance is not allowed.

Another improvement we made is to shorten the typing of text a bit.

```
@Override
public void typeText(String text) {
    Thread.sleep(500);
    webElement.clear();
    webElement.sendKeys(text);
}
```

If you return to the previous sections and look at the tests' code, you will notice that almost always, these two lines go together. If you are not proficient with the WebDriver syntax (for example, the `sendKeys` method), it may be hard for you to understand that you type text in the fields. On top of removing code duplication, using this new method will make our tests a little bit more readable.

NOTE

We will talk much more about test readability in *Chapter 4 Test Readability.*

Let’s remember what the letter O stands for in the SOLID - **Open/Closed principle** - "*software entities (classes, modules, functions, etc.) should be open for extension but closed for modification*". Imagine that we want to add logging after we perform a particular action in the `WebCoreElement` class. You can open the class and add the logic there, but we will break the principle by doing so. To implement it correctly without modifying the existing code, we will create a decorator for the element component.

```
public class ElementDecorator extends Element {
    protected final Element element;

    protected ElementDecorator(Element element) {
        Element = element;
    }

    @Override
    public By getBy() {
```

```
        return element.getBy();
    }

    @Override
    public String getText() {
        return element.getText();
    }

    @Override
    public Boolean isEnabled() {
        return element.isEnabled();
    }

    @Override
    public Boolean isDisplayed() {
        return element.isDisplayed();
    }

    @Override
    public void typeText(String text) {
        element.typeText(text);
    }

    @Override
    public void click() {
        element.click();
    }

    @Override
    public String getAttribute(String attributeName) {
        return element.getAttribute(attributeName);
    }
}
```

A few things to notice here. First, we derive from the abstract `Element` class. Next, we hold an instance of the wrapped element, and for all methods and properties, we call the methods of the wrapped element.

Now let's create our concrete decorator that will create the log entries for each action.

```
public class LogElement extends ElementDecorator {
    protected LogElement(Element element) {
        super(element);
    }

    @Override
    public By getBy() {
        return element.getBy();
    }

    @Override
    public String getText() {
        System.out.print(String.format("Element Text = %s", Element.getText()));
```

```
        return element.getText();
    }

    @Override
    public Boolean isEnabled() {
        System.out.print(String.format("Element Enabled = %b", Element.isEnabled()));
        return element.isEnabled();
    }

    @Override
    public Boolean isDisplayed() {
        System.out.print(String.format("Element Displayed = %b", Element.isDisplayed()));
        return element.isDisplayed();
    }

    @Override
    public void typeText(String text) {
        System.out.print(String.format("Type Text = = %s", text));
        element.typeText(text);
    }

    @Override
    public void click() {
        System.out.print("Element Clicked");
        element.click();
    }

    @Override
    public String getAttribute(String attributeName) {
        System.out.print("Element Clicked");
        return element.getAttribute(attributeName);
    }
}
```

As you can see, the code is similar to the one of the abstract base decorator. However, the parent class is `ElementDecorator`, and in the overridden properties and methods, we added the logging. Also, each decorator is an element object. This means we can nest an unlimited number of decorators, where each layer will add additional logic to the default element action. You will see how we will use it in the tests in a minute, but before that, we need to create a similar decorator for the `WebDriver` interface.

Decorator Design Pattern Implementation for WebDriver

Again, we first need to create the abstract component that defines the default actions.

```
public abstract class Driver {
    public abstract void start(Browser browser);
    public abstract void quit();
    public abstract void goToUrl(String url);
    public abstract Element findElement(By locator);
```

```
    public abstract List<Element> findElements(By locator);
}
```

> **NOTE**
>
> We will need to change `driver.navigate().to(…)` to `driver.goToUrl(…)`, which will improve the readability of our tests.

Next, we will create a class called `WebCoreDriver` that will derive from the abstract `Driver` class. We will develop a significant improvement because instead of calling the findElement method directly, we will first use the WebDriverWait class to wait for the elements to exist and then return them using the `findElement` method. Another enhancement is creating a `WebDriver` instance through a factory method called `start`, which will initialize the correct browser driver based on the `Browser` enumeration argument.

```
public enum Browser {
    CHROME,
    FIREFOX,
    EDGE,
    OPERA,
    SAFARI,
    INTERNET_EXPLORER
}
```

> **NOTE**
>
> The Simple Factory design pattern is a factory class in its simplest form (compared to Factory Method or Abstract Factory design patterns). In this creational design pattern, our class has a method that returns different types of objects based on a given input. The creational design patterns are design patterns that deal with object creation mechanisms, trying to create objects suitably. The basic form of object creation could cause design problems or added complexity to the design. Creational design patterns solve this problem by somehow controlling this object creation.

```
public class WebCoreDriver extends Driver {
    private org.openqa.selenium.WebDriver webDriver;
    private WebDriverWait webDriverWait;

    @Override
    public void start(Browser browser) {
        switch (browser)
```

```
    {
        case CHROME:
            WebDriverManager.chromedriver().setup();
            webDriver = new ChromeDriver();
            break;
        case FIREFOX:
            WebDriverManager.firefoxdriver().setup();
            webDriver = new FirefoxDriver();
            break;
        case EDGE:
            WebDriverManager.edgedriver().setup();
            webDriver = new EdgeDriver();
            break;
        case OPERA:
            WebDriverManager.operadriver().setup();
            webDriver = new OperaDriver();
            break;
        case SAFARI:
            webDriver = new SafariDriver();
            break;
        case INTERNET_EXPLORER:
            WebDriverManager.iedriver().setup();
            webDriver = new InternetExplorerDriver();
            break;
        default:
            throw new IllegalArgumentException(browser.name());
    }

    webDriverWait = new WebDriverWait(webDriver, 30);
}

@Override
public void quit() {
    webDriver.quit();
}

@Override
public void goToUrl(String url) {
    webDriver.navigate().to(url);
}

@Override
public Element findElement(By locator) {
    var nativeWebElement =
            webDriverWait.until(ExpectedConditions.presenceOfElementLocated(locator));
    Element element = new WebCoreElement(webDriver, nativeWebElement, locator);

    // If we use a log decorator.
    Element logElement = new LogElement(element);

    return logElement;
}

@Override
```

```
    public List<Element> findElements(By locator) {
        List<WebElement> nativeWebElements =

webDriverWait.until(ExpectedConditions.presenceOfAllElementsLocatedBy(locator));
        var elements = new ArrayList<Element>();
        for (WebElement nativeWebElement:nativeWebElements) {
            Element element = new WebCoreElement(webDriver, nativeWebElement, locator);
            Element logElement = new LogElement(element);
            elements.add(logElement);
        }

        return elements;
    }
}
```

Please, pay special attention to the `findElement` and `findElements` methods. First, we use `webDriverWait` to wait for the element to exist. After that, we initialize our `WebCoreElement`, and then we pass it to its decorator `LogElement`. If you create another decorator of the `Element` class later, you just need to add it here, and its behavior will be added to the other two.

How about adding a similar logging capability for the `WebCoreDriver` class, as we did with the `WebCoreElement`? To do it right, we need to implement a `DriverDecorator` class.

```
public class DriverDecorator extends Driver {
    protected final Driver driver;

    public DriverDecorator(Driver driver) {
        this.driver = driver;
    }

    @Override
    public void start(Browser browser) {
        driver.start(browser);
    }

    @Override
    public void quit() {
        driver.quit();
    }

    @Override
    public void goToUrl(String url) {
        driver.goToUrl(url);
    }

    @Override
    public Element findElement(By locator) {
        return driver.findElement(locator);
    }

    @Override
    public List<Element> findElements(By locator) {
```

```
        return driver.findElements(locator);
    }
}
```

It inherits the abstract `Driver` and holds it as a protected variable, using composition. After that, again, we override all actions and call the wrapped driver instance. Last, let us create the concrete logging decorator for our `Driver` class.

```
public class LoggingDriver extends DriverDecorator {
    public LoggingDriver(Driver driver) {
        super(driver);
    }

    @Override
    public void start(Browser browser) {
        System.out.print(String.format("start browser = %s", browser.name()));
        driver.start(browser);
    }

    @Override
    public void quit() {
        System.out.print("close browser");
        driver.quit();
    }

    @Override
    public void goToUrl(String url) {
        System.out.print(String.format("go to url = %s", url));
        driver.goToUrl(url);
    }

    @Override
    public Element findElement(By locator) {
        System.out.print("find element");
        return driver.findElement(locator);
    }

    @Override
    public List<Element> findElements(By locator) {
        System.out.print("find elements");
        return driver.findElements(locator);
    }
}
```

NOTE

The most popular feature introduced in Java 12 is the **Switch Expressions**. New switch statements are not only more compact and readable. They also remove the need for break statements. The code execution will not fall through after the first match. Another notable difference is that we can assign a switch statement directly to the variable. It was impossible previously.

```
webDriver = switch (browser) {
    case CHROME -> {
        WebDriverManager.chromedriver().setup();
        yield new ChromeDriver();
    }
    case FIREFOX -> {
        WebDriverManager.firefoxdriver().setup();
        yield new FirefoxDriver();
    }
    case EDGE -> {
        WebDriverManager.edgedriver().setup();
        yield new EdgeDriver();
    }
    case OPERA -> {
        WebDriverManager.operadriver().setup();
        yield new OperaDriver();
    }
    case SAFARI -> new SafariDriver();
    case INTERNET_EXPLORER -> {
        WebDriverManager.iedriver().setup();
        yield  new InternetExplorerDriver();
    }
    default-> {
        WebDriverManager.chromedriver().setup();
        yield new ChromeDriver();
    }
};
```

In Java 13, using `yield`, we can now effectively return values from a `switch` expression.

Decorator Design Pattern in Tests

After so much code, why not see how we will integrate our new element and driver decorators in our automated tests?

```
private Driver driver;

@BeforeMethod
public void testInit() {
    driver = new LoggingDriver(new WebCoreDriver());
    driver.start(Browser.CHROME);
}

@AfterMethod
public void testCleanup() {
    driver.quit();
}
```

```
@Test(priority=1)
public void completePurchaseSuccessfully_whenNewClient() {
    driver.goToUrl("http://demos.bellatrix.solutions/");
    var addToCartFalcon9 = driver.findElement(By.cssSelector("[data-product_id*='28']"));
    addToCartFalcon9.click();
    var viewCartButton = driver.findElement(By.cssSelector("[class*='added_to_cart wc-
forward']"));
    viewCartButton.click();

    var couponCodeTextField = driver.findElement(By.id("coupon_code"));
    couponCodeTextField.typeText("happybirthday");
    var applyCouponButton = driver.findElement(By.cssSelector("[value*='Apply coupon']"));
    applyCouponButton.click();
    Thread.sleep(4000);
    var messageAlert = driver.findElement(By.cssSelector("[class*='woocommerce-message']"));
    Assert.assertEquals(messageAlert.getText(), "Coupon code applied successfully.");

    var quantityBox = driver.findElement(By.cssSelector("[class*='input-text qty text']"));
    quantityBox.typeText("2");

    var updateCart = driver.findElement(By.cssSelector("[value*='Update cart']"));
    updateCart.click();
    Thread.sleep(4000);
    var totalSpan = driver.findElement(By.xpath("//*[@class='order-total']//span"));
    Assert.assertEquals("114.00€", totalSpan.getText());

    var proceedToCheckout = driver.findElement(By.cssSelector("[class*='checkout-button
button alt wc-forward']"));
    proceedToCheckout.click();

    var billingFirstName = driver.findElement(By.id("billing_first_name"));
    billingFirstName.typeText("Anton");
    var billingLastName = driver.findElement(By.id("billing_last_name"));
    billingLastName.typeText("Angelov");
    var billingCompany = driver.findElement(By.id("billing_company"));
    billingCompany.typeText("Space Flowers");
    var billingCountryWrapper = driver.findElement(By.id("select2-billing_country-
container"));
    billingCountryWrapper.click();
    var billingCountryFilter = driver.findElement(By.className("select2-search__field"));
    billingCountryFilter.typeText("Germany");
    var germanyOption = driver.findElement(By.xpath("//*[contains(text(),'Germany')]"));
    germanyOption.click();
    var billingAddress1 = driver.findElement(By.id("billing_address_1"));
    billingAddress1.typeText("1 Willi Brandt Avenue Tiergarten");
    var billingAddress2 = driver.findElement(By.id("billing_address_2"));
    billingAddress2.typeText("Lotzowplatz 17");
    var billingCity = driver.findElement(By.id("billing_city"));
    billingCity.typeText("Berlin");
    var billingZip = driver.findElement(By.id("billing_postcode"));
    billingZip.typeText("10115");
    var billingPhone = driver.findElement(By.id("billing_phone"));
    billingPhone.typeText("+00498888999281");
```

```
    var billingEmail = driver.findElement(By.id("billing_email"));
    billingEmail.typeText("info@berlinspaceflowers.com");

    // This pause will be removed when we introduce a logic for waiting for AJAX requests.
    Thread.sleep(5000);
    var placeOrderButton = driver.findElement(By.id("place_order"));
    placeOrderButton.click();

    Thread.sleep(10000);
    var receivedMessage =
driver.findElement(By.xpath("/html/body/div[1]/div/div/div/main/div/header/h1"));
    Assert.assertEquals(receivedMessage.getText(), "Order received");
}
```

In the `testInit` method, we create an instance of our `LoggingDriver` driver decorator - the line below invokes the `start` method to initialize a new Chrome driver instance. When we call the `findElement` method in the tests, it returns an instance of the `LogElement` class. Because of that, you have access to the `typeText` method. When you call the `click` method, the decorator waits for the element to be clickable before performing the actual click. And all of that achieved without changing the code of the tests. How cool is that?

Now that we have looked at the **Decorator design pattern**, would you like to review another essential principle?

Test Independence- Isolation Principle

The principle states that each test should be independent and self-sufficient. Any dependency on other tests or third-party services that cannot be controlled should be avoided at all costs. We get access to many benefits if we integrate the principle in developing our automated test:

- **Resilience** - developing our tests in a non-dependent way makes them more resilient if some other tests or 3rd party services fail to setup/delete the required data or leave the system in a not expected state.
- **Faster test development** - speed up the long-term maintenance and test development since we don't need to make a long analysis session, wondering what will happen if we change/delete this test.
- **Random run order** - allows us to run the tests in random order and in different subsets.
- **Parallel testing** - connected to the previous point, we can run the tests in random order, and we can run them in parallel, which cannot happen where the tests should be run in a particular order because they depend on each other to set up required data.

Refactoring Tests to Follow Test Independence- Isolation Principle

If we want to improve our three tests further, so they don't depend on each other, we can do a few things. If you run the first test that creates an order with a new user, you will notice that it will fail on the second run, stating that you cannot complete the purchase with this client unless you authenticate since you already have an account. To fix the problem, we can generate a unique email every time by using a method like the following.

```
private String generateUniqueEmail() {
    return String.format("%s@berlinspaceflowers.com", UUID.randomUUID().toString());
}
```

NOTE

UUID (Universally Unique Identifier), also known as GUID (Globally Unique Identifier), represents a 128-bit long value unique for all practical purposes. The standard representation of the UUID uses hex digits: **123e4567-e89b-12d3-a456-556642440000**

The randomUUID() method creates a version 4 UUID which is the most convenient way of creating a UUID. The UUID v4 implementation uses random numbers as the source. The Java implementation is SecureRandom – which uses an unpredictable value as the seed to generate random numbers to reduce collisions.

The newly developed method solves the problem with the first test. For the next two, instead of getting data from the other tests, they can use the data we created in the test environment. An even better approach would be to generate the data (orders and users) using internal API services before each test is run.

Summary

In this chapter, we created our first automated real-world tests. At first, we applied no complex design patterns but used directly a simple **WebDriver** syntax. However, as you saw, the tests weren't very stable, nor readable. Because of that, we refactored them by using the `WebDriverWait` class. After that, we investigated how you can reuse the improvements in future tests by incorporating them by implementing the **Decorator design pattern**. We even enhanced the test readability and API usability through the usage of the **Simple Factory design pattern**. Also, at the end of the chapter, we discussed briefly the **Test Independence-Isolation principle** and how you can apply it.
After we stabilized our tests, in the next chapter, we will further optimize them so they can be faster and less brittle. First, we will create an optimization plan to refactor the login mechanism and remove the hard-coded pauses. After that, we will investigate the **Observer design pattern** and how it can help us to optimize the browser initialization.

Questions

1. Can you describe the common problems in automated tests using the simple WebDriver syntax?
2. How would you use the `WebDriverWait` class to wait for an element to exist on a web page?
3. How would you wait for an element to be clickable?
4. Can you describe the participants in the Decorator design pattern?
5. Can you explain what is the difference between implicit and explicit wait in WebDriver?
6. Can you list the benefits of the Test Independence-Isolation principle?

Chapter 3. Strategies for Speeding-up the Tests

In the previous chapter, we created a test suite validating our e-commerce website. At first, the tests weren't very stable, but we managed to stabilize them. However, they can be further optimized, so they can even be faster and less flaky. First, we will look at how we can instrument our code to find and define various improvement points. Next, we will investigate how we can speed up the tests by refactoring the login method.

Next, we will deal with the outstanding hard-coded pauses needed for handling the asynchronous loading of various forms. After that, we will further enhance our code by creating a better solution for browser initialization. We will look into how to make our code parallelizable since this is the most powerful way to execute our tests faster. Last, we will talk about how the so-called **Black Hole Proxy** approach can be used to optimize our tests.
In the chapter after this one, we will make the test library easier to use and maintain. We will strive for the tests to be easier to read and understand.

An essential part of decreasing the effort for developing new tests is to build the test library in a way so it is easy to add new features - without breaking existing logic and tests- a.k.a. **Extensibility**.

These topics will be covered in this chapter:

- Instrumenting the Test Code to Find Possible Points for Optimization
- Optimize Authentication
- How to Wait for AJAX in tests?
- Optimize Browser Initialization- Observer Design Pattern
- Isolated Browser Initialization for Each Test
- Running Tests in Parallel
- Black Hole Proxy Approach

Instrumenting the Test Code to Find Possible Points for Optimization

Our tests should be fast, so we can integrate them in CI and find problems in our products promptly. If you remember the examples from the last chapter, even in the latest stable version of the test suite, there were many places we can further optimize. To locate possible optimization points, we will instrument our code with few statements that will measure how much time we spent performing them.

```
private Driver driver;
private static Stopwatch stopwatch;

@BeforeMethod
public void testInit() {
    stopwatch = Stopwatch.createStarted();
    driver = new LoggingDriver(new WebCoreDriver());
    driver.start(Browser.CHROME);
    System.out.printf("end browser init: %d", stopwatch.elapsed(TimeUnit.SECONDS));
}

@AfterMethod
public void testCleanup() {
    driver.quit();
    System.out.printf("afterTest: %d", stopwatch.elapsed(TimeUnit.SECONDS));
    stopwatch.stop();
}

@Test(priority=1)
public void completePurchaseSuccessfully_whenNewClient() {
    System.out.printf("start completePurchaseSuccessfully_whenNewClient: %d",
stopwatch.elapsed(TimeUnit.SECONDS));
    // test's code
    System.out.printf("end completePurchaseSuccessfully_whenNewClient: %d",
stopwatch.elapsed(TimeUnit.SECONDS));
}

@Test(priority=2)
public void completePurchaseSuccessfully_whenExistingClient() {
    System.out.printf("start completePurchaseSuccessfully_whenExistingClient: %d",
stopwatch.elapsed(TimeUnit.SECONDS));
    // test's code
    System.out.printf("end completePurchaseSuccessfully_whenExistingClient: %d",
stopwatch.elapsed(TimeUnit.SECONDS));
}
```

We use the special Java class called `Stopwatch` to measure the time between different statement executions. Through the line `System.out.printf("afterTest: %d",` `stopwatch.elapsed(TimeUnit.SECONDS));` we print to the console how many seconds have passed since the start.

After running the tests a few times, we will have a few key measurements.

The time needed to initialize a new instance of a browser was ~2 seconds. The login to the website took ~5 seconds. Also, if we sum up the seconds in the hard-coded pauses, we get 12 additional seconds. Our first test was completed in ~40 seconds. This means if we optimize the previous points, we can save from 10 to 15 seconds, or our tests can become ~25-40% faster.

Optimize Authentication

In most websites, the login is one of the most critical areas. Most tests will need to log in first to make their verifications. However, 99% don't test the login functionality but rather something different. This means we can have a test suite only for validating that our login is working well and integrating with all others, but beyond these tests, all others need not load this page every time, type the username and password, and so on. A common optimization is to authenticate on the website through the automatic creation of the authentication cookie. Usually, we call an internal web API to generate the value of the cookie, which executes the logic behind the login itself.

NOTE

There are cases where you cannot merely generate the authentication cookie. Examine how the authentication process works and try to accomplish it using API calls instead of the UI. You may need to bypass the captcha if there is one.

NOTE

Don't worry if you don't know how to implement this yourself. Just mention to your developers what you need, and they will be happy to help you to optimize your tests.

If we implement such logic for our tests, we will save ~2 seconds for each test. For 1000 tests, this will be equal to over 30 saved minutes.

How to Wait for Asynchronous Requests to Finish in Tests?

As you saw in the optimization plan, one of the biggest bottlenecks is the hard-coded pauses we use to handle the asynchronous loading of forms. How about reviewing how we can delete them and wait no longer than the time needed?

The modern method being adopted by the industry is to load web elements asynchronously. In this method, JavaScript code is processed in parallel to rendering the page content. This means even if a component is slow to respond or load, this will not freeze the rest of the page. Before this era, after a button click, the whole page was reloaded, then the test could safely execute a verification. However, thanks to AJAX, the element we need to work with may be missing from the page after the page load and show up after a few seconds, causing the check or interaction to fail. So, we need to prepare our code adequately from the very beginning.

Two of the places where we have such requests in our test cases are when applying the discount coupon and increasing the product quantity.

```
// increase product quantity
var quantityBox = driver.findElement(By.cssSelector("[class*='input-text qty text']"));
quantityBox.typeText("2");
Thread.sleep(2000);
var updateCart = driver.findElement(By.cssSelector("[value*='Update cart']"));
updateCart.click();
Thread.sleep(4000);
var totalSpan = driver.findElement(By.xpath("//*[@class='order-total']//span"));
Assert.assertEquals(totalSpan.getText() , "114.00€");

// apply coupon
var couponCodeTextField = driver.findElement(By.id("coupon_code"));
couponCodeTextField.typeText("happybirthday");
var applyCouponButton = driver.findElement(By.cssSelector("[value*='Apply coupon']"));
applyCouponButton.click();
Thread.sleep(2000);
var messageAlert = driver.findElement(By.cssSelector("[class*='woocommerce-message']"));
Assert.assertEquals(messageAlert.getText() , "Coupon code applied successfully.");
```

This is what appears on the screen when we apply the code:

Depending on the environment where our tests are being executed, this loading can stay for a few milliseconds up to a couple of seconds. However, since we used a hard-coded pause, we will always wait for this time. We need to improve our test library to handle these AJAX requests by detecting and waiting for them.

Waiting for All AJAX Requests Completion

Many JavaScript libraries ease the work with asynchronous JavaScript. One of the most popular ones is jQuery. We will use some of its methods to get the total count of the currently active async requests. `jQuery.active` returns 0 if the page is fully loaded. It will return a positive number if there are still executing requests.

WebDriver provides an API for executing JavaScript code within the current web page. It happens through the `executeScript` method. Would you like to look at a sample implementation of the `waitForAjax` method?

```
@Override
public void waitForAjax() {
    var javascriptExecutor = (JavascriptExecutor) webDriver;
    webDriverWait.until(d -> (Boolean)javascriptExecutor.executeScript("return window.jQuery
!= undefined && jQuery.active == 0"));
}
```

NOTE

The code is coupled to the jQuery library, and because of that, it won't work on websites that don't use it. Also, it must be used after the load event. Otherwise, it will throw an exception if jQuery is not defined- "Uncaught TypeError: Cannot read property 'active' of undefined."

In WebDriver, the until method in the Wait class is simply a loop that executes the contents of the code block passed to it until the code returns a true value. We ask JavaScript to return jQuery.active count. With the waitForAjax method, the exit loop condition is reached when there are 0 active AJAX requests. If the conditional returns true, all the AJAX requests have finished, and we are ready to move onto to the next step.

Now, we can simply use the waitForAjax method anywhere we need our tests to wait for async requests. We will be replacing the hard-coded sleep method added earlier, as shown here:

```
// increase product quantity
var quantityBox = driver.findElement(By.cssSelector("[class*='input-text qty text']"));
quantityBox.typeText("2");
driver.waitForAjax();
var updateCart = driver.findElement(By.cssSelector("[value*='Update cart']"));
updateCart.click();
driver.waitForAjax();
var totalSpan = driver.findElement(By.xpath("//*[@class='order-total']//span"));
Assert.assertEquals(totalSpan.getText() , "114.00€");

// apply coupon
var couponCodeTextField = driver.findElement(By.id("coupon_code"));
couponCodeTextField.typeText("happybirthday");
var applyCouponButton = driver.findElement(By.cssSelector("[value*='Apply coupon']"));
applyCouponButton.click();
driver.waitForAjax();
var messageAlert = driver.findElement(By.cssSelector("[class*='woocommerce-message']"));
Assert.assertEquals(messageAlert.getText() , "Coupon code applied successfully.");
```

We have conquered the AJAX menace. Now, it's time to move on to another way we can improve the test execution time - optimizing the browser initialization.

There is one more place where we need a more special wait logic to remove the pauses. It is just after we click the '**Proceed to checkout**' button. There we need to wait for the entire page to load. Since there aren't asynchronous requests, the WaitForAjax method won't work in this case. Therefore, we can add one more helper function to our WebCoreDriver decorator. Here is the code:

```
@Override
public void waitUntilPageLoadsCompletely() {
    var javascriptExecutor = (JavascriptExecutor) webDriver;
    webDriverWait.until(d -> javascriptExecutor.executeScript("return
document.readyState").toString().equals("complete"));
}
```

Via JavaScript, we wait for the ready state of the document to be "complete". This is how we use our completePurchaseSuccessfully_whenNewClient test:

```
var proceedToCheckout = driver.findElement(By.cssSelector("[class*='checkout-button button
alt wc-forward']"));
proceedToCheckout.click();
driver.waitUntilPageLoadsCompletely();
```

Optimize Browser Initialization- Observer Design Pattern

Looking into our optimization points list, we get to the next thing that slows down our tests. Specifically, repeating, and time-consuming browser initialization, which can take up to 2 seconds per test.

```
@BeforeMethod
public void testInit() {
    driver = new LoggingDriver(new WebCoreDriver());
    driver.start(Browser.CHROME);
}

@AfterMethod
public void testCleanup() {
    driver.quit();
}
// Tests' code starts here
```

We start and close the browser for each test. A smarter solution might be to reuse the browser - start it at the beginning of the whole test suite and close it after all tests have finished their execution. This will bring us considerable execution time improvements, but what if we still need to restart the browser before some tests? Because of that, we will need a smarter solution, where you can configure this behavior per test class or test method. For the job, we will implement the **Observer design pattern**.

Observer Design Pattern

The **Observer design pattern** defines a one-to-many relation between objects, so when one object changes its state, all dependents are automatically notified and updated.

- Strives for loosely coupled designs between objects that interact.
- Allows you to send data to many other objects in a very efficient manner.
- No modification needs to be done to the subject if you need to add new observers.
- You can add and remove observers at any time.

- The order of Observer notifications is unpredictable.

Abstract UML Class Diagram

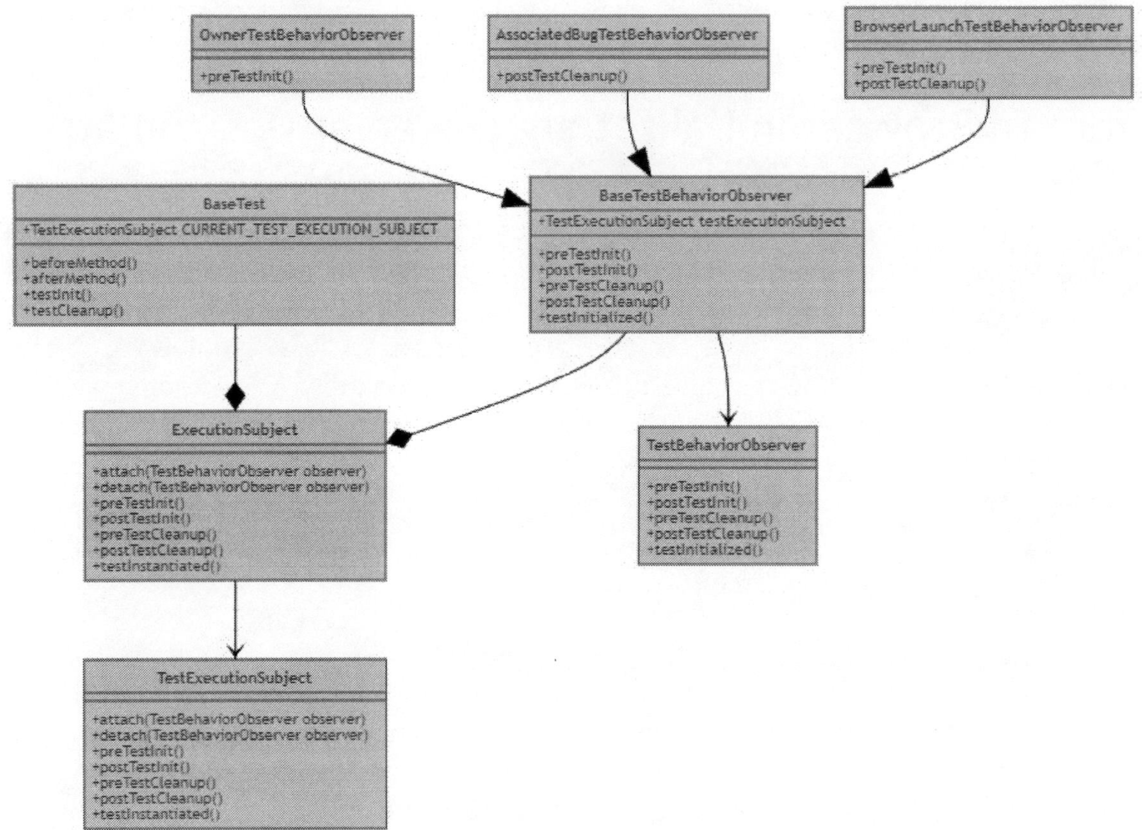

The participants in this pattern are:

- **TestExecutionSubject** - Objects use this interface to register as observers and to remove themselves from being observers.
- **ExecutionSubject** - The concrete subject always implements the `TestExecutionSubject` interface. In addition, to `attach` and `detach` methods, the specific subject implements different notification methods to update all the subscribed observers whenever the state changes.
- **TestBehaviorObserver** - All potential observers need to implement the observer interface. The methods of this interface are called at different points when the subject's state changes.

- **OwnerTestBehaviorObserver** - A concrete observer can be any class that implements `TestBehaviorObserver` interface. Each observer registers with a specific subject to receive updates.
- **BaseTest** - The parent class for all test classes in the framework. Uses the `TestExecutionSubject` to extend its test execution capabilities via test method/class level defined attributes and concrete observers.

Observer Design Pattern Implementation

We will provide an easy way for automation engineers to add additional logic to the current test execution via class/test level attributes with our implementation. For example, start and reuse the browser if the previous test hasn't failed.
The `Subject` is the object that contains the state and controls it. So, there is only one subject with a state. The observers use the state, even though they don't own it. There are many observers, and they rely on the `Subject` to tell them when its state changes. Consequently, there is a relationship between the one subject and the many observers. Why not first look at the `TestExecutionSubject` interface?

```
public interface TestExecutionSubject {
    void attach(TestBehaviorObserver observer);
    void detach(TestBehaviorObserver observer);
    void preTestInit(ITestResult result, Method memberInfo);
    void postTestInit(ITestResult result, Method memberInfo);
    void preTestCleanup(ITestResult result, Method memberInfo);
    void postTestCleanup(ITestResult result, Method memberInfo);
    void testInstantiated(Method memberInfo);
}
```

The `attach` and `detach` methods are used by the observer classes to associate themselves with the subject. The rest of the methods are invoked in the steps of the test execution workflow to notify the observers about changes in the subject's state. To notify the observers, they need to implement the `TestBehaviorObserver` interface, where all notification methods are defined.

```
public interface TestBehaviorObserver {
    void preTestInit(ITestResult testResult, Method memberInfo);
    void postTestInit(ITestResult testResult, Method memberInfo);
    void preTestCleanup(ITestResult testResult, Method memberInfo);
    void postTestCleanup(ITestResult testResult, Method memberInfo);
    void testInstantiated(Method memberInfo);
}
```

After that, a concrete subject class should be created.

```java
public class ExecutionSubject implements TestExecutionSubject {
    private final List<TestBehaviorObserver> testBehaviorObservers;

    public ExecutionSubject() {
        testBehaviorObservers = new ArrayList<>();
    }

    @Override
    public void attach(TestBehaviorObserver observer) {
        testBehaviorObservers.add(observer);
    }

    @Override
    public void detach(TestBehaviorObserver observer) {
        testBehaviorObservers.remove(observer);
    }

    @Override
    public void preTestInit(ITestResult result, Method memberInfo) {
        for (var currentObserver: testBehaviorObservers) {
            currentObserver.preTestInit(result, memberInfo);
        }
    }

    @Override
    public void postTestInit(ITestResult result, Method memberInfo) {
        for (var currentObserver: testBehaviorObservers) {
            currentObserver.postTestInit(result, memberInfo);
        }
    }

    @Override
    public void preTestCleanup(ITestResult result, Method memberInfo) {
        for (var currentObserver: testBehaviorObservers) {
            currentObserver.preTestCleanup(result, memberInfo);
        }
    }

    @Override
    public void postTestCleanup(ITestResult result, Method memberInfo) {
        for (var currentObserver: testBehaviorObservers) {
            currentObserver.postTestCleanup(result, memberInfo);
        }
    }

    @Override
    public void testInstantiated(Method memberInfo) {
        for (var currentObserver: testBehaviorObservers) {
            currentObserver.testInstantiated(memberInfo);
        }
    }
}
```

The specific subject knows nothing about the implementations of the observers. It is working with a list of `TestBehaviorObserver` objects. The `attach` and `detach` methods add and remove observers to/from the collection. In this classic implementation of the observer design pattern, the observers are responsible for associating themselves with the subject class.

Not all the observers need to implement all the notification methods. To support this requirement, we will add a base class to implement the `TestBehaviorObserver` interface.

```
public class BaseTestBehaviorObserver implements TestBehaviorObserver {
    public BaseTestBehaviorObserver(TestExecutionSubject testExecutionSubject) {
        testExecutionSubject.attach(this);
    }

    @Override
    public void preTestInit(ITestResult testResult, Method memberInfo) {
    }

    @Override
    public void postTestInit(ITestResult testResult, Method memberInfo) {
    }

    @Override
    public void preTestCleanup(ITestResult testResult, Method memberInfo) {
    }

    @Override
    public void postTestCleanup(ITestResult testResult, Method memberInfo) {
    }

    @Override
    public void testInstantiated(Method memberInfo) {
    }
}
```

As all notification methods are empty, the child class only needs to override the necessary ones. Also, the base class constructor requires a `TestExecutionSubject` parameter to associate the current observer to the subject.

Configure Browser Behavior via Attribute

Finally, we are ready to develop our solution for optimizing the browser initialization flow. Shall we review what our tests will look like if they use it?

```
@ExecutionBrowser(browser = Browser.CHROME, browserBehavior =
BrowserBehavior.RESTART_EVERY_TIME)
public class ProductPurchaseTests extends BaseTest {
    @Test(priority=1)
    public void completePurchaseSuccessfully_whenNewClient() {
        // the test's code
```

```
    }

    @Test(priority=2)
    @ExecutionBrowser(browser = Browser.FIREFOX, browserBehavior =
BrowserBehavior.REUSE_IF_STARTED)
    public void completePurchaseSuccessfully_whenExistingClient() {
       // the test's code
    }
    // the rest of the code
}
```

In the example, the new annotation is used to configure the tests to use the Chrome browser for all tests in the class. However, the test method attribute will override the value at the method level. So, before the `completePurchaseSuccessfully_whenExistingClient` test starts, the browser initialized will be Firefox—instead of Chrome.

```
@Target( { ElementType.TYPE, ElementType.METHOD } )
@Retention(RetentionPolicy.RUNTIME)
public @interface ExecutionBrowser {
    BrowserBehavior browserBehavior() default BrowserBehavior.RESTART_EVERY_TIME;
    Browser browser() default Browser.CHROME;
}
```

There is nothing special about the `ExecutionBrowser`; it only holds two getters. The first one holds the `BrowserBehavior` enum, which controls the behavior of the browser.

```
public enum BrowserBehavior {
    NOT_SET,
    REUSE_IF_STARTED,
    RESTART_EVERY_TIME,
    RESTART_ON_FAIL,
}
```

The second getter returns the browser to be started through the `Browser` enum.

The `ExecutionBrowser` annotation is configured to be available on the test class and method level through the `Target` annotation.

The browser controlling and the extraction of the attributes' information occurs in the concrete observer implementation called `BrowserLaunchTestBehaviorObserver`. It inherits our base observer `BaseTestBehaviorObserver` class.

```
public class BrowserLaunchTestBehaviorObserver extends BaseTestBehaviorObserver {
    private final Driver driver;
    private BrowserConfiguration currentBrowserConfiguration;
    private BrowserConfiguration previousBrowserConfiguration;

    public BrowserLaunchTestBehaviorObserver(TestExecutionSubject testExecutionSubject,
Driver driver) {
        super(testExecutionSubject);
```

```
        this.driver = driver;
    }

    @Override
    public void preTestInit(ITestResult testResult, Method memberInfo) {
        currentBrowserConfiguration = getBrowserConfiguration(memberInfo);

        Boolean shouldRestartBrowser = ShouldRestartBrowser(currentBrowserConfiguration);

        if (shouldRestartBrowser) {
            restartBrowser();
        }

        previousBrowserConfiguration = currentBrowserConfiguration;
    }

    @Override
    public void postTestCleanup(ITestResult testResult, Method memberInfo)  {
        if (currentBrowserConfiguration.getBrowserBehavior() ==
                BrowserBehavior.RESTART_ON_FAIL && testResult.getStatus() ==
ITestResult.FAILURE) {
            restartBrowser();
        }
    }

    private void restartBrowser() {
        driver.quit();
        driver.start(currentBrowserConfiguration.getBrowser());
    }

    private Boolean ShouldRestartBrowser(BrowserConfiguration browserConfiguration)  {
        if (previousBrowserConfiguration == null)  {
            return true;
        }

        Boolean shouldRestartBrowser =
                browserConfiguration.getBrowserBehavior() ==
BrowserBehavior.RESTART_EVERY_TIME || browserConfiguration.getBrowser() == Browser.NOT_SET;

        return shouldRestartBrowser;
    }

    private BrowserConfiguration getBrowserConfiguration(Method memberInfo)  {
        BrowserConfiguration result = null;
        var classBrowserType =
getExecutionBrowserClassLevel(memberInfo.getDeclaringClass());
        var methodBrowserType = getExecutionBrowserMethodLevel(memberInfo);
        if (methodBrowserType != null)  {
            result = methodBrowserType;
        }  else if (classBrowserType != null)  {
            result = classBrowserType;
        }

        return result;
```

```
    }

    private BrowserConfiguration getExecutionBrowserMethodLevel(Method memberInfo)  {
        var executionBrowserAnnotation =
(ExecutionBrowser)memberInfo.getDeclaredAnnotation(ExecutionBrowser.class);
        if (executionBrowserAnnotation == null)  {
            return null;
        }

        return new BrowserConfiguration(executionBrowserAnnotation.browser(),
executionBrowserAnnotation.browserBehavior());
    }

    private BrowserConfiguration getExecutionBrowserClassLevel(Class<?> type)  {
        var executionBrowserAnnotation =
(ExecutionBrowser)type.getDeclaredAnnotation(ExecutionBrowser.class);
        if (executionBrowserAnnotation == null)  {
            return null;
        }

        return new BrowserConfiguration(executionBrowserAnnotation.browser(),
executionBrowserAnnotation.browserBehavior());
    }
}
```

Many things are happening here so why not discuss them one by one? The values from the annotations are extracted via the Java Reflection API.

```
var executionBrowserAnnotation =
(ExecutionBrowser)type.getDeclaredAnnotation(ExecutionBrowser.class);
```

In the `preTestInit` and `postTestCleanup` methods, we call the method `shouldRestart` to determine whether we should restart the current browser instance.

```
private Boolean shouldRestartBrowser(BrowserConfiguration browserConfiguration)  {
    if (previousBrowserConfiguration == null)  {
        return true;
    }

    Boolean shouldRestartBrowser =
            browserConfiguration.getBrowserBehavior() == BrowserBehavior.RESTART_EVERY_TIME
|| browserConfiguration.getBrowser() == Browser.NOT_SET;

    return shouldRestartBrowser;
}
```

If the method is called for the first time the `previousBrowserConfiguration` variable is still `null`, so the method will return `true`. For the rest of the flow, we check the values of the `BrowserBehavior` enum of the current browser configuration.

Also, in the `postTestCleanup` method, we check whether the test has failed or not. If it has failed, we will restart the browser, since it may have been left in an inconsistent state.

```
@Override
public void postTestCleanup(ITestResult testResult, Method memberInfo) {
    if (currentBrowserConfiguration.getBrowserBehavior() ==
            BrowserBehavior.RESTART_ON_FAIL && testResult.getStatus() ==
ITestResult.FAILURE)  {
        restartBrowser();
    }
}
```

NOTE

Before Java 8, developers had to carefully validate values they referred to because of the possibility of throwing the `NullPointerException` (NPE). All these checks demanded an annoying and error-prone boilerplate code.
Java 8 `Optional<T>` class can help handle situations where there is a possibility of getting the NPE. It works as a container for type T. It can return a value of this object if this value is not null. When the value inside this container is null, it allows some predefined actions instead of throwing NPE.

Without `Optional<T>`:

```
private BrowserConfiguration getBrowserConfiguration(Method memberInfo) {
    BrowserConfiguration result = null;
    var classBrowserType = getExecutionBrowserClassLevel(memberInfo.getDeclaringClass());
    var methodBrowserType = getExecutionBrowserMethodLevel(memberInfo);
    if (methodBrowserType != null) {
        result = methodBrowserType;
    } else if (classBrowserType != null) {
        result = classBrowserType;
    }

    return result;
}
```

With `Optional<T>`:

```
private BrowserConfiguration getBrowserConfiguration(Method memberInfo) {
    return Optional.ofNullable(getExecutionBrowserMethodLevel(memberInfo)).
            orElse(getExecutionBrowserClassLevel(memberInfo.getDeclaringClass()));
}
```

The last part of the puzzle is to combine all these classes. This happens in the `BaseTest` class.

```
public class BaseTest {
```

```java
private static final TestExecutionSubject executionSubject;
private static final Driver driver;
private ITestResult result;

static {
    executionSubject = new ExecutionSubject();
    driver = new LoggingDriver(new WebCoreDriver());
    new BrowserLaunchTestBehaviorObserver(executionSubject, driver);
}

public String getTestName() {
    return getTestResult().getTestName();
}

public void setTestResult(ITestResult result) {
    this.result = result;
}

public ITestResult getTestResult() {
    return result;
}

public Driver getDriver() {
    return driver;
}

@AfterSuite
public void afterSuite() {
    if (driver != null) {
        driver.quit();
    }
}

@BeforeMethod
public void beforeMethod(ITestResult result) {
    setTestResult(result);
    var testClass = this.getClass();
    var methodInfo = testClass.getMethod(getTestResult().getMethod().getMethodName());
    executionSubject.preTestInit(getTestResult(), methodInfo);
    testInit();
    executionSubject.postTestInit(getTestResult(), methodInfo);
}

@AfterMethod
public void afterMethod() {
    var testClass = this.getClass();
    var methodInfo = testClass.getMethod(getTestResult().getMethod().getMethodName());
    executionSubject.preTestCleanup(getTestResult(), methodInfo);
    testCleanup();
    executionSubject.postTestCleanup(getTestResult(), methodInfo);
}

protected void testInit() {
}
```

```
    protected void testCleanup() {
    }
}
```

> **NOTE**
>
> Constant names use CONSTANT_CASE: all uppercase letters, with each word separated from the next by a single underscore. But what is a constant, exactly? I will quote the Google Java Style Guide: "Constants are static final fields whose contents are deeply immutable and whose methods have no detectable side effects. This includes primitives, Strings, immutable types, and immutable collections of immutable types. If any of the instance's observable state can change, it is not a constant." I checked many online discussions, and I would add that a final field to be a constant should be marked as public. In other cases, most probably, you intend to make the private field immutable rather than communicating to the users of your API that your class provides constants. Thus, many developers don't count private final static/non-static fields as constants, me including. Through the book, I treat these fields as standard private fields, no matter if they are marked as final, so they are named as regular private fields. There are various coding styles, and no approach is right or wrong. Feel free to use another convention if you like.
>
> You will read more about the Google Java Style Guide and other coding standards in *Chapter 4. Test Readability*.

Before the explanations of the code's logic, I want to make a note about the naming of constants. As you can see, I marked the `executionSubject` variable as `private static final`. However, it still follows the naming conventions for private variables because I don't consider it a constant.

If the test classes need to add its `BeforeMethod` or `AfterMethod` logic, they will now have to override the `testInit` and `testCleanup` methods, instead of using the `BeforeMethod` and `AfterMethod` annotations.

Three important methods are invoked in the base `beforeMethod` method. First, we invoke the `preTestInit` method of the current subject class, which must invoke `preTestInit` for each observer. After that, the `testInit` method executes or its overridden version. Finally, all observers' `postTestInit` methods are invoked through the current subject again. The same flow is valid for the cleanup methods.

```
driver = new LoggingDriver(new WebCoreDriver());
new BrowserLaunchTestBehaviorObserver(executionSubject, driver);
```

In the constructor are created the instances of all desired observers through passing them the current subject as a parameter. There we moved the creation of our `WebCoreDriver` decorator which we pass as an argument to the `BrowserLaunchTestBehaviorObserver`.

After the base constructor is executed, the `ITestResult` variable is populated from the TestNG execution engine. It is used to retrieve the currently executed test's `Method` meta information.

```
@AfterSuite
public void afterSuite() {
    if (DRIVER != null) {
        DRIVER.quit();
    }
}
```

Since all our tests may reuse the current browser, we need to make sure that we will close the browser at the end of the test run. We do that in the `afterSuite` method, executed after all tests.

NOTE

Most test frameworks contain similar methods to execute custom logic at specific points of the test execution. Another popular test framework for Java is JUnit. Its representation of TestNG's @BeforeMethod and @AfterMethod are @BeforeEach and @AfterEach. To execute code after all tests in the class, you need to annotate the method with @AfterAll. In TestNG, it is called @AfterClass.

NOTE

Through the book, I follow the naming convention to name the classes using the design pattern's name they implement. To ease the reading, I included the prefix **'Base'** for some core classes. However, in the real world, sometimes, it is smarter to provide context-specific shorter names. For example, in the open-sourced test automation framework I developed called **BELLATRIX**, I named the `BaseTest` for the web - `WebTest`, in the context of desktop - `DesktopTest`. Instead of using the long `BehaviorObserver` suffix, I use the word **'Plugin'**. `BrowserLaunchTestBehaviorObserver` is called there `BrowserLaunchPlugin`. However, as we mentioned, sometimes it is helpful to use the design pattern's names because they are universal and used as a shared dictionary between software developers. I decided that it is more important for the code to be concise and easier to read in the framework.

Isolated Browser Initialization for Each Test

There still is a problem with our new solution. You may notice it if you have run the tests. Depending on which test runs first, a weird behavior may occur. For example, suppose the tests with authentication in the website are executed first. In that case, the test with anonymous user purchases will fail since we reuse the browser and the login session. Also, because of this dependency, we broke the **Hermetic test pattern**.

One way to handle this situation is to extend our solution to clear the cache and cookies of the browser in case we reuse it - that way, we would have a clean session for each test.

First, we need to add a new method for deleting all cookies to our `WebCoreDriver` concrete component class.

```
@Override
public void deleteAllCookies() {
    webDriver.manage().deleteAllCookies();
}
```

After that we need to change the preTestInit and postTestCleanup method of the BrowserLaunchTestBehaviorObserver class.

```
@Override
public void postTestCleanup(ITestResult testResult, Method memberInfo) {
    if (currentBrowserConfiguration.getBrowserBehavior() ==
            BrowserBehavior.RESTART_ON_FAIL && testResult.getStatus() ==
ITestResult.FAILURE) {
        restartBrowser();
    }
    else {
        driver.deleteAllCookies();
    }
}
```

If we are reusing the browser, we delete all cookies, ensuring that we won't mess up with the state of the next test.

Running Tests in Parallel

Maybe the most powerful way to run your tests faster is to execute them in parallel. If we want to run the examples in parallel, we need to change the code slightly. On purpose, I haven't done that through the remaining example code snippets because it would make the code harder to comprehend. To make the tests parallelizable, we will be using the `ThreadLocal`

construct from the `java.lang` package. This gives us the ability to store data individually for the current thread – and wrap it within a particular type of object.
The core update should be done in the `BaseTest` class and `BrowserLaunchTestBehaviorObserver` classes.

```
public class BaseTest {
    private static final ThreadLocal<TestExecutionSubject> executionSubject;
    private static final ThreadLocal<Driver> driver;
    private ITestResult result;

    static {
        executionSubject = new ThreadLocal<>();
        executionSubject.set(new ExecutionSubject());
        driver = new ThreadLocal<>();
        driver.set(new LoggingDriver(new WebCoreDriver()));
        new BrowserLaunchTestBehaviorObserver(executionSubject.get(), driver.get());
    }

    public String getTestName() {
        return getTestResult().getTestName();
    }

    public void setTestResult(ITestResult result) {
        this.result = result;
    }

    public ITestResult getTestResult() {
        return result;
    }

    public Driver getDriver() {
        return driver.get();
    }

    @AfterSuite
    public void afterSuite() {
        if (driver.get() != null) {
            driver.get().quit();
        }
    }

    @BeforeMethod
    public void beforeMethod(ITestResult result) {
        setTestResult(result);
        var testClass = this.getClass();
        var methodInfo = testClass.getMethod(getTestResult().getMethod().getMethodName());
        executionSubject.get().preTestInit(getTestResult(), methodInfo);
        testInit();
        executionSubject.get().postTestInit(getTestResult(), methodInfo);
    }

    @AfterMethod
    public void afterMethod() {
```

```
        var testClass = this.getClass();
        var methodInfo = testClass.getMethod(getTestResult().getMethod().getMethodName());
        executionSubject.get().preTestCleanup(getTestResult(), methodInfo);
        testCleanup();
        executionSubject.get().postTestCleanup(getTestResult(), methodInfo);
    }

    protected void testInit() {
    }

    protected void testCleanup() {
    }
}
```

We wrap `TestExecutionSubject` and `Driver` instances in the `ThreadLocal` class. We initialize the `ThreadLocal` variables in the constructor and use the set method to add the current thread's subject and driver. To access them in the code later, we used the `ThreadLocal's` method `get`. We need to perform similar changes to the `BrowserLaunchTestBehaviorObserver` class. I will leave them to you as an exercise.

Black Hole Proxy Approach

The **Black Hole Proxy approach** tries to reduce test instability by getting rid of many third-party uncertainties. Modern websites have a lot of third-party content loaded on every page. There are social networking buttons, images coming from CDNs, tracking pixels, analytics, and much more. All these items can destabilize our tests at any point. **Black Hole Proxy** takes all HTTP requests going to third-party websites and blocks them as if the request was sucked into a black hole.

Implementing the Black Hole Proxy

Our website integrates with a couple of third-party user tracking services that collect analytics data and use others to download the fonts. We may not need to test these services in all our tests to use the **Black Hole Proxy approach** to block them.

We will be taking advantage of the HTTP proxy settings that all browsers use. Our tests will send all the HTTP traffic to a fake proxy that will swallow all the requests and send only the relevant ones.

NOTE

For Java, we will use a lightweight HTTP(S) proxy server called **BrowserMob**. You need to install the BrowserMob through the Maven dependency called **browsermob-core**. The project is open-source, and you can find the full source code on GitHub - https://bit.ly/38I4vcQ. BrowserMob Proxy allows you to manipulate HTTP requests and responses, capture HTTP content, and export performance data as a HAR file. BMP works well as a standalone proxy server.

```
public class CaptureHttpTrafficTests {
    private WebDriver driver;
    private BrowserMobProxyServer proxyServer;

    @BeforeMethod
    public void testInit() {
        WebDriverManager.chromedriver().setup();
        proxyServer = new BrowserMobProxyServer();
        proxyServer.start();

        proxyServer.enableHarCaptureTypes(CaptureType.REQUEST_CONTENT,
CaptureType.RESPONSE_CONTENT);
        proxyServer.newHar();
        String proxyDetails = "127.0.0.1:" + proxyServer.getPort();
        final Proxy proxyConfig = new Proxy().
                setHttpProxy(proxyDetails).
                setSslProxy(proxyDetails);

        final ChromeOptions options = new ChromeOptions();
        options.setProxy(proxyConfig);
        options.setAcceptInsecureCerts(true);
        driver = new ChromeDriver(options);
        driver.manage().timeouts().implicitlyWait(10, TimeUnit.SECONDS);
        proxyServer.blacklistRequests("(http(s?):)([/|.|\\w|\\s|-])*\\.(?:jpg|gif|png)",
400);
    }

    @AfterMethod
    public void testCleanup() {
        driver.quit();
        proxyServer.abort();
    }

    @Test
    public void completePurchaseSuccessfully_whenNewClient() {
        driver.navigate().to("http://demos.bellatrix.solutions/");
    }
}
```

The preceding code performs these actions:

- Before each test in the class, we start the proxy server.

- It creates an instance of the `ChromeOptions` class.
- It configures the HTTP proxy to point to a non-existing proxy on 127.0.0.1 with the port of the created proxy server.
- We connect the proxy server with the browser created through the `ChromeOptions setProxy` method.
- We configure the browser to accept insecure certificates because of the proxy through the method `setAcceptInsecureCerts`.

In the example, I configured the proxy server to block all image requests passing a special Regex expression to the `blackListrequests` method. After that, when you load a new web page through the driver's created instance, the proxy will block these requests, and we won't spend time waiting for them.

> **NOTE**
>
> A regular expression is a sequence of characters that forms a search pattern. When you search for data in a text, you can use this search pattern to describe what you are searching for. Java does not have a built-in Regular Expression class, but we can import the `java.util.regex` package to work with regular expressions.

Our tests can speed up significantly through the Black Hole Proxy pattern by not waiting for 3rd-party services to load. The tests will be more hermetically sealed by blocking the third-party requests, reducing the external dependencies that often cause test failures.

> **NOTE**
>
> The code can be further integrated into our browser initialization solution through attributes. I will leave this to you as an exercise.

Summary

In this chapter, we investigated how we can speed up our test suite. First, we started by instrumenting our code so we can list all potential optimization points. Next, I showed you how you could improve the login processes by using API calls. Next, we talked about how to handle async requests and thus eliminating all hard-coded pauses. Next, we created a comprehensive solution for browser initialization using the **Observer design pattern** to reuse the existing browser, saving a couple of seconds for each test. After that, we looked into how to make our code parallelizable. Last, we discussed the benefits of the **Black Hole Proxy approach** by blocking irrelevant for the test 3rd-party services.

In the next chapter, we will work towards making our tests easier to read and maintain. We will introduce some new design patterns and discuss how to establish high-quality code standards.

Questions

1. How would you decide which part of your code should be optimized?
2. What is the typical approach for speeding up the login process?
3. How can you use WebDriver API to handle asynchronous forms?
4. Can you list the main participants in the Observer design pattern?
5. Can you create the Observer design pattern UML diagram?
6. Which WebDriver method can be used to ensure that each test is not depending on the previous one if we reuse the browser?
7. What are the advantages of using the Black Hole Proxy approach?

Chapter 4. Test Readability

At this point, our tests are passing, we have improved their speed, removed the need for hard-coded waits. The next step is to make the test library easier to use and maintain. Also, we will strive for the tests to be easier to read and understand. An important part of decreasing the effort for developing new tests is to build the test library, so it is easy to add new features without breaking existing logic and tests - a.k.a. **Extensibility**.

First, we will discuss how to hide nitty-gritty low-level WebDriver API details in the so-called page objects. Next, we will step on this foundation and make the tests more readable through a few improvements. In the second part of the chapter, we will discuss coding standards - naming the action and assertion methods right, and variables and parameters. At the end of the section, we will discuss various tools that can help us enforce all coding guidelines we agreed to use.

These topics will be covered in this chapter:

- Page Object Model Design Pattern
- Handling Common Page Elements and Actions
- Page Object Model Design Pattern - Sections
- High Quality Code - Use Meaningful Names
- Naming the Methods, The Right Way
- Follow Coding Standards – Tools

Page Object Model Design Pattern

One of the most popular patterns in web automation is the so-called **Page Object Model design pattern**. To understand the primary goal of the pattern, first you need to think about what your web automation tests are doing. They navigate to different web pages and perform actions against various elements, right? The page object wraps all elements, actions, and validations happening on a page in a single object.

Page Object Model Design Pattern with PageFactory

Let's review how to create page object models with the WebDriver built-in factory class.

```java
public class SearchEngineMainPage {
    private final WebDriver driver;
    private final String url = " https://www.google.com/";

    public SearchEngineMainPage(WebDriver browser) {
        driver = browser;
        PageFactory.initElements(browser, this);
    }

    @FindBy(id = "sb_form_q")
    public WebElement searchBox;
    @FindBy(xpath = "//label[@for='sb_form_go']")
    public WebElement goButton;
    @FindBy(css = "b_tween")
    public WebElement resultsCountDiv;

    public void navigate() {
        driver.navigate().to(url);
    }

    public void search(String textToType) {
        searchBox.clear();
        searchBox.sendKeys(textToType);
        goButton.click();
    }
}
```

First, to locate the different web elements, we used the `FindsBy` annotation to specify the finding strategy - by id, class, xpath, etc. and then assigning the actual locator to the property used. For all the web elements to be populated on page load, you had to call the `initElements` methods of the `PageFactory` class.

NOTE

To use the built-in Page Object Pattern Factory feature of the framework, you need to install an additional Maven dependency – **selenium-support**

NOTE

It is untrue that this way of creating page object models is deprecated. Even in the .NET world, many people think it was obsolete, but this isn't true either. It was just moved to another GitHub project and NuGet package. I don't recommend using it because there are ways to precisely control how the elements are found and make the tests more readable. Even Simon Stewart, Selenium project lead and creator of the `PageFactory`, recommends against using the built-in page `PageFactory` because of the lack of Java annotations' extensibility. You can listen to his statement at the 2017 Selenium Conference here https://bit.ly/3tskxiZ, talking about PageFactory from 25:19 to 29:30.

Page Object Model Design Pattern without PageFactory

If you look closely at the previous code, you will notice you couldn't integrate `PageFactory` with the `WebDriverWait` class, so more complex scenarios can be handled. Lucky for us, we can reuse the code we have created to stabilize and optimize our shopping cart tests. Instead of using the `WebDriver` directly, we can locate the elements through our decorated version and return decorated web elements. Why not quickly recall how our tests looked without the usage of page objects?

```
@Test(priority=1)
public void completePurchaseSuccessfully_whenNewClient() {
    driver.goToUrl("http://demos.bellatrix.solutions/");
    var addToCartFalcon9 = driver.findElement(By.cssSelector("[data-product_id*='28']"));
    addToCartFalcon9.click();
    var viewCartButton = driver.findElement(By.cssSelector("[class*='added_to_cart wc-
forward']"));
    viewCartButton.click();

    var couponCodeTextField = driver.findElement(By.id("coupon_code"));
    couponCodeTextField.typeText("happybirthday");
    var applyCouponButton = driver.findElement(By.cssSelector("[value*='Apply coupon']"));
    applyCouponButton.click();
    driver.waitForAjax();
    var messageAlert = driver.findElement(By.cssSelector("[class*='woocommerce-message']"));
    Assert.assertEquals(messageAlert.getText(), "Coupon code applied successfully.");

    var quantityBox = driver.findElement(By.cssSelector("[class*='input-text qty text']"));
    quantityBox.typeText("2");
    driver.waitForAjax();

    var updateCart = driver.findElement(By.cssSelector("[value*='Update cart']"));
    updateCart.click();
    driver.waitForAjax();
    var totalSpan = driver.findElement(By.xpath("//*[@class='order-total']//span"));
    Assert.assertEquals("114.00€", totalSpan.getText());

    var proceedToCheckout = driver.findElement(By.cssSelector("[class*='checkout-button
button alt wc-forward']"));
    proceedToCheckout.click();
    driver.waitUntilPageLoadsCompletely();

    var billingFirstName = driver.findElement(By.id("billing_first_name"));
    billingFirstName.typeText("Anton");
    var billingLastName = driver.findElement(By.id("billing_last_name"));
    billingLastName.typeText("Angelov");
    var billingCompany = driver.findElement(By.id("billing_company"));
    billingCompany.typeText("Space Flowers");
```

```
    var billingCountryWrapper = driver.findElement(By.id("select2-billing_country-
container"));
    billingCountryWrapper.click();
    var billingCountryFilter = driver.findElement(By.className("select2-search__field"));
    billingCountryFilter.typeText("Germany");
    var germanyOption = driver.findElement(By.xpath("//*[contains(text(),'Germany')]"));
    germanyOption.click();
    var billingAddress1 = driver.findElement(By.id("billing_address_1"));
    billingAddress1.typeText("1 Willi Brandt Avenue Tiergarten");
    var billingAddress2 = driver.findElement(By.id("billing_address_2"));
    billingAddress2.typeText("Lotzowplatz 17");
    var billingCity = driver.findElement(By.id("billing_city"));
    billingCity.typeText("Berlin");
    var billingZip = driver.findElement(By.id("billing_postcode"));
    billingZip.typeText("10115");
    var billingPhone = driver.findElement(By.id("billing_phone"));
    billingPhone.typeText("+00498888999281");
    var billingEmail = driver.findElement(By.id("billing_email"));
    billingEmail.typeText("info@berlinspaceflowers.com");
    driver.waitForAjax();
    var placeOrderButton = driver.findElement(By.id("place_order"));
    placeOrderButton.click();

    driver.waitForAjax();
    var receivedMessage =
driver.findElement(By.xpath("/html/body/div[1]/div/div/div/main/div/header/h1"));
    Assert.assertEquals(receivedMessage.getText(), "Order received");
}
```

To use the **Page Object Model design pattern**, we need to refactor the code and create 5 page objects for each specific page. We will develop the first two pages together, but you can download the source code and exercise yourself for the next ones.

The first page object will be a representation of the main page of our website.

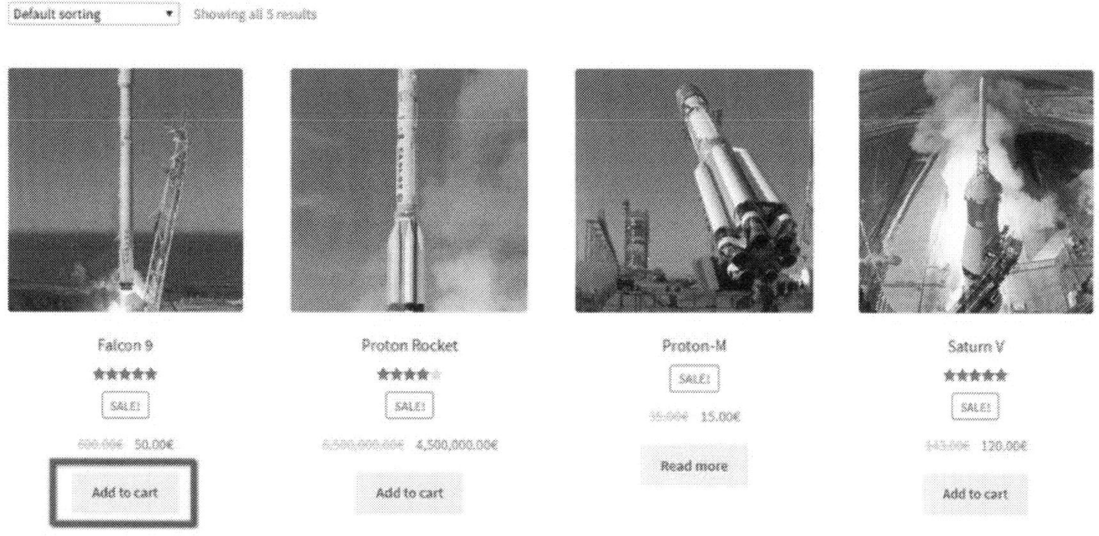

We will move all the existing code related to this page to a page object class called `MainPage`.

```
public class MainPage {
    private final Driver driver;
    private final String url = "http://demos.bellatrix.solutions/";

    public MainPage(Driver driver) {
        this.driver = driver;
    }

    private Element addToCartFalcon9() {
        return driver.findElement(By.cssSelector("[data-product_id*='28']"));
    }

    private Element viewCartButton() {
        return driver.findElement(By.cssSelector("[class*='added_to_cart wc-forward']"));
    }

    public void addRocketToShoppingCart() {
        driver.goToUrl(url);
        addToCartFalcon9().click();
        viewCartButton().click();
    }
```

```
}
```

As you can see, instead of using the `WebDriver` interface directly to locate the elements, we used the previously created improved version - the `Driver` decorator. When you call the `findElement` method, it will return the web element decorated version `Element`. Also, we moved the `addRocketToShoppingCart` private method as a publicly accessible method of our first page object.

The next page object we can create is the one representing the shopping cart page.

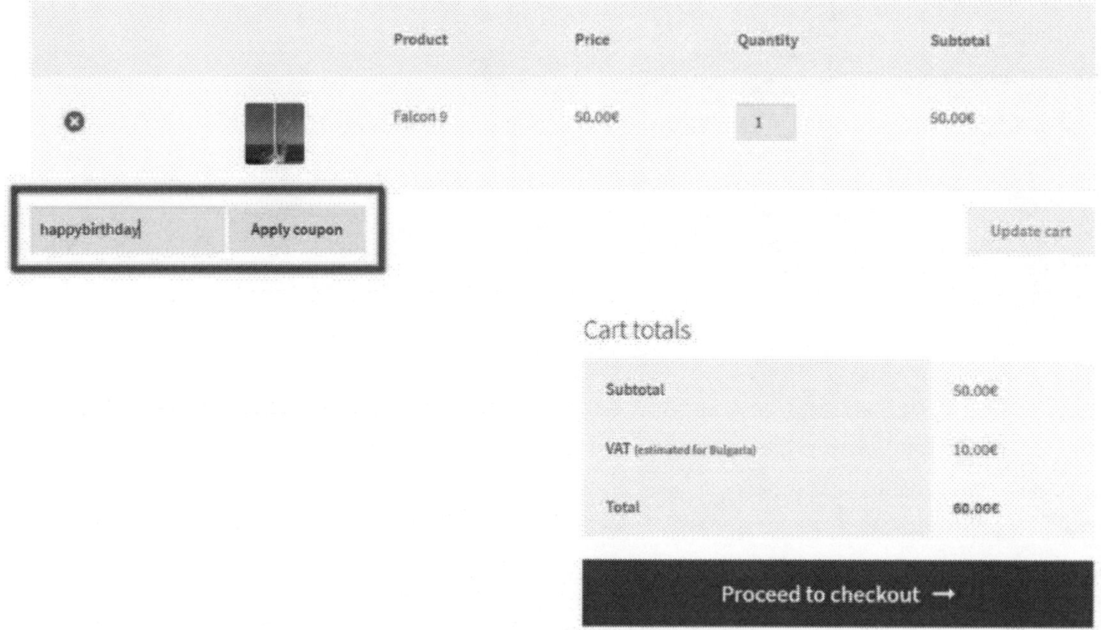

Let us implement the class `CartPage`.

```
public class CartPage {
    private final Driver driver;

    public CartPage(Driver driver) {
        this.driver = driver;
    }

    public void applyCoupon(String coupon) {
        couponCodeTextField().typeText(coupon);
        applyCouponButton().click();
        driver.waitForAjax();
```

```
    }

    public void increaseProductQuantity(int newQuantity) {
        quantityBox().typeText(String.valueOf(newQuantity));
        updateCart().click();
        driver.waitForAjax();
    }

    public void clickProceedToCheckout() {
        proceedToCheckout().click();
        driver.waitUntilPageLoadsCompletely();
    }

    public String getTotal() {
        return totalSpan().getText();
    }


    public String getMessageNotification() {
        return messageAlert().getText();
    }

    private Element couponCodeTextField() {
        return driver.findElement(By.id("coupon_code"));
    }

    private Element applyCouponButton() {
        return driver.findElement(By.cssSelector("[value*='Apply coupon']"));
    }

    private Element quantityBox() {
        return driver.findElement(By.cssSelector("[class*='input-text qty text']"));
    }

    private Element updateCart() {
        return driver.findElement(By.cssSelector("[value*='Update cart']"));
    }

    private Element messageAlert() {
        return driver.findElement(By.cssSelector("[class*='woocommerce-message']"));
    }

    private Element totalSpan() {
        return driver.findElement(By.xpath("//*[@class='order-total']//span"));
    }

    private Element proceedToCheckout() {
        return driver.findElement(By.cssSelector("[class*='checkout-button button alt wc-
forward']"));
    }
}
```

Again, all elements are represented here as private getters to not be accessed outside the page object. The page object exposes only a few public methods representing the so-called DSL, making the tests more readable. Also, I like to add the type of web elements as a suffix. This gives more context about what actions are available for the specific component. For example, it doesn't make sense to call the `typeText` method of a button or click <span> elements.

> **NOTE**
>
> I didn't completely follow the naming conventions for getters. If I did, I had to name the elements' getters – `getTotalSpan` and `getMessageAlert`. This leads to improved readability and API usability of the library. We will talk much more about enhancing API Usability in Chapter 6.
>
> **NOTE**
>
> Domain-specific languages (DSLs) are languages developed to solve problems in a specific domain, which distinguishes them from general purpose languages (GPLs). One characteristic of DSLs is they support a restricted set of concepts, limited to the domain.

Page Object Model Usage in Tests

How about reviewing how our tests can become more readable and concise if we use the page object models?

```
public class ProductPurchaseTestsWithPageObjects {
    private Driver driver;
    private static String purchaseEmail;
    private static String purchaseOrderNumber;
    private static MainPage mainPage;
    private static CartPage cartPage;

    @BeforeMethod
    public void testInit() {
        driver = new LoggingDriver(new WebCoreDriver());
        driver.start(Browser.CHROME);
        mainPage = new MainPage(driver);
        cartPage = new CartPage(driver);
    }

    @AfterMethod
    public void testCleanup() {
        driver.quit();
    }
```

```
    @Test(priority=1)
    public void completePurchaseSuccessfully_whenNewClient() {
        mainPage.addRocketToShoppingCart();
        cartPage.applyCoupon("happybirthday");

        Assert.assertEquals(cartPage.getMessageNotification(), "Coupon code applied
successfully.");

        cartPage.increaseProductQuantity(2);

        Assert.assertEquals("114.00€", cartPage.getTotal());

        cartPage.clickProceedToCheckout();

        var receivedMessage = driver.findElement(By.xpath("//h1"));
        Assert.assertEquals(receivedMessage.getText(), "Checkout");
    }
   // rest of the code
}
```

We create the page objects during the class initialize phase, and we can use them directly in our tests. As you can see, their usage has improved the readability of our tests significantly. All the low-level WebDriver details and finding of web elements are hidden from us. Moreover, the maintainability is also improved significantly, since if some locators change over time, we can go directly in the page object and change it in a single place.

We can apply the same technique for the rest of the tests, so I encourage you to download the source code and refactor the tests by creating the rest of the page objects.

Handling Common Page Elements and Actions

As you will see, maintainability and readability are closely related. With the upcoming changes to our tests, we will make them easier to maintain and read simultaneously. Why not start by understanding the common page elements?

Defining Common Page Elements

In the first implemented version of the **Page Object Model design pattern**, we grouped the elements and actions based on the physical web pages, e.g. home page, cart page, billing page, etc. However, there are many parts of the pages where certain elements are repeated with the same HTML markup and functionality they provide. Let us look closely at our shop's home page.

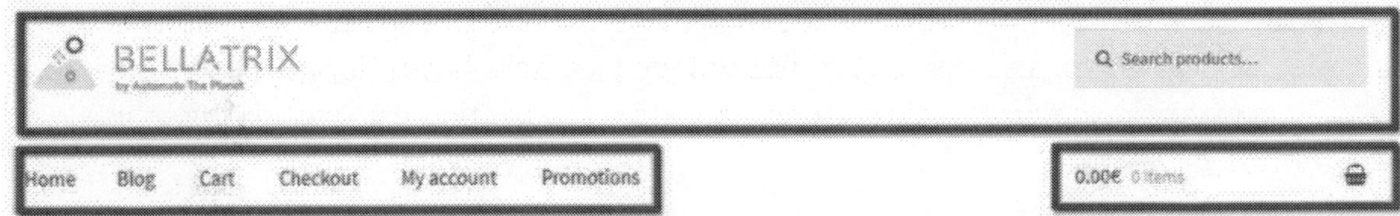

Shop

The first such group is the logo and the search bar. The next one is the main navigation. After that, the cart icon and current cart price label. We also have the unique functionality of the page related to the eshop - displaying all items that the user can purchase. Last, there is one more common section - the footer.
Why not examine our next page - the cart?

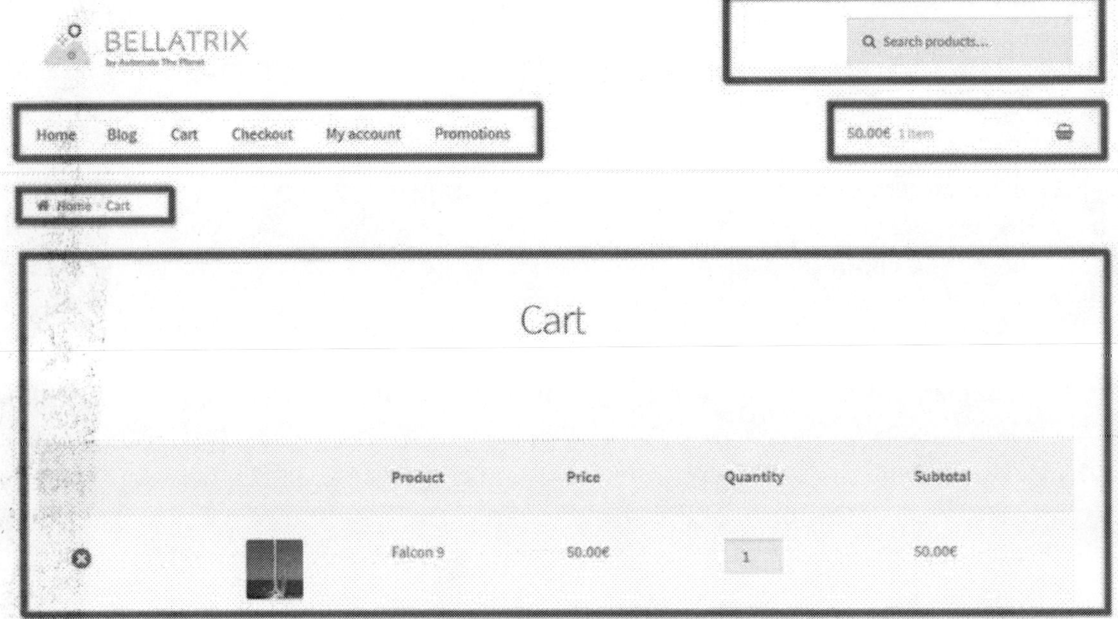

Common sections with the home page are the top section - logo and search input, the navigation, the cart info, and the footer. The unique part here is positioned below the cart title; that is one new section that is common only to this and following cart pages - the breadcrumb.

After we analyzed the sections of our page, we found that some are shared between many pages. We can allow the users to use the search on the pages or click on the menu with the current design of our page objects. This means we will have a duplicated logic between our pages, which is in most cases a bad practice since with each copied code the maintainability costs rise. The pages will do more than one thing, so we won't follow the **Single Responsibility Principle** discussed in chapter one.

> **NOTE**
>
> **DRY- Do Not Repeat Yourself Principle** - A well-implemented and Page Objects library has only one way to accomplish any action. This prevents duplicate implementation of the same `searchItem` or `fillBillingInfo` methods.

Non-DRY Page Objects

To ease the comparison, we will review what the first two page objects will look like if we just transfer all elements and logic available on the pages.

```
public class MainPage {
    private final Driver driver;
    private final String url = "http://demos.bellatrix.solutions/";

    public MainPage(Driver driver) {
        this.driver = driver;
    }

    private Element addToCartFalcon9() {
        return driver.findElement(By.cssSelector("[data-product_id*='28']"));
    }

    private Element viewCartButton() {
        return driver.findElement(By.cssSelector("[class*='added_to_cart wc-forward']"));
    }

    private Element searchField() {
        return driver.findElement(By.id("woocommerce-product-search-field-0"));
    }

    private Element homeLink() {
```

```
        return driver.findElement(By.linkText("Home"));
    }

    private Element blogLink() {
        return driver.findElement(By.linkText("Blog"));
    }

    private Element cartLink() {
        return driver.findElement(By.linkText("Cart"));
    }

    private Element checkoutLink() {
        return driver.findElement(By.linkText("Checkout"));
    }

    private Element myAccountLink() {
        return driver.findElement(By.linkText("My Account"));
    }

    private Element promotionsLink() {
        return driver.findElement(By.linkText("Promotions"));
    }

    private Element cartIcon() {
        return driver.findElement(By.className("cart-contents"));
    }

    private Element cartAmount() {
        return driver.findElement(By.className("amount"));
    }
    // methods
}
```

Since the elements are marked as private, which means we need additional action methods so we can perform the desired actions, such as searching for an item or opening a specific page. Here are the methods part of the page object.

```
public void addRocketToShoppingCart() {
    driver.goToUrl(url);
    addToCartFalcon9().click();
    viewCartButton().click();
}

public void searchForItem(String searchText) {
    searchField().typeText(searchText);
}

public void openHomePage() {
    homeLink().click();
}

public void openBlogPage() {
    blogLink().click();
```

```
}

public void openMyAccountPage() {
    myAccountLink().click();
}

public void openPromotionsPage() {
    promotionsLink().click();
}

public String getCurrentAmount() {
    return cartAmount().getText();
}

public void openCart() {
    cartIcon().click();
}
```

Most common elements are part of the cart page with some additional ones such as the breadcrumb.

```
public class CartPage {
    // constructor
    private Element couponCodeTextField() {
        return driver.findElement(By.id("coupon_code"));
    }

    private Element applyCouponButton() {
        return driver.findElement(By.cssSelector("[value*='Apply coupon']"));
    }

    private Element quantityBox() {
        return driver.findElement(By.cssSelector("[class*='input-text qty text']"));
    }

    private Element updateCart() {
        return driver.findElement(By.cssSelector("[value*='Update cart']"));
    }

    private Element messageAlert() {
        return driver.findElement(By.cssSelector("[class*='woocommerce-message']"));
    }

    private Element totalSpan() {
        return driver.findElement(By.xpath("//*[@class='order-total']//span"));
    }

    private Element proceedToCheckout() {
        return driver.findElement(By.cssSelector("[class*='checkout-button button alt wc-
forward']"));
    }

    private Element searchField() {
```

```java
        return driver.findElement(By.id("woocommerce-product-search-field-0"));
    }

    private Element homeLink() {
        return driver.findElement(By.linkText("Home"));
    }

    private Element blogLink() {
        return driver.findElement(By.linkText("Blog"));
    }

    private Element cartLink() {
        return driver.findElement(By.linkText("Cart"));
    }

    private Element checkoutLink() {
        return driver.findElement(By.linkText("Checkout"));
    }

    private Element myAccountLink() {
        return driver.findElement(By.linkText("My Account"));
    }

    private Element promotionsLink() {
        return driver.findElement(By.linkText("Promotions"));
    }

    private Element cartIcon() {
        return driver.findElement(By.className("cart-contents"));
    }

    private Element cartAmount() {
        return driver.findElement(By.className("amount"));
    }

    private Element breadcrumb() {
        return driver.findElement(By.className("woocommerce-breadcrumb"));
    }
    // methods
}
```

As discussed, almost half of the page object's code is duplicated, so if we need to change the behavior, fix a locator, or something similar, we must do it in at least two places. With the next page, the effort will be tripled, and so on. I hope you see why this is not a viable solution, so shall we explore what can be done about it?

First Version of Reusing Common Elements

A simple first attempt to solve the problem is to create a base class that will hold all common elements and related actions. Let's try to follow the KISS principle, starting with something simple.

> **NOTE**
>
> KISS refers to the famous acronym "Keep it Simple, Stupid". It can also mean "Keep it Short and Simple" or "Keep it Simple and Straightforward". It is tightly connected to the DRY principle we discussed earlier. As programmers, we are sometimes tempted to think of very smart and complex solutions upfront, thinking about the future that may never come. This often leads to overly complex, hard to maintain, and understand code. So, the principle reminds us to start with the shortest and simplest solution first, and then, if it is not working for us, we can try to enhance it.

```
public abstract class BaseEShopPage {
    protected final Driver driver;

    public BaseEShopPage(Driver driver) {
        this.driver = driver;
    }

    private Element searchField() {
        return driver.findElement(By.id("woocommerce-product-search-field-0"));
    }

    private Element homeLink() {
        return driver.findElement(By.linkText("Home"));
    }

    private Element blogLink() {
        return driver.findElement(By.linkText("Blog"));
    }

    private Element cartLink() {
        return driver.findElement(By.linkText("Cart"));
    }

    private Element checkoutLink() {
        return driver.findElement(By.linkText("Checkout"));
    }

    private Element myAccountLink() {
        return driver.findElement(By.linkText("My Account"));
    }

    private Element promotionsLink() {
        return driver.findElement(By.linkText("Promotions"));
    }
```

```java
    private Element cartIcon() {
        return driver.findElement(By.className("cart-contents"));
    }

    private Element cartAmount() {
        return driver.findElement(By.className("amount"));
    }

    private Element breadcrumb() {
        return driver.findElement(By.className("woocommerce-breadcrumb"));
    }

    protected abstract String getUrl();

    public void open() {
        driver.goToUrl(getUrl());
    }

    public void searchForItem(String searchText) {
        searchField().typeText(searchText);
    }

    public void openHomePage() {
        homeLink().click();
    }

    public void openBlogPage() {
        blogLink().click();
    }

    public void openMyAccountPage() {
        myAccountLink().click();
    }

    public void openPromotionsPage() {
        promotionsLink().click();
    }

    public String getCurrentAmount() {
        return cartAmount().getText();
    }

    public void openCart() {
        cartIcon().click();
    }

    public void openBreadcrumbItem(String itemToOpen) {
        breadcrumb().findElement(By.linkText(itemToOpen)).click();
    }
}
```

You can see how much shorter the page became. The shorter it is, the easier it is to read and understand.

```
public class CartPage extends BaseEShopPage {
    public CartPage(Driver driver) {
        super(driver);
    }

    @Override
    protected String getUrl() {
        return "http://demos.bellatrix.solutions/cart/";
    }

    private Element couponCodeTextField() {
        return driver.findElement(By.id("coupon_code"));
    }

    private Element applyCouponButton() {
        return driver.findElement(By.cssSelector("[value*='Apply coupon']"));
    }

    private Element quantityBox() {
        return driver.findElement(By.cssSelector("[class*='input-text qty text']"));
    }

    private Element updateCart() {
        return driver.findElement(By.cssSelector("[value*='Update cart']"));
    }

    private Element messageAlert() {
        return driver.findElement(By.cssSelector("[class*='woocommerce-message']"));
    }

    private Element totalSpan() {
        return driver.findElement(By.xpath("//*[@class='order-total']//span"));
    }

    private Element proceedToCheckout() {
        return driver.findElement(By.cssSelector("[class*='checkout-button button alt wc-
forward']"));
    }

    public void applyCoupon(String coupon) {
        couponCodeTextField().typeText(coupon);
        applyCouponButton().click();
        driver.waitForAjax();
    }

    public void increaseProductQuantity(int newQuantity) {
        quantityBox().typeText(String.valueOf(newQuantity));
        updateCart().click();
        driver.waitForAjax();
    }

    public void clickProceedToCheckout() {
        proceedToCheckout().click();
        driver.waitUntilPageLoadsCompletely();
```

```
    }

    public String getTotal() {
        return totalSpan().getText();
    }

    public String getMessageNotification() {
        return messageAlert().getText();
    }
}
```

The cart page is twice as short compared to before. However, our simplest solution has a drawback. We moved the breadcrumb logic to the base class. Even though the breadcrumb is displayed on the cart pages, you can access it from the `MainPage` as well. This could mislead someone to use it on a page where the breadcrumb does not exist.

In the next part of the chapter, we will examine a much better approach to solve such problems.

Creating Common Page Section Page Objects

If you review the images of the pages and the code examples, you will distinct four logical groups of elements:

- Search
- Main menu
- Cart info
- Breadcrumb

Having such groups, we can create four page objects that will keep each group's elements and operations. Since they are not entire pages, I will name them with the suffix - **Section** instead of **Page**.

```
public class SearchSection {
    private final Driver driver;

    public SearchSection(Driver driver) {
        this.driver = driver;
    }

    private Element searchField() {
        return driver.findElement(By.id("woocommerce-product-search-field-0"));
    }

    public void searchForItem(String searchText) {
```

```
        searchField().typeText(searchText);
    }
}
```

The `SearchSection` includes only a single method called `searchForItem`, allowing us to search for items on the page.

The next group `MainMenuSection` consists of methods that open the pages of the website.

```
public class MainMenuSection {
    private final Driver driver;

    public MainMenuSection(Driver driver) {
        this.driver = driver;
    }

    private Element homeLink() {
        return driver.findElement(By.linkText("Home"));
    }

    private Element blogLink() {
        return driver.findElement(By.linkText("Blog"));
    }

    private Element cartLink() {
        return driver.findElement(By.linkText("Cart"));
    }

    private Element checkoutLink() {
        return driver.findElement(By.linkText("Checkout"));
    }

    private Element myAccountLink() {
        return driver.findElement(By.linkText("My Account"));
    }

    private Element promotionsLink() {
        return driver.findElement(By.linkText("Promotions"));
    }

    public void openHomePage() {
        homeLink().click();
    }

    public void openBlogPage() {
        blogLink().click();
    }

    public void openMyAccountPage() {
        myAccountLink().click();
    }

    public void openPromotionsPage() {
```

```
        promotionsLink().click();
    }
}
```

The `CartInfoSection` exposes two methods. They are:

- One for opening the cart through the cart icon
- One for getting the current cart amount

```
public class CartInfoSection {
    private final Driver driver;

    public CartInfoSection(Driver driver) {
        this.driver = driver;
    }

    private Element cartIcon() {
        return driver.findElement(By.className("cart-contents"));
    }

    private Element cartAmount() {
        return driver.findElement(By.className("amount"));
    }

    public String getCurrentAmount() {
        return cartAmount().getText();
    }

    public void openCart() {
        cartIcon().click();
    }
}
```

Last, we have the `BreadcrumbSection`, which is responsible for opening breadcrumb items.

```
public class BreadcrumbSection {
    private final Driver driver;

    public BreadcrumbSection(Driver driver) {
        this.driver = driver;
    }

    private Element breadcrumb() {
        return driver.findElement(By.className("woocommerce-breadcrumb"));
    }

    public void openBreadcrumbItem(String itemToOpen) {
        breadcrumb().findElement(By.linkText(itemToOpen)).click();
    }
}
```

After we created all common section page objects, let's see how we will integrate them into the existing page objects.

Page Sections Usage in Page Objects - Version One

The simplest way to use the sections is to add them as public getters where needed- eliminating, for now, the base classes.

```
public class MainPage {
    private final Driver driver;
    private final String url = "http://demos.bellatrix.solutions/";

    public MainPage(Driver driver) {
        this.driver = driver;
    }

    private Element addToCartFalcon9() {
        return driver.findElement(By.cssSelector("[data-product_id*='28']"));
    }

    private Element viewCartButton() {
        return driver.findElement(By.cssSelector("[class*='added_to_cart wc-forward']"));
    }

    public MainMenuSection mainMenuSection() {
        return new MainMenuSection(driver);
    }

    public CartInfoSection cartInfoSection() {
        return new CartInfoSection(driver);
    }

    public SearchSection searchSection() {
        return new SearchSection(driver);
    }

    public void addRocketToShoppingCart() {
        driver.goToUrl(url);
        addToCartFalcon9().click();
        viewCartButton().click();
    }
}
```

For the `MainPage`, I added only three sections since, as mentioned before, we shouldn't allow access to the breadcrumb from it.

```
public class CartPage {
    private final Driver driver;

    public CartPage(Driver driver) {
        this.driver = driver;
```

```
    }
   // elements' getters
    public BreadcrumbSection breadcrumbSection() {
        return new BreadcrumbSection(driver);
    }

    public MainMenuSection mainMenuSection() {
        return new MainMenuSection(driver);
    }

    public CartInfoSection cartInfoSection() {
        return new CartInfoSection(driver);
    }

    public SearchSection searchSection() {
        return new SearchSection(driver);
    }
    // methods
}
```

I did almost the same refactoring to the `CartPage`, except for the added `BreadcrumbSection`.

More or less, this version is much closer to the desired outcome. However, if you look closely, you will notice some duplicated code between the pages. The first three sections should be present on all pages. So, with each addition of a new page, I must copy these three properties and their initialization. To fix this, we will bring back the base class we created earlier.

Page Sections Usage in Page Objects - Version Two

We can move the shared sections and their initialization to a base class.

```
public abstract class BaseEShopPage {
    protected final Driver driver;

    public BaseEShopPage(Driver driver) {
        this.driver = driver;
    }

    public MainMenuSection mainMenuSection() {
        return new MainMenuSection(driver);
    }

    public CartInfoSection cartInfoSection() {
        return new CartInfoSection(driver);
    }

    public SearchSection searchSection() {
        return new SearchSection(driver);
    }

    protected abstract String getUrl();
```

```
    public void open() {
        driver.goToUrl(getUrl());
    }
}
```

Just like before, I added additional logic for navigating to the page. Moreover, the class is marked as **abstract** since we shouldn't be allowed to create an instance. The `Driver` instance is now **protected** instead of **private,** so that instead of defining **private** variables in each child page object, we will use the **protected** instance from the base class.

So, what would our pages look like if they used the base class?

```
public class MainPage extends BaseEShopPage {

    public MainPage(Driver driver) {
        super(driver);
    }

    private Element addToCartFalcon9() {
        return driver.findElement(By.cssSelector("[data-product_id*='28']"));
    }

    private Element viewCartButton() {
        return driver.findElement(By.cssSelector("[class*='added_to_cart wc-forward']"));
    }

    @Override
    protected String getUrl() {
        return "http://demos.bellatrix.solutions/";
    }

    public void addRocketToShoppingCart() {
        open();
        addToCartFalcon9().click();
        viewCartButton().click();
    }
}
```

Now, all the `MainPage` code is being reused, and it is much easier to understand, read, and maintain.

I did the same refactoring to `CartPage` as well. The only difference is that we added a public getter for the `BreadcrumbSection` since it is a unique part of the cart pages, and we didn't include it in the base class.

```
public class CartPage extends BaseEShopPage {
    public CartPage(Driver driver) {
        super(driver);
    }
```

```
    @Override
    protected String getUrl() {
        return "http://demos.bellatrix.solutions/cart/";
    }

    private Element couponCodeTextField() {
        return driver.findElement(By.id("coupon_code"));
    }

    private Element applyCouponButton() {
        return driver.findElement(By.cssSelector("[value*='Apply coupon']"));
    }

    private Element quantityBox() {
        return driver.findElement(By.cssSelector("[class*='input-text qty text']"));
    }

    private Element updateCart() {
        return driver.findElement(By.cssSelector("[value*='Update cart']"));
    }

    private Element messageAlert() {
        return driver.findElement(By.cssSelector("[class*='woocommerce-message']"));
    }

    private Element totalSpan() {
        return driver.findElement(By.xpath("//*[@class='order-total']//span"));
    }

    private Element proceedToCheckout() {
        return driver.findElement(By.cssSelector("[class*='checkout-button button alt wc-
forward']"));
    }

    public BreadcrumbSection breadcrumbSection() {
        return new BreadcrumbSection(driver);
    }
    // methods
}
```

Page Sections Usage in Tests

After so much struggle to create reusable and readable page objects through page sections, let us see how we can use them in our tests.

```
public class ProductPurchaseTestsWithPageObjects {
    private Driver driver;
    private static MainPage mainPage;
    private static CartPage cartPage;

    @BeforeMethod
    public void testInit() {
```

```java
        driver = new LoggingDriver(new WebCoreDriver());
        driver.start(Browser.CHROME);
        mainPage = new MainPage(driver);
        cartPage = new CartPage(driver);

        mainPage.open();
    }

    @AfterMethod
    public void testCleanup() {
        driver.quit();
    }

    @Test
    public void openBlogPage() {
        mainPage.mainMenuSection().openBlogPage();
        // verify page title
    }

    @Test
    public void searchForItem() {
        mainPage.searchSection().searchForItem("Falcon 9");
        // add the item to cart
    }

    @Test
    public void openCart() {
        mainPage.cartInfoSection().openCart();
        // verify items in the cart
    }
}
```

We need to use the new section getters to use their publicly exposed logic. This further improves the readability since you can assume where on the page the action will be performed.

High-Quality Code - Meaningful Names

A big part of the role of the readable code is to communicate its intent to the reader with no huge comments. In the following section, we will talk about various guidelines you can follow while naming multiple parts of your code, and by doing so, to make your code much easier to understand and comprehend.

General Naming Guidelines

Always use English. Avoid abbreviations:

- `buttonsCnt` vs `butonsCount`
- `usrLt` vs `usersList`
- `cdCrdsNums` vs `creditCardNumbers`
- `dtenRegExPtrn` vs `dateTimeEnglishRegExPattern`

Always prefer names that are meaningful to short ones. It is more critical for your names to be readable than brief. Do not use words that most users of your code won't know. Their meaning should come off the top of your head, instead of making people ask colleagues or searching in specialized dictionaries. The names should answer a couple of questions.
What does this class do?
What is the intent of this variable?
What is this variable used for?
What would this method return?

Correct

`DiscountsCalculator, buttonsCount, Math.PI, fileNames, generateInvoice`

Incorrect

`d, d8, d6, u33, HCJ, anchor3, variable, temp, tmp, temp__var, something, someValue`

Whether a name is meaningful or not depends on the context where you are using it. Let's look at a few examples below.

Correct

- `generate()` in the class `DiscountsGenerator`
- `find(String item)` in the class `ItemFinder`
- `createInvoice(Double amount)` in the class `Account`

Incorrect

- `createInvoice()` in the class `Program`
- `search(String item)` in the class `DiscountsGenerator`

Naming Classes

Class names are written in UpperCamelCase. Class names are typically nouns or noun phrases.

Do not use Hungarian notation. Do not use underscores, hyphens, or any other non-alphanumeric characters. Avoid using names that conflict with keywords such as **new**, **class** and so on.

> **NOTE**
>
> Hungarian notation is a naming convention in programming, in which the name of a variable or method indicates its intention and type—for example, `bBusy` for `Boolean` or `iSize` for `Integer`.

Do not use abbreviations or acronyms as part of the names, especially if they are not widely accepted, and even if they are, use them only when necessary—for example, `getWindow` rather than `getWin`.

Correct

```
SalesOrdersInvoiceCreator salesOrdersInvoiceCreator;
SuggestedOrdersInvoiceCreator suggestedOrdersInvoiceCreator;
```

Incorrect

```
InvoiceCreator1 creator1;
InvoiceCreator2 creator2;
```

Classes are named starting with the name of the class they are testing, and ending with Test(s) if we are talking about unit tests.

Correct: `OrderCalculatorTests`, `InvoiceCreatorTests`

Incorrect: `Orders`, `ScreenshotCapture`

With UI, system, API, and similar test classes, you can start the class's name with a short description of the context they are covering.

Correct: `ProductPurchaseWithoutPagesObjectsTests`, `SearchEngineTests`

Incorrect: `PerformSearches`, `MakeOrders`

If you create an exception class, its name should end with the suffix '`Exception`'.

Correct: `NumberFormatException`, `StaleElementException`

Incorrect: `ElementNotFound`, `StaleElement`

How long can the name be? As long as required. Do not abbreviate the names. As mentioned, opt for readability over brevity. The modern programming IDEs have features easing the work with long names.

Correct: `createOrderWithActiveCustomerViaShoppingCart`, `ClientSupportInvoiceService`
Incorrect: `createOrdActiveCustViaSC`, `CustSprInvSrvc`

Naming New Versions of Existing API

Sometimes adding new behavior to an existing class is impossible, and a new version should be created. This means that a new type should be introduced that will live with the original class. In this situation, you need to find a proper new name.

It is better to use names close to the existing API. Opt for using a suffix than a prefix to differentiate both types. Previously, we mentioned that it is not a good practice to use numbers in the class names. However, sometimes no other meaningful suffix can be used for the new API version other than just adding a numeric suffix. In such cases, it is OK to use a numeric suffix—for example, `X509Certificate` and `X509Certificate2`.

It is a good practice not to delete the old versions of the API immediately. Instead, give your users time to migrate their code to the new versions by marking the old API with the `Deprecated` annotation and explaining why the code is deprecated and what should be used instead.

Here is an example from the official WebDriver Java bindings GitHub repository.

```
/**
  * @deprecated Use {@link #implicitlyWait(Duration)}
  * Specifies the amount of time the driver should wait when searching for an element if it
is
  * not immediately present.
  * <p>
  * @param time The amount of time to wait.
  * @param unit The unit of measure for {@code time}.
  * @return A self reference.
*/
@Deprecated
Timeouts implicitlyWait(Long time, TimeUnit unit);
```

Naming the Methods - The Right Way

Another essential step in the quest for readable code is naming your methods the right way.

General Naming Guidelines

Like the classes, they should answer a specific question, in this case- "**What does this method do?**". If you cannot answer it, this usually means that the method does more than one thing and should be refactored. Since methods perform actions, their names should include **verbs** or **verb phrases.**

Correct: `findItem`, `loadPage`, `placePurchase`, `createInvoice`

Incorrect: `method1`, `doSomething`, `handleStuff`, `sampleMethod`, `somewhere`

Follow formats **[Verb], [Verb] + [Noun],[Verb] + [Adjective] + [Noun]**.

> **NOTE**
>
> The suggested "case" may vary based on which programming language you use. The examples in the book are for Java.

Correct: `generate`, `loadConfigurationFile`, `findItemByPattern`, `toString`, `printItemsList`

Incorrect: `student`, `creator`, `counter`, `black`, `mathUtilities`

Just like in other parts of the code, do not use underscores in the names of the methods. Except for the names of the tests.

Correct

```
public performActionKeys(Keyboard keyboard, String keysToSend) {
    //...
}
```

Incorrect

```
public perform_Action_Keys(Keyboard keyboard, String keysToSend) {
    //...
}
```

Using Meaningful Method Names

If you cannot answer the question "**What does this method do?**", then your method most probably has more than one purpose. Therefore, it doesn't follow the **Single Responsibility principle**. It should be refactored and divided into multiple methods.

Correct

```
int count = getCountByItemId(client, itemId);
```

Incorrect

```
getAllByItemCount(client, itemCount);
```

The rules about the length of the method names are applicable here. They should not be abbreviated and should be as long as they need to be. Otherwise, the code can become much harder to understand and comprehend.

Correct

```
loadClientSupportInvoiceService, createAnnualDiscountsReport
```

Incorrect

```
loadClnSuppInvSrvc, createMonthDiscReport
```

Best Practices for Method Parameters

Use a short list of method parameters. The more parameters you add, the harder it will be for the library's users to understand your code. If you need to pass more than 4 parameters to your method, maybe you should think about grouping them in a separate class and using it as a single parameter.

Correct

```
public void createInvoiceReport(
    LocalDate startDate,
    LocalDate endDate,
    Integer limit,
    Boolean isForExistingClients) {
     //..
}
```

Incorrect

```
public void createInvoiceReport(
    LocalDate startDate,
    LocalDateTime endDate,
    Integer limit,
    Boolean isForExistingClients,
    Boolean isForMonthlyBucket,
    Double requestedAmount,
    Double dependentClientAmount,
    Double futureCustomerDemand,
    Double upperClientLevelAmount,
    Double dependentClusterAmount) {
     //..
}
```

As method names, there is a preferable format for naming the parameters- **[Noun] or [Adjective] + [Noun]**. They should be in camelCase, and the parameter's unit should be visible from the name, as shown.

Correct: `lastName`, `reportName`, `supportTicket`, `recurringBillingOrder`, `timeInSeconds`

Incorrect: `d`, `d1`, `d2`, `generate`, `FirstName`, `first_name`, `convertFormat`

After we discussed some of the best practices for naming identifiers, methods, and parameters. In the next section, we will talk about automatically enforcing these guidelines to your code.

> **NOTE**
>
> There is one provided by Oracle called "**Code Conventions for the Java Programming Language**". You can find it here - https://bit.ly/3bRkpDL However, when you open the page, you will see the notice: "*This page is not being actively maintained. Links within the documentation may not work, and the information itself may no longer be valid. The last revision to this document was made on April 20, 1999*" I believe most of the standards are still valid, but still you can refer to newer documents.
>
> Another alternative I use often is the "**Google Java Style Guide**" - https://bit.ly/3bMyemP
>
> A third option is the "**Spring Framework Code Style**" - https://bit.ly/38DElYH

Follow Coding Standards - Tools

Depending on which programming language and programming IDE you use, the tools for enforcing coding standards may be different. Here, I will mention two of the most popular ones in the Java world, but you can find similar alternatives for all popular programming languages. Also, the way these tools work is almost identical. The examples we will review are for IntelliJ.

> **NOTE**
>
> Coding standards are guidelines, best practices, programming styles, and conventions that

developers adhere to when writing the source code for a project.

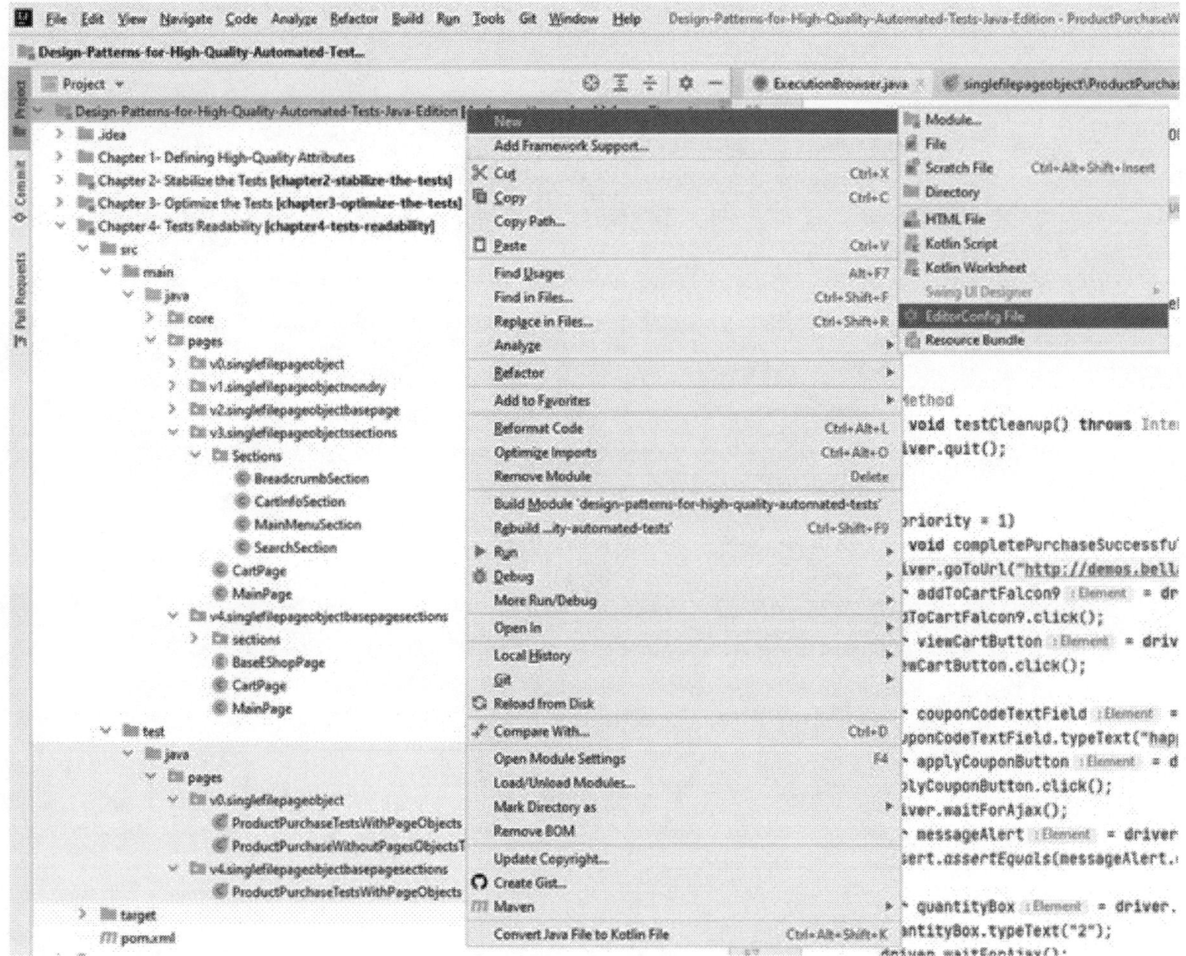

Enforcing Coding Standards Using EditorConfig

EditorConfig helps programmers to define shared coding styles between different editors. The project consists of a file format for determining coding styles that will be followed and a collection of text editor plugins that enable IDEs to read the file format. After that, warning messages are displayed if non-adherence occurs.

In the **Project** view, right-click a source directory containing the files whose code style you want to define and choose **New | EditorConfig** from the context menu. Select EditorConfig standard.

You can override the global settings through a **.editorconfig** file placed on the project level.

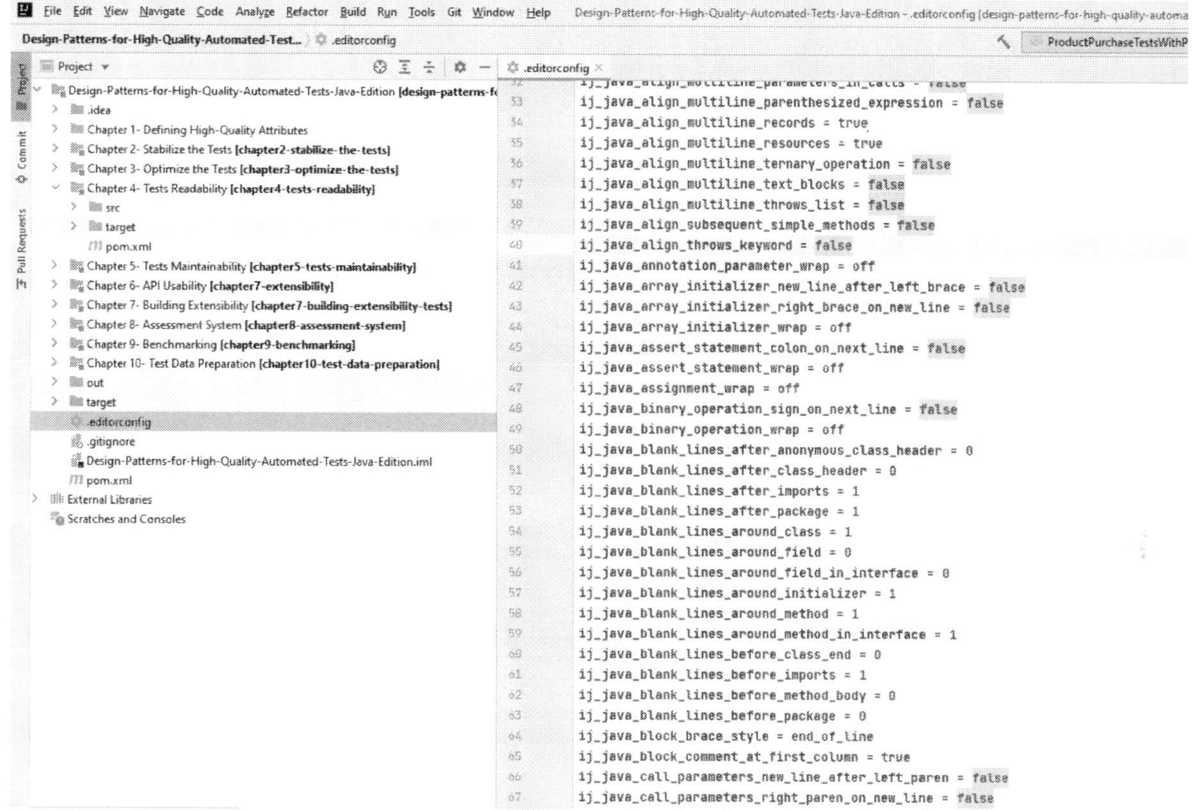

When some library users don't follow some of the defined rules, the editor displays warnings.

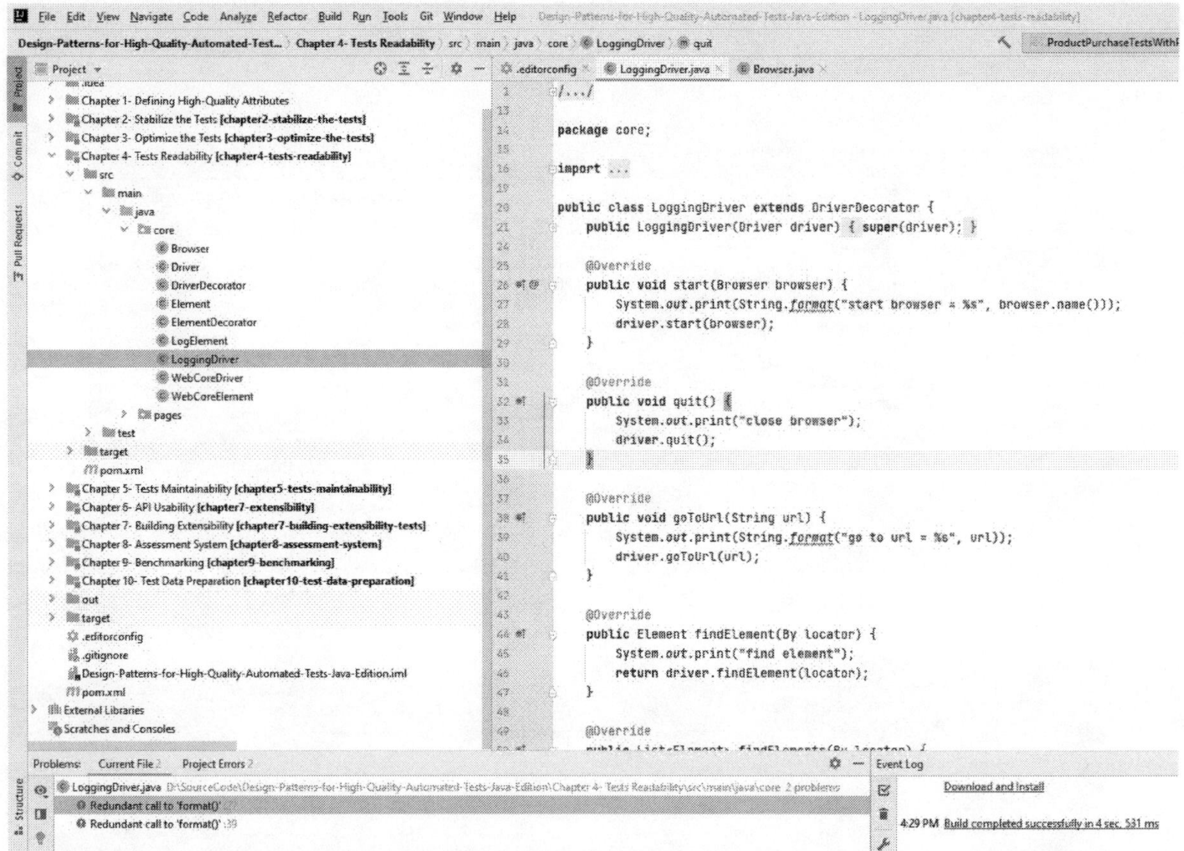

For Java projects, you can change the project's settings, so all warnings are treated as errors. By doing so, all users will be forced to fix the errors immediately instead of ignoring the warnings for years.

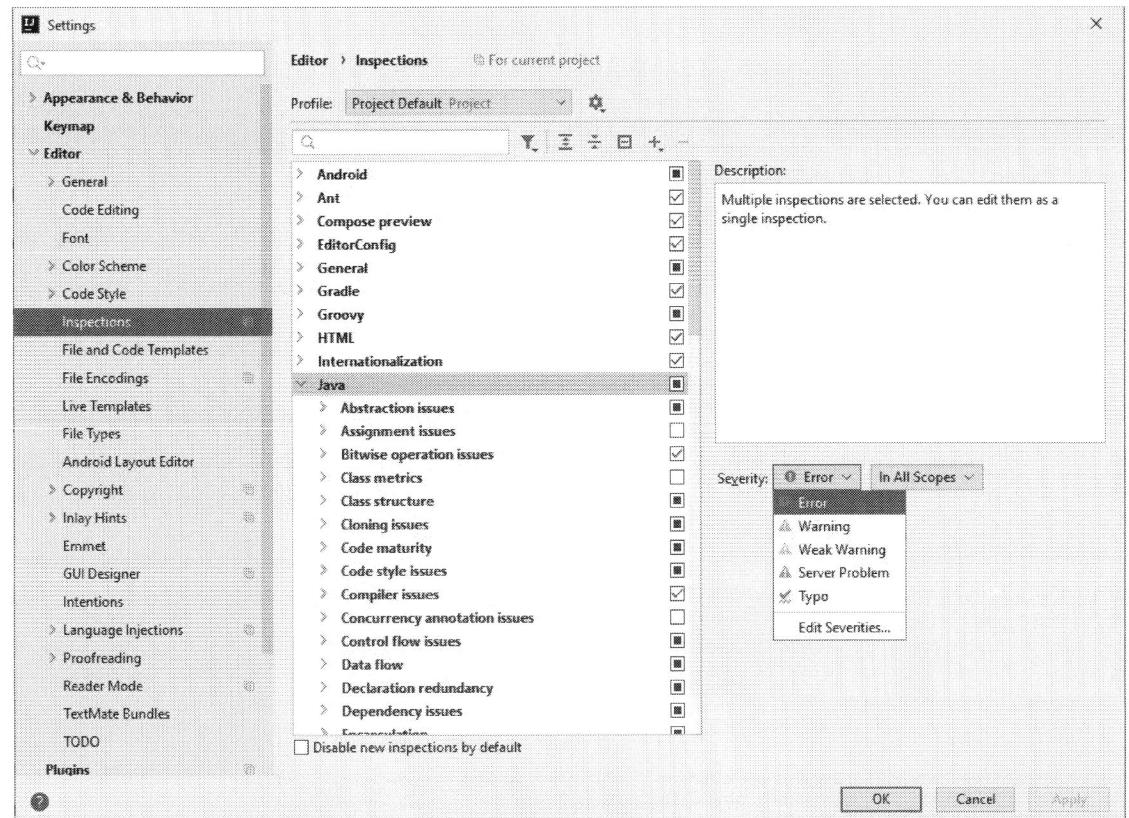

Another popular solution for applying coding standards for IntelliJ is the **CheckStyle-IDEA plug-in**.

Enforcing Coding Standards Using CheckStyle-IDEA Plug-in

This plugin provides both real-time and on-demand scanning of Java files with CheckStyle from within IDEA. Go to **File | Settings | Plugins** and search for **CheckStyle-IDEA**.

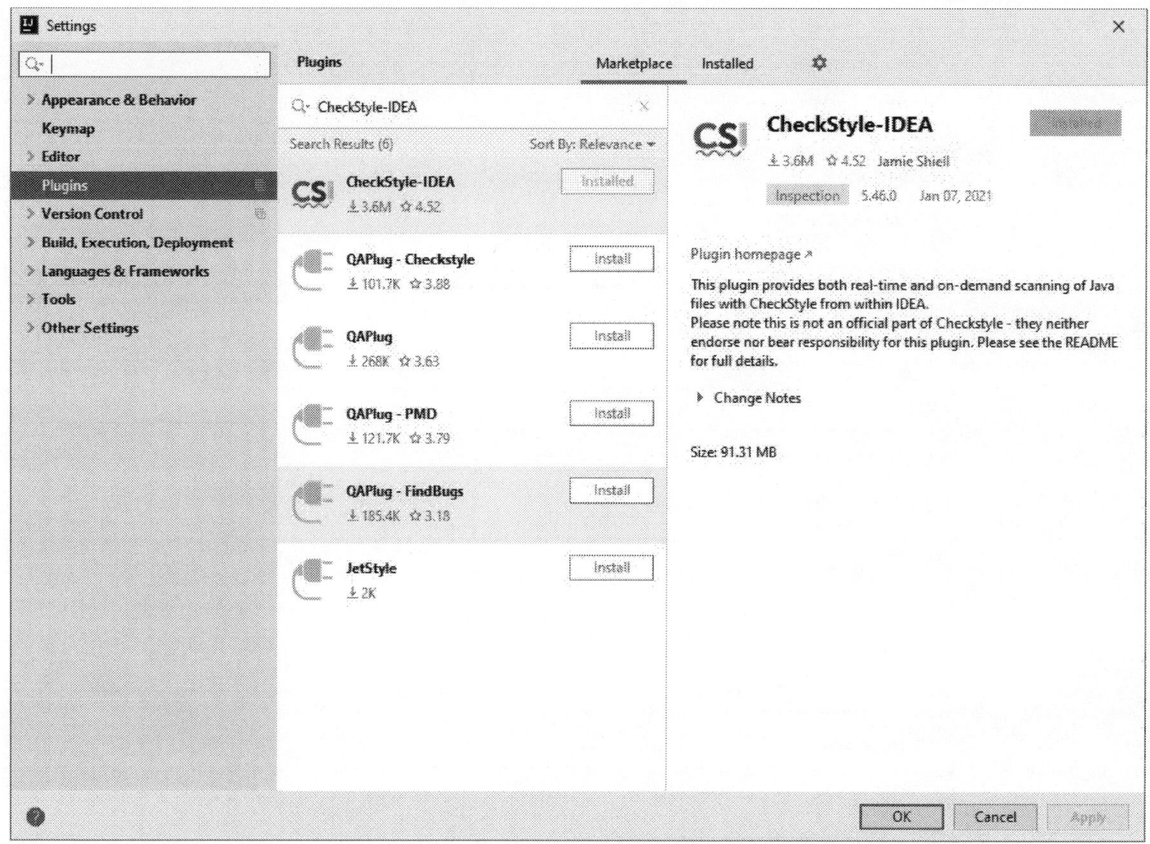

To configure the plug-in, restart IntelliJ after the installation. Go to **File | Settings | Tools | Checkstyle**. Select the desired configuration file. I suggest using the **Google Checks** one. Click **Apply**. If you want the warnings to be treated as errors, check the **'Treat Checkstyle errors as warnings'** checkbox.

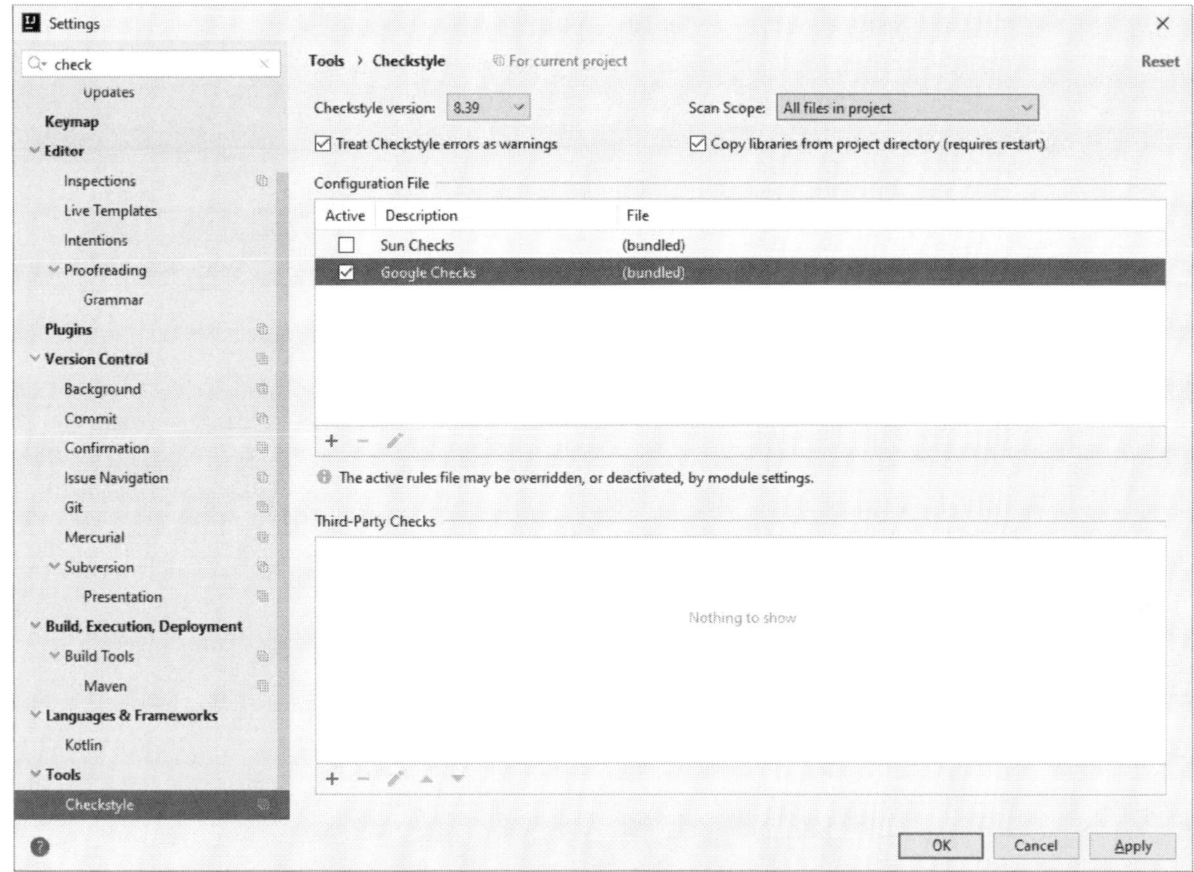

After you rebuild your projects, the new warnings will be displayed.

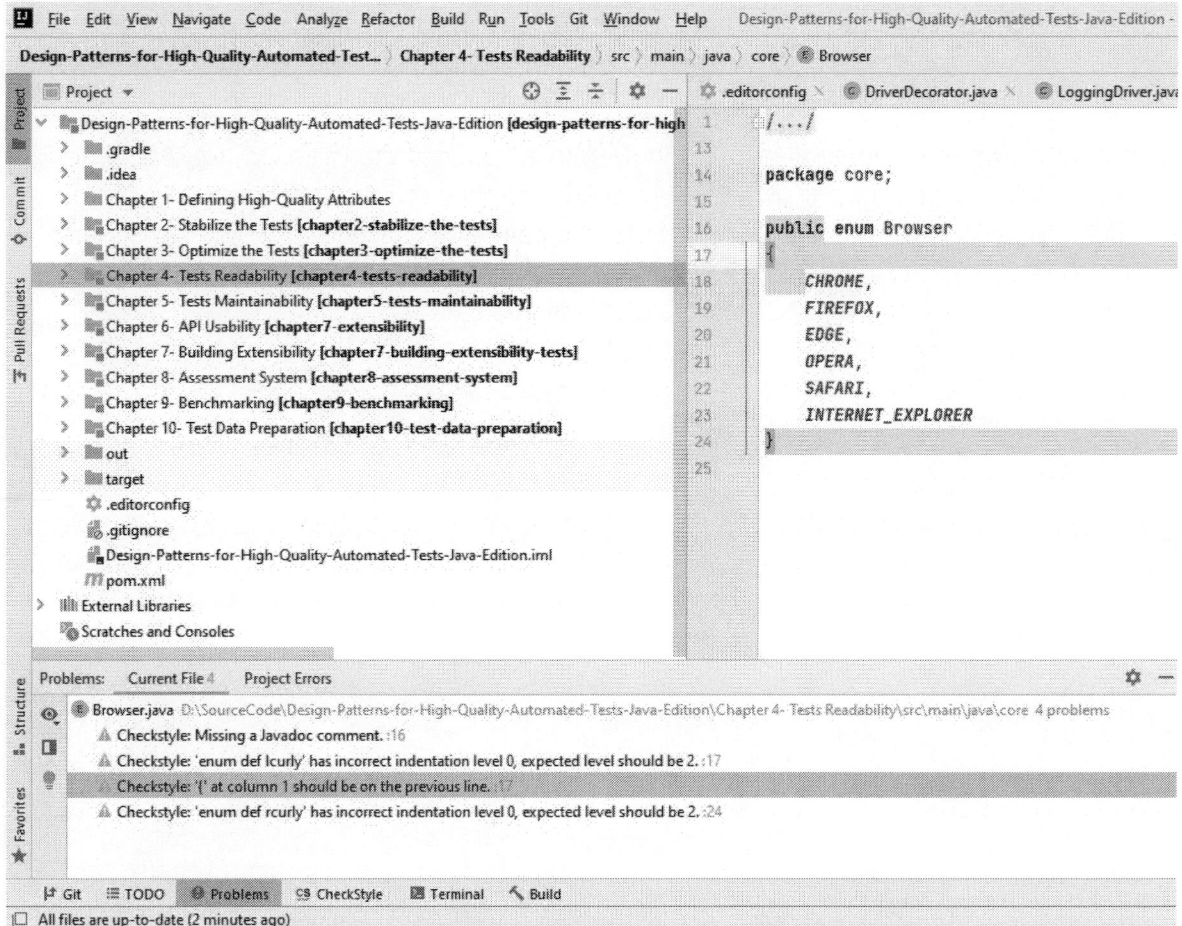
File Edit View Navigate Code Analyze Refactor Build Run Tools Git Window Help Design-Patterns-for-High-Quality-Automated-Tests-Java-Edition -
Design-Patterns-for-High-Quality-Automated-Test... Chapter 4- Tests Readability src main java core Browser
Project
.editorconfig DriverDecorator.java LoggingDriver.java
Design-Patterns-for-High-Quality-Automated-Tests-Java-Edition [design-patterns-for-high
.gradle
.idea
Chapter 1- Defining High-Quality Attributes
Chapter 2- Stabilize the Tests [chapter2-stabilize-the-tests]
Chapter 3- Optimize the Tests [chapter3-optimize-the-tests]
Chapter 4- Tests Readability [chapter4-tests-readability]
Chapter 5- Tests Maintainability [chapter5-tests-maintainability]
Chapter 6- API Usability [chapter7-extensibility]
Chapter 7- Building Extensibility [chapter7-building-extensibility-tests]
Chapter 8- Assessment System [chapter8-assessment-system]
Chapter 9- Benchmarking [chapter9-benchmarking]
Chapter 10- Test Data Preparation [chapter10-test-data-preparation]
out
target
.editorconfig
.gitignore
Design-Patterns-for-High-Quality-Automated-Tests-Java-Edition.iml
pom.xml
External Libraries
Scratches and Consoles
/.../
package core;
public enum Browser
{
CHROME,
FIREFOX,
EDGE,
OPERA,
SAFARI,
INTERNET_EXPLORER
}
Problems: Current File 4 Project Errors
Browser.java D:\SourceCode\Design-Patterns-for-High-Quality-Automated-Tests-Java-Edition\Chapter 4- Tests Readability\src\main\java\core 4 problems
Checkstyle: Missing a Javadoc comment. :16
Checkstyle: 'enum def lcurly' has incorrect indentation level 0, expected level should be 2. :17
Checkstyle: '{' at column 1 should be on the previous line. :17
Checkstyle: 'enum def rcurly' has incorrect indentation level 0, expected level should be 2. :24
Git TODO Problems CheckStyle Terminal Build
All files are up-to-date (2 minutes ago)

Summary

In this chapter, we made lots of improvements. We introduced the **Page Object Model design pattern**. Then we further improved our page objects so they can reuse and group common elements and logic. After these improvements, the page objects are more closely following the **Single Responsibility principle,** and they became much more maintainable and easier to read. In the second part of the chapter, we discussed various naming guidelines that can further improve your automated tests' readability. We reviewed some automated ways for enforcing the defined coding standards that will ensure constant quality and styling across all our projects.

In the next chapter, we will continue the topic about maintainability and reusability by further enhancing our page objects through the **Template design pattern.** We will add one more level of abstraction, so the **Single Responsibility principle** is followed more closely. We will also introduce one more design pattern to our list called **Facade design pattern** that will help us reuse common test workflows.

Questions

1. What are the primary advantages of the Page Object Model design pattern?
2. What does a page object class consist of?
3. How do you use page objects in the tests?
4. Can you define the common sections of your company's website?
5. Can you explain what composition means in the context of computer programming?
6. Why is it always much better to use sections through composition instead of inheritance?
7. What are the coding standards?
8. Why is it important to enforce them in an automated way?

Chapter 5. Enhancing the Test Maintainability and Reusability

We will see how to reuse more code among page objects through the **Template Method design pattern**. Also, we will see the 3rd type of page object, where the assertions and elements will be used as getter methods instead of coming from base classes. This will demonstrate the benefits of the composition over the inheritance principle. However, we will have a separate section discussing how we can reuse both through generics and reflection.

In the second part of the chapter, we will discuss how to reuse common test workflows through the **Facade design pattern**. We will discuss how the **Template Method design pattern** will help us test different versions of the same web page (new and old) with maximum code reuse.

These topics will be covered in this chapter:

- Navigatable Page Objects - Template Method Design Pattern
- Composition Principle for Assertions and Elements of Page Objects
- Reuse Elements and Assertions via Base Pages
- Reuse Test Workflows - Facade Design Pattern
- Test Different Page Versions - Facades Combined with Template Method Design Pattern

Navigatable Page Objects- Template Method Design Pattern

In the previous chapter, we looked at how we can reuse common elements and actions of the website in our page objects, so we don't duplicate code. We achieved it through sections, which made the tests' code more readable and easier to maintain. After that, we used a base class to hold some of the common website sections such as `Navigation` and `Search`.

We added a navigation method called `open` in the base class to help us navigate directly to our pages. There are specific web pages, such as a shopping cart process or support ticket submission. They are part of a workflow, but you cannot navigate directly even if you have the URL.

This is why we will further refactor our tests so we will have two base classes - one for pages that can be accessed directly (navigatable pages) and others that cannot.

Non-refactored Version Page Objects

Here is how our base class looks now.

```
public abstract class BaseEShopPage {
    protected final Driver driver;

    public BaseEShopPage(Driver driver) {
        this.driver = driver;
    }

    public MainMenuSection mainMenuSection() {
        return new MainMenuSection(driver);
    }

    public CartInfoSection cartInfoSection() {
        return new CartInfoSection(driver);
    }

    public SearchSection searchSection() {
        return new SearchSection(driver);
    }

    protected abstract String getUrl();

    public void open()  {
        driver.goToUrl(getUrl());
    }
}
```

This is how we use it in page objects. Since it is an abstract class, we need to implement the `Url` property to navigate to the page.

```
public class CartPage extends BaseEShopPage {
    public CartPage(Driver driver) {
        super(driver);
    }

    @Override
    protected String getUrl() {
        return "http://demos.bellatrix.solutions/cart/";
    }
    // web elements and methods
}
```

Create Separate Base Classes for Navigatable and Non-navigatable Pages

Let's create two separate base classes - one for the pages you can navigate directly and another for the ones you cannot. So why not begin with the code of the non-navigatable page? It only contains the properties providing access to the common web page sections and the driver.

```
public abstract class EShopPage {
    protected final Driver driver;

    public EShopPage(Driver driver) {
        this.driver = driver;
    }

    public MainMenuSection mainMenuSection() {
        return new MainMenuSection(driver);
    }

    public CartInfoSection cartInfoSection() {
        return new CartInfoSection(driver);
    }

    public SearchSection searchSection() {
        return new SearchSection(driver);
    }
}
```

We will now look at the navigatable base page. The only difference in this page is that it holds the logic for navigating directly to the page.

```
public abstract class NavigatableEShopPage extends EShopPage {
    public NavigatableEShopPage(Driver driver) {
        super(driver);
    }

    protected abstract String getUrl();

    public void open() {
        driver.goToUrl(getUrl());
    }
}
```

To make the tests more stable and maintainable, we can improve the `open` method. Sometimes the page opens fast, but not all elements are fully loaded. If you try to perform an action on them while still loading - an error will occur.

A standard way to handle the situation is to wait for an element, which takes the most time to load on the page, and wait for it to be visible before performing any actions. However, we cannot put this logic in the base class since each page's unique element is different. To handle this, we can use the **Template Method design pattern**.

Template Method Design Pattern

Definition: Template Method
The Template Method design pattern defines a skeleton/structure of an algorithm in a base class and then leaves its specific implementation to the child classes.

Abstract UML Class Diagram

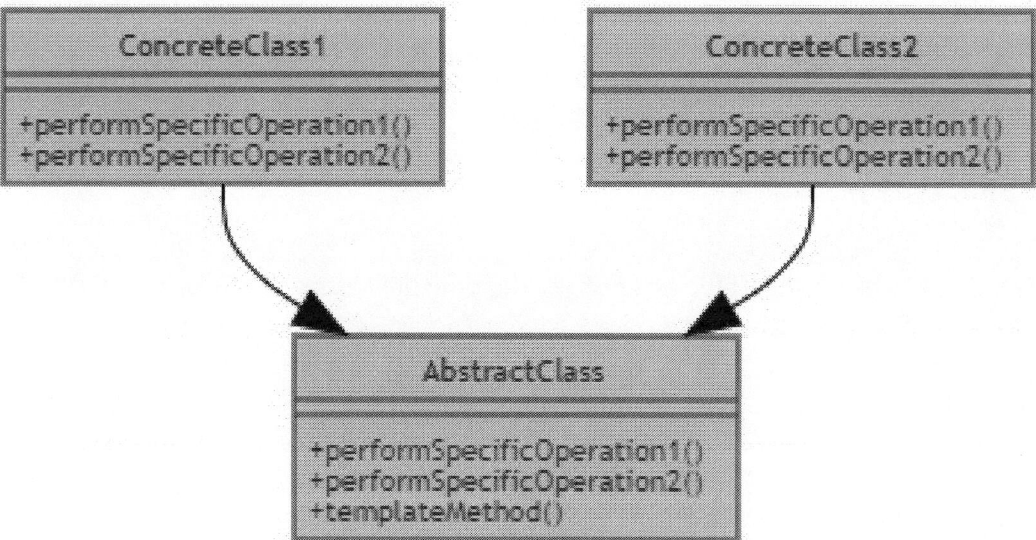

Participants

The objects participating in this pattern are:

- **Abstract Class** - defines the algorithm's structure and usually uses abstract protected methods and a public method containing the algorithm.
- **Concrete Class** - inherits the abstract class and implements the abstract methods as part of the defined algorithm.

Template Method Design Pattern Implementation

To incorporate the **Template Method design pattern**, we can include an abstract method in the navigatable page class. Its child classes can implement it and wait for their specific element to be displayed.

```
public abstract class NavigatableEShopPage extends EShopPage {
    public NavigatableEShopPage(Driver driver) {
        super(driver);
    }

    protected abstract String getUrl();

    public void open()  {
        driver.goToUrl(getUrl());
        waitForPageLoad();
    }

    protected abstract void waitForPageLoad();
}
```

The main page looks like this.

```
public class MainPage extends NavigatableEShopPage {
    public MainPage(Driver driver)  {
        super(driver);
    }

    private Element addToCartFalcon9() {
        return driver.findElement(By.cssSelector("[data-product_id*='28']"));
    }

    private Element viewCartButton() {
        return driver.findElement(By.cssSelector("[class*='added_to_cart wc-forward']"));
    }

    @Override
    protected String getUrl() {
        return "http://demos.bellatrix.solutions/";
    }

    @Override
    protected void waitForPageLoad() {
        addToCartFalcon9().waitToExists();
    }

    public void addRocketToShoppingCart()  {
        open();
        addToCartFalcon9().click();
        viewCartButton().click();
    }
}
```

We implement the abstract method `waitForPageLoad` and wait for the `addToCartFalcon9` link to be visible before doing something else. Also, we need to define the `waitToExists` method in the `Element` class and its children.

```
@Override
public void waitToExists()  {
    var webDriverWait = new WebDriverWait(webDriver, 30);
    webDriverWait.until(ExpectedConditions.presenceOfElementLocated(by));
}
```

The method is similar to the approach we used in the `findElement` and `findElements` methods. The difference is that we only wait for the element by the specified locator and not return it.

Separating the base page class into two separate classes made our tests much more maintainable. But why? The maintainability is connected with the future costs of fixing broken tests and adding new logic for automating a new website feature. The refactoring that we made will ease the addition of new logic. If we had left the previous implementation, this would mean that each time you need to change the navigation logic, you would change a single base class and affect all pages that should not be able to be opened directly. The changes helped us to follow the **Single Responsibility Principle** more closely as well.

NOTE

In real-world scenarios, you may decide to have only one base class for all page types, even if there are cases where it makes little sense to navigate to a particular page. Initially, in the framework I invented, many people gave me feedback that it is hard to orient which base class to use. My team and I combined these base classes, even if this meant violating some principles stated in the book. Sometimes, we need to sacrifice something to gain another benefit. Here, we surrendered following some of the suggested practices in the book to improve API usability and the framework users' understandability.

NOTE

Some developers relate code maintainability to the time needed to change a piece of code (meet new requirements, correct defects) or to the risk of breaking something. Code readability and coupling are tightly connected to it. Related terms are evolvability, modifiability, technical debt, and code smells. An official metric called maintainability index is calculated using lines of code measures, McCabe, and Halstead complexity measures.

Using Composition Principle

Another maintainability problem you may have spotted is that right now, our page objects are still not following the **Single Responsibility principle** precisely. They have more than one reason to change. What will happen if we need to update the element locators due to design change, figure out new page action, or add a new assertion method? We have at least three reasons to change our page class. Similar to how we handled the navigation issue, we can do something similar here.

However, we cannot create more base classes since this will be impractical, but we can use **composition**. We looked into what the **composition** was in the previous chapter when we introduced the web sections. We can use it again here to separate the actions, elements, assertions, and make our page objects much more maintainable - by giving them only a single reason to change.

Non-refactored Version Page Objects without Composition

Let us take a short look at how our pages look now without composition.

```
public class CartPage extends NavigatableEShopPage {
    public CartPage(Driver driver) {
        super(driver);
    }

    @Override
    protected String getUrl() {
        return "http://demos.bellatrix.solutions/cart/";
    }

    @Override
    protected void waitForPageLoad() {
        couponCodeTextField().waitToExists();
    }

    private Element couponCodeTextField() {
        return driver.findElement(By.id("coupon_code"));
    }

    private Element applyCouponButton() {
        return driver.findElement(By.cssSelector("[value*='Apply coupon']"));
    }

    private Element quantityBox() {
        return driver.findElement(By.cssSelector("[class*='input-text qty text']"));
    }
```

```
    private Element updateCart() {
        return driver.findElement(By.cssSelector("[value*='Update cart']"));
    }

    private Element messageAlert() {
        return driver.findElement(By.cssSelector("[class*='woocommerce-message']"));
    }

    private Element totalSpan() {
        return driver.findElement(By.xpath("//*[@class='order-total']//span"));
    }

    private Element proceedToCheckout() {
        return driver.findElement(By.cssSelector("[class*='checkout-button button alt wc-
forward']"));
    }

    public BreadcrumbSection breadcrumbSection() {
        return new BreadcrumbSection(driver);
    }

    public void applyCoupon(String coupon) {
        couponCodeTextField().typeText(coupon);
        applyCouponButton().click();
        driver.waitForAjax();
    }

    public void increaseProductQuantity(int newQuantity) {
        quantityBox().typeText(String.valueOf(newQuantity));
        updateCart().click();
        driver.waitForAjax();
    }

    public void clickProceedToCheckout() {
        proceedToCheckout().click();
        driver.waitUntilPageLoadsCompletely();
    }

    public String getTotal() {
        return totalSpan().getText();
    }

    public String getMessageNotification() {
        return messageAlert().getText();
    }
}
```

First, we define the elements we will use in the action and assertion methods. After that, the page holds all actions and assertions you can perform on the web page. To use **composition**, we can move the elements and assertions into separate classes, and later, they can be exposed through properties.

Elements and Assertions - Composition Implementation

Wonder how our main page will look after we do the mentioned refactoring? We create a separate class that contains all elements. This will be its only responsibility.

```
public class MainPageElements {
    private final Driver driver;

    public MainPageElements(Driver driver) {
        this.driver = driver;
    }

    public Element addToCartFalcon9() {
        return driver.findElement(By.cssSelector("[data-product_id*='28']"));
    }

    public Element viewCartButton() {
        return driver.findElement(By.cssSelector("[class*='added_to_cart wc-forward']"));
    }

    public Element getProductBoxByName(String name) {
        return driver.findElement(By.xpath(String.format("//h2[text()='%s']/parent::a[1]",
name)));
    }
}
```

If we need to change an element locator, we will do it here. This improves the maintainability significantly by making the localization of the elements much faster because the files will contain fewer lines of code.
Create a separate class for the assertions. The same notes are valid for it as well.

```
public class MainPageAssertions {
    private final MainPageElements elements;

    public MainPageAssertions(MainPageElements mainPageElements) {
        elements = mainPageElements;
    }

    public void assertProductBoxLink(String name, String expectedLink) {
        var actualLink = elements.getProductBoxByName(name).getAttribute("href");
        Assert.assertEquals(actualLink, expectedLink);
    }
}
```

Now in the primary main page class, we expose the previous two as getters.

```
public class MainPage extends NavigatableEShopPage {

    public MainPage(Driver driver) {
        super(driver);
    }
```

```java
    public MainPageElements elements() {
        return new MainPageElements(driver);
    }

    public MainPageAssertions assertions() {
        return new MainPageAssertions(elements());
    }

    @Override
    protected String getUrl() {
        return "http://demos.bellatrix.solutions/";
    }

    @Override
    protected void waitForPageLoad() {
        elements().addToCartFalcon9().waitToExists();
    }

    public void addRocketToShoppingCart() {
        open();
        elements().addToCartFalcon9().click();
        elements().viewCartButton().click();
    }
}
```

As you can see, now only the action methods are left in the class. We use the `elements` getter to access the elements and the `assertions` to access the assertion methods. Would you like to see how the usage of the pages looks in tests?

NOTE

Again, I didn't completely follow the naming conventions for getters. If I did, I had to name the new getters - `getElements` and `getAssertions`. I did the same for the get methods returning the web elements. This leads to improved readability and API usability of the library.

NOTE

If you follow the "**Google Java Style Guide**" it suggests arranging all members based on their modifiers – "*Class and member modifiers, when present, appear in the order recommended by the Java Language Specification: public protected private abstract default static final transient volatile synchronized native strictfp*". However, you will notice I don't follow this suggestion for the page object models. There I group the methods by meaning to improve the readability. First, I put the protected `getUrl` and `waitForPageLoad`. Then I place the elements and assertions getters or the private elements getters. They are followed by page actions and, eventually, assertion methods if any are not placed in a separate class. Note that this is completely OK, depending on which standards you follow. I will quote the "**Oracle Code Conventions for the Java Programming Languag**e" file organization section - "*The methods should be grouped by functionality rather than by scope or accessibility. For example, a private class method can be in between two public instance methods. The goal is to make reading and understanding the code easier*".

Using Composition in Tests

This is how our code looked like before the change.

```
public class ProductPurchaseTestsWithPageObjects {
    private Driver driver;
    private static MainPage mainPage;
    private static CartPage cartPage;

    @BeforeMethod
    public void testInit() {
        driver = new LoggingDriver(new WebCoreDriver());
        driver.start(Browser.CHROME);
        mainPage = new MainPage(driver);
        cartPage = new CartPage(driver);

        mainPage.open();
    }

    @AfterMethod
    public void testCleanup() {
        driver.quit();
    }

    @Test
    public void falcon9LinkAddsCorrectProduct() {
        mainPage.open();

        mainPage.assertProductBoxLink("Falcon 9",
"http://demos.bellatrix.solutions/product/falcon-9/");
    }

    @Test
    public void saturnVLinkAddsCorrectProduct() {
        mainPage.open();

        mainPage.assertProductBoxLink("Saturn V",
"http://demos.bellatrix.solutions/product/saturn-v/");
    }
}
```

As you can see, we access the assertion methods and the publicly exposed elements directly from the page. This is how we are accessing them now:

```
public class ProductPurchaseTestsWithPageObjects {
    private Driver driver;
    private static MainPage mainPage;
    private static CartPage cartPage;

    @BeforeMethod
    public void testInit() {
        driver = new LoggingDriver(new WebCoreDriver());
        driver.start(Browser.CHROME);
        mainPage = new MainPage(driver);
        cartPage = new CartPage(driver);

        mainPage.open();
    }

    @AfterMethod
    public void testCleanup() {
        driver.quit();
    }

    @Test
    public void falcon9LinkAddsCorrectProduct() {
        mainPage.open();

        mainPage.assertions().assertProductBoxLink("Falcon 9",
"http://demos.bellatrix.solutions/product/falcon-9/");
    }

    @Test
    public void saturnVLinkAddsCorrectProduct() {
        mainPage.open();

        mainPage.assertions().assertProductBoxLink("Saturn V",
"http://demos.bellatrix.solutions/product/saturn-v/");
    }
}
```

After the refactoring, we need to use the `assertions` to access the assertion methods and the `elements` getter to access the elements. With these changes, the readability decreased slightly, but the writing experience has improved since you type '.' after the page instance name, the list of available options is now decreased significantly. Following a naming convention for the elements and assertions getters, you will always know which getters you should use to access them.

NOTE

As you can see from the above examples, there are no perfect solutions. Some changes improve maintainability and reusability but decrease readability and understandability. The third part of the book will be dedicated to an evaluation system that can help you assess which design is the most appropriate in a particular situation.

Reuse Elements and Assertions via Base Pages

Since this chapter is about code reuse, you have probably noticed that we defined, again and again, the `elements` and `assertions` getters till now for every page. Let's look into a solution where we can move these methods to our base classes. We will use generic classes and Reflection API. The code will be more complicated. In the next chapters, we will return to more simplistic implementations, even breaking the DRY pattern, sometimes it is better to follow the KISS principle instead, e.g., choosing the more straightforward solution.
For sure, the code that follows is everything but not simple.

NOTE

Generics were added to Java to ensure type safety. To ensure that generics wouldn't cause an overhead at runtime, the compiler applies a type erasure process on generics at compile time. Type erasure removes all type parameters and replaces them with their bounds or Object if the type parameter is unbounded. Thus, the bytecode after compilation contains only standard classes, interfaces, and methods, thus ensuring that no new types are produced.

Let's review again how we defined the elements and assertions getters till now.

```
public class MainPage extends NavigatableEShopPage {
    public MainPage(Driver driver) {
        super(driver);
    }

    public MainPageElements elements() {
        return new MainPageElements(driver);
    }

    public MainPageAssertions assertions() {
        return new MainPageAssertions(elements());
    }
    // rest of the code
```

```
}
```

For the `MainPageElements` and `MainPageAssertions`, we had to declare a variable to the `Driver` and the page elements, followed by a constructor.

```
public class MainPageElements {
    private final Driver driver;

    public MainPageElements(Driver driver) {
        this.driver = driver;
    }
    // rest of the code
}

public class MainPageAssertions {
    private final MainPageElements elements;

    public MainPageAssertions(MainPageElements mainPageElements) {
        elements = mainPageElements;
    }
    // rest of the code
}
```

> **NOTE**
>
> The Java bytecode is the instruction set for the Java Virtual Machine. It acts similar to an assembler, which is an alias representation of a C++ code. As soon as a Java program is compiled, the Java bytecode is generated. It is a machine code in the form of a .class file. Through it, we achieve platform independence. When we compile a Java program, the compiler compiles it and produces bytecode. After that, we can run it on any platform. The Java Virtual Machine can run it, considering the current processor, so we only need to have a basic Java installation on any platform.
>
> **NOTE**
>
> The Reflection API is used to examine or modify the behavior of methods, classes, and interfaces at runtime. The required classes for reflection are provided under `java.lang.reflect` package. It gives us information about the class to which an object belongs and the methods of that class that can be executed using the object. We can invoke methods at runtime despite the access specifier used with them.

Base Elements and Assertions Classes

To eliminate some of the repetitive code and ease the upcoming upgrade to our base page classes, I will create two base classes, one for all element classes and a second one for the assertions ones.

```
public abstract class BaseElements {
    protected final Driver driver;

    public BaseElements(Driver driver) {
        this.driver = driver;
    }
}
```

The first one is simple. By deriving from it we will eliminate the declaration of the `Driver` variable to every concrete elements' class.

```
public abstract class BaseAssertions<ElementsT extends BaseElements> {
    protected ElementsT elements() {
        try {
            var elementsClass =
(Class<ElementsT>)((ParameterizedType)getClass().getGenericSuperclass()).getActualTypeArgume
nts()[0];
            return elementsClass.getDeclaredConstructor().newInstance();
        } catch (Exception e) {
            return null;
        }
    }
}
```

We are casting the first generic type argument `ElementsT` of the class `BaseAssertions` to a class of its type. In Java, type parameters cannot be instantiated directly, so we need to use Reflection API to instantiate the class from the type parameter. The type parameters are being erased when the code is compiled. Since the parameter doesn't have a constructor yet, the methods `getDeclaredConstructor` and `newInstance` give us warnings about an unhandled exception, so we need to wrap it in a try-catch block. It is not the best practice to return null in the catch block, but we may never get to this point anyway. When derived, this generic class will provide direct access to the element map.

> **NOTE**
>
> Sometimes you will need to restrict the types allowed to be passed to a type of parameter. For example, in the above code, we limit the generic type to only a class derived from the base class `BaseElements`. This is what bounded parameters are for. To declare a bounded type parameter, list the type parameter's name, followed by the `extends` keyword, followed by its upper bound.

BaseElements and BaseAssertions Usage

The usage of our new base classes is straightforward. We need to extend the `BaseElements` class.

```
public class MainPageElements extends BaseElements {
    public MainPageElements(Driver driver) {
       super(driver);
    }

    public Element addToCartFalcon9() {
        return driver.findElement(By.cssSelector("[data-product_id*='28']"));
    }
    // rest of the code
}
```

We need to derive from the `BaseElements` class and pass the `Driver` parameter to the `super` constructor method. Notice we don't have the `Driver` variable anymore.
The `BaseAssertions` abstract class usage is even simpler because we don't need to define a constructor. Just make sure to provide the proper elements' class as a generic parameter. After that, you can freely use the derived `elements` getter method without explicitly defining it every time in every assertion class.

```
public class MainPageAssertions extends BaseAssertions<MainPageElements> {
    public void assertProductBoxLink(String name, String expectedLink) {
        var actualLink = elements().getProductBoxByName(name).getAttribute("href");
        Assert.assertEquals(actualLink, expectedLink);
    }
}
```

We are far from done. To use these classes in our page objects, we need to upgrade our two base page classes - `EShopPage` and `NavigatableEShopPage`. Let's review the first version of the `EShopPage`.

```
public abstract class EShopPage<ElementsT extends BaseElements, AssertionsT extends
BaseAssertions<ElementsT>> {
    protected final Driver driver;

    public EShopPage(Driver driver) {
        this.driver = driver;
    }

  public AssertionsT assertions() {
        try {
            var assertionsClass =
(Class<AssertionsT>)((ParameterizedType)getClass().getGenericSuperclass()).getActualTypeArgu
ments()[1];
            return assertionsClass.getDeclaredConstructor().newInstance();
        } catch (Exception e) {
            return null;
        }
```

```
    }

    protected ElementsT elements() {
        try {
            var elementsClass =
(Class<ElementsT>)((ParameterizedType)getClass().getGenericSuperclass()).getActualTypeArgume
nts()[0];
            return elementsClass.getDeclaredConstructor().newInstance();
        } catch (Exception e) {
            return null;
        }
    }

    public MainMenuSection mainMenuSection() {
        return new MainMenuSection(driver);
    }

    public CartInfoSection cartInfoSection() {
        return new CartInfoSection(driver);
    }

    public SearchSection searchSection() {
        return new SearchSection(driver);
    }
}
```

The first thing to notice is that the class now requires two generic parameters `ElementsT` to derive from our new `BaseElements` and `AssertionsT`, which should extend the `BaseAssertions` abstract class. Similarly, to `BaseAssertions`, we have two important new methods: `elements` and `assertions`. The first one is marked as protected since we don't want to expose the getter to the public, meaning your library's user won't access the page's web elements.
For the `NavigatableEShopPage` upgrade, we need only to put the generic parameters, bounded type parameters, and extend another abstract base class, `EShopPage`.

```
public abstract class NavigatableEShopPage<ElementsT extends BaseElements, AssertionsT
extends BaseAssertions<ElementsT>> extends EShopPage<ElementsT, AssertionsT> {
    public NavigatableEShopPage(Driver driver) {
        super(driver);
    }

    protected abstract String getUrl();

    public void open() {
        driver.goToUrl(getUrl());
        waitForPageLoad();
    }

    protected abstract void waitForPageLoad();
}
```

One huge drawback of this approach is that all child pages should provide both elements' and assertions' implementations. However, this is not the case with most pages. Some perform no assertions and thus don't force us to create an additional class. An example of this is the `CartPage`.

```
public class CartPage extends NavigatableEShopPage<CartPageElements, CartPageAssertions> {
    public CartPage(Driver driver) {
        super(driver);
    }
    // the rest of the code
}

public class CartPageAssertions extends BaseAssertions<CartPageElements> {
}
```

As you can see, the `CartPageAssertions` class is empty, and the declaration of the `CartPage` just got more complicated for almost nothing. We can fix this problem by creating separate types for the cases, e.g., one containing assertions and another without them. Let's discuss how we can do that.

Defining AssertableEShopPage and NavigatableAssertableEShopPage

First, let's delete the `EShopPage` base class's assertions method since we won't need it in cases like `CartPage`, where we don't need to perform any verifications.

```
public abstract class EShopPage<ElementsT extends BaseElements> {
    protected final Driver driver;

    public EShopPage(Driver driver) {
        this.driver = driver;
    }

    protected ElementsT elements() {
        try {
            var elementsClass =
(Class<ElementsT>)((ParameterizedType)getClass().getGenericSuperclass()).getActualTypeArgume
nts()[0];
            return elementsClass.getDeclaredConstructor().newInstance();
        } catch (Exception e) {
            return null;
        }
    }

    public MainMenuSection mainMenuSection() {
        return new MainMenuSection(driver);
    }

    public CartInfoSection cartInfoSection() {
        return new CartInfoSection(driver);
    }
```

```
    public SearchSection searchSection() {
        return new SearchSection(driver);
    }
}
```

Next, we can create a successor where we can add the assertions, we can call it `AssertableEShopPage`.

```
public abstract class AssertableEShopPage<ElementsT extends BaseElements, AssertionsT
extends BaseAssertions<ElementsT>> extends EShopPage<ElementsT> {
    public AssertableEShopPage(Driver driver) {
        super(driver);
    }

    public AssertionsT assertions() {
        try {
            var assertionsClass =
(Class<AssertionsT>)((ParameterizedType)getClass().getGenericSuperclass()).getActualTypeArgu
ments()[1];
            return assertionsClass.getDeclaredConstructor().newInstance();
        } catch (Exception e) {
            return null;
        }
    }
}
```

We will create two corresponding versions for the `NavigatableEShopPage` as well. The first one will extend the `EShop<ElementsT>`.

```
public abstract class NavigatableEShopPage<ElementsT extends BaseElements> extends
EShopPage<ElementsT> {
    public NavigatableEShopPage(Driver driver) {
        super(driver);
    }

    protected abstract String getUrl();

    public void open() {
        driver.goToUrl(getUrl());
        waitForPageLoad();
    }

    protected abstract void waitForPageLoad();
}
```

All successors to this class won't have the `assertions` method. The second version will provide it.

```
public abstract class NavigatableAssertableEShopPage<ElementsT extends BaseElements,
AssertionsT extends BaseAssertions<ElementsT>> extends AssertableEShopPage<ElementsT,
AssertionsT> {
    public NavigatableAssertableEShopPage(Driver driver) {
        super(driver);
```

```
    }

    protected abstract String getUrl();

    public void open() {
        driver.goToUrl(getUrl());
        waitForPageLoad();
    }

    protected abstract void waitForPageLoad();
}
```

> **NOTE**
>
> I realize this declaration is hard to "parse" and comprehend with all these bounded type parameters, generics, inheritance, but it is the "necessary evil". As I mentioned, we will stick to the more straightforward non-generic implementations for the rest of the book's examples, even if this means copying a method or two.

AssertableEShopPage and NavigatableAssertableEShopPage Usage

Now, we can delete the `CartPageAssertions` empty class and simplify the `CartPage` definition.

```
public class CartPage extends NavigatableEShopPage<CartPageElements> {
    public CartPage(Driver driver) {
        super(driver);
    }
   // rest of the code
}
```

For the rest of the page object models where we perform verifications, we can use one of our new base classes - `AssertableEShopPage` or `NavigatableAssertableEShopPage` if we need to navigate to the web page.

```
public class MainPage extends NavigatableAssertableEShopPage<MainPageElements,
MainPageAssertions> {
    public MainPage(Driver driver) {
        super(driver);
    }

    @Override
    protected String getUrl() {
        return "http://demos.bellatrix.solutions/";
    }

    @Override
    protected void waitForPageLoad() {
        elements().addToCartFalcon9().waitToExists();
```

```
    }

    public void addRocketToShoppingCart() {
        open();
        elements().addToCartFalcon9().click();
        elements().viewCartButton().click();
    }
}
```

As you can see from the example, the `MainPage` definition is much shorter, and we have access to both `elements` and `assertions` getter methods without explicitly defining them.

Final Code Reuse with NewInstanceFactory

If you check the code of the elements and assertions getter methods, you will notice that some complicated Reflection code is repeated.

```
    protected ElementsT elements() {
        try {
            var elementsClass =
(Class<ElementsT>)((ParameterizedType)getClass().getGenericSuperclass()).getActualTypeArgume
nts()[0];
            return elementsClass.getDeclaredConstructor().newInstance();
        } catch (Exception e) {
            return null;
        }
    }

    public AssertionsT assertions() {
        try {
            var assertionsClass =
(Class<AssertionsT>)((ParameterizedType)getClass().getGenericSuperclass()).getActualTypeArgu
ments()[1];
            return assertionsClass.getDeclaredConstructor().newInstance();
        } catch (Exception e) {
            return null;
        }
    }
```

We can move this logic to a separate class called `NewInstanceFactory` containing a single generic method called `createByTypeParameter`.

```
public class NewInstanceFactory {
    public static <T> T createByTypeParameter(Class parameterClass, int index) {
        try {
            var elementsClass =
(Class)((ParameterizedType)parameterClass.getGenericSuperclass()).getActualTypeArguments()[i
ndex];
            return (T)elementsClass.getDeclaredConstructor().newInstance();
        } catch (Exception e) {
            return null;
        }
```

```
    }
}
```

Its usage is straightforward. We need to specify as a generic parameter the type we want to create an instance of, provide as a parameter our current class, and the number of the generic type in the class definition. The index is 0 because it is the first generic parameter of the current class. If it was the second generic parameter, then we would have set 1.

```
public abstract class BaseAssertions<ElementsT extends BaseElements> {
    protected ElementsT elements() {
        return NewInstanceFactory.<ElementsT>createByTypeParameter(getClass(), 0);
    }
}
```

Reuse Test Workflows - Facade Design Pattern

The second part of the chapter will focus on another common problem in automated tests - test workflows. The workflow is actions and assertions that need to happen always in almost identical order. In our case with the shopping cart, we have the purchase order workflow. There may be one test verifying **product1**, another for **product2** and one more for a discount $ coupon - this can go on and on. Let us see the naive implementation of such tests.

Test Workflows Naive Implementation

We have two tests with the exact same workflow, but we use different data.

```
public class ProductPurchaseTestsWithPageObjects {
    private Driver driver;
    private static MainPage mainPage;
    private static CartPage cartPage;
    private static CheckoutPage checkoutPage;

    @BeforeMethod
    public void testInit() {
        driver = new LoggingDriver(new WebCoreDriver());
        driver.start(Browser.CHROME);
        mainPage = new MainPage(driver);
        cartPage = new CartPage(driver);
        checkoutPage = new CheckoutPage(driver);
    }

    @AfterMethod
    public void testCleanup() {
        driver.quit();
    }
```

```java
    }

    @Test
    public void purchaseFalcon9WithoutFacade() {
        mainPage.open();
        mainPage.addRocketToShoppingCart("Falcon 9");
        cartPage.applyCoupon("happybirthday");
        cartPage.assertions().assertCouponAppliedSuccessfully();
        cartPage.increaseProductQuantity(2);
        cartPage.assertions().assertTotalPrice("114.00€");
        cartPage.clickProceedToCheckout();

        var purchaseInfo = new PurchaseInfo();
        purchaseInfo.setEmail("info@berlinspaceflowers.com");
        purchaseInfo.setFirstName("Anton");
        purchaseInfo.setLastName("Angelov");
        purchaseInfo.setCompany("Space Flowers");
        purchaseInfo.setCountry("Germany");
        purchaseInfo.setAddress1("1 Willi Brandt Avenue Tiergarten");
        purchaseInfo.setAddress2("Lotzowplatz 17");
        purchaseInfo.setCity("Berlin");
        purchaseInfo.setZip("10115");
        purchaseInfo.setPhone("+00498888999281");

        checkoutPage.fillBillingInfo(purchaseInfo);
        checkoutPage.assertions().assertOrderReceived();
    }

    @Test
    public void purchaseSaturnVWithoutFacade() {
        mainPage.open();
        mainPage.addRocketToShoppingCart("Saturn V");
        cartPage.applyCoupon("happybirthday");
        cartPage.assertions().assertCouponAppliedSuccessfully();
        cartPage.increaseProductQuantity(3);
        cartPage.assertions().assertTotalPrice("355.00€");
        cartPage.clickProceedToCheckout();

        var purchaseInfo = new PurchaseInfo();
        purchaseInfo.setEmail("info@berlinspaceflowers.com");
        purchaseInfo.setFirstName("Anton");
        purchaseInfo.setLastName("Angelov");
        purchaseInfo.setCompany("Space Flowers");
        purchaseInfo.setCountry("Germany");
        purchaseInfo.setAddress1("1 Willi Brandt Avenue Tiergarten");
        purchaseInfo.setAddress2("Lotzowplatz 17");
        purchaseInfo.setCity("Berlin");
        purchaseInfo.setZip("10115");
        purchaseInfo.setPhone("+00498888999281");

        checkoutPage.fillBillingInfo(purchaseInfo);
        checkoutPage.assertions().assertOrderReceived();
    }
}
```

When we need to test a new product or a new discount code, we will copy one of the existing tests and change the data. There is one massive drawback of such a solution. If the workflow changes, for example, we move the step with the discount coupon to the last page or add a new discount type, we need to go through the code and rearrange the steps for all tests.

We can solve the problem more elegantly through the usage of the **Facade design pattern**.

Facade Design Pattern

> **Definition: Facade Design Pattern**
>
> Facades are classes that ease the use of a large chunk of dependent code—usually, providing a simplified interface- a couple of methods with fewer parameters, instead of tons of initializations of objects. They hide the complexity of the underlying dependent components and expose only the methods that the user needs.

Abstract UML Class Diagram

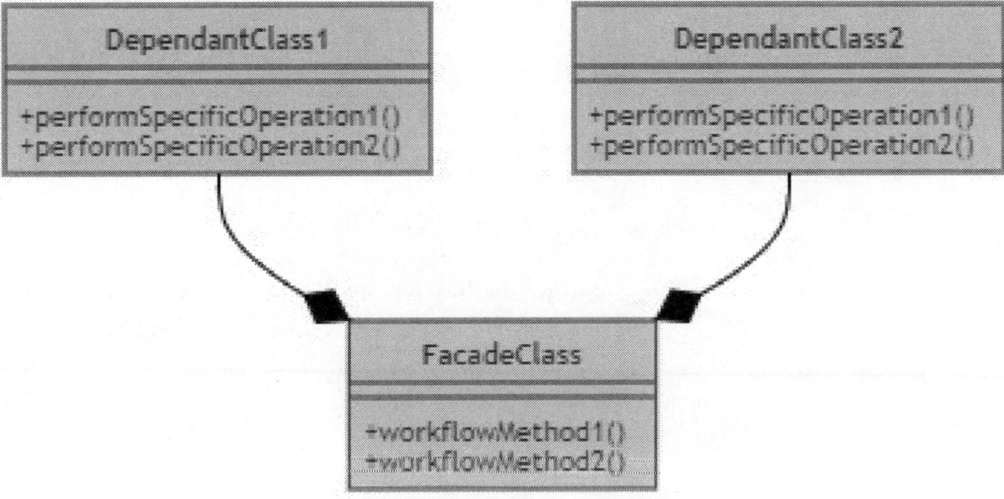

Participants

The classes and objects participating in this pattern are:

- **Facade Class** - the main class that the user will use to access the simplified API. It usually contains public methods which use the dependent classes' logic.

- **Dependent Classes** - they hold specific logic later used in the facade. They are usually used as parameters in the facade.

Facade Design Pattern Implementation

In our scenario, we can create a facade for creating purchases. It will contain a single method called `verifyItemPurchase` that will call the pages' methods in the right order.

```
public class PurchaseFacade {
    private final MainPage mainPage;
    private final CartPage cartPage;
    private final CheckoutPage checkoutPage;

    public PurchaseFacade(MainPage mainPage, CartPage cartPage, CheckoutPage checkoutPage) {
        this.mainPage = mainPage;
        this.cartPage = cartPage;
        this.checkoutPage = checkoutPage;
    }

    public void verifyItemPurchase(String rocketName, String couponName, int quantity,
String expectedPrice, PurchaseInfo purchaseInfo) {
        mainPage.open();
        mainPage.addRocketToShoppingCart(rocketName);
        cartPage.applyCoupon(couponName);
        cartPage.assertions().assertCouponAppliedSuccessfully();
        cartPage.increaseProductQuantity(quantity);
        cartPage.assertions().assertTotalPrice(expectedPrice);
        cartPage.clickProceedToCheckout();
        checkoutPage.fillBillingInfo(purchaseInfo);
        checkoutPage.assertions().assertOrderReceived();
    }
}
```

We use composition again to hold the dependent pages. We initialize the page objects in the constructor. Also, all data required for the workflow is supplied in the form of facade methods' parameters.

> **NOTE**
>
> To make the examples simpler, the method doesn't follow all best practices. In theory, it is OK to have methods up to 5-7 parameters. Here, we may consider moving them all to a new class, as I usually do when I have over 4 parameters.
>
> **NOTE**

It is a matter of preference whether to include or not assertion methods in the facade's methods. It is OK to move them outside of the facades, making the tests more understandable. We will talk much more about comparing different architecture variants in *Chapter 8. Assessment System for Tests' Architecture Design*.

Also, we make assertions inside the function, which may seem to break the Single Responsibility Principle. However, we define the test structure, which is the primary purpose of the method. A better name may be - `verifyPurchaseOfItem` or something similar. You may move the assertion methods to separate facade methods. However, I prefer my facade methods to be more concise since we perform a few verifications after some actions, not just at the end of the test.

Shall we examine how the tests will look if we use the new facade?

```
public class ProductPurchaseTestsWithPageObjects {
    private Driver driver;
    private static MainPage mainPage;
    private static CartPage cartPage;
    private static CheckoutPage checkoutPage;
    private static PurchaseFacade purchaseFacade;

    @BeforeMethod
    public void testInit() {
        driver = new LoggingDriver(new WebCoreDriver());
        driver.start(Browser.CHROME);
        mainPage = new MainPage(driver);
        cartPage = new CartPage(driver);
        checkoutPage = new CheckoutPage(driver);
        purchaseFacade = new PurchaseFacade(mainPage, cartPage, checkoutPage);
    }

    @AfterMethod
    public void testCleanup() {
        driver.quit();
    }

    @Test
    public void purchaseFalcon9WithFacade() {
        var purchaseInfo = new PurchaseInfo();
        purchaseInfo.setEmail("info@berlinspaceflowers.com");
        purchaseInfo.setFirstName("Anton");
        purchaseInfo.setLastName("Angelov");
        purchaseInfo.setCompany("Space Flowers");
        purchaseInfo.setCountry("Germany");
        purchaseInfo.setAddress1("1 Willi Brandt Avenue Tiergarten");
        purchaseInfo.setAddress2("Lotzowplatz 17");
        purchaseInfo.setCity("Berlin");
        purchaseInfo.setZip("10115");
        purchaseInfo.setPhone("+00498888999281");
```

```
        purchaseFacade.verifyItemPurchase("Falcon 9", "happybirthday", 2, "114.00€",
purchaseInfo);
    }

    @Test
    public void purchaseSaturnVWithFacade() {
        var purchaseInfo = new PurchaseInfo();
        purchaseInfo.setEmail("info@berlinspaceflowers.com");
        purchaseInfo.setFirstName("Anton");
        purchaseInfo.setLastName("Angelov");
        purchaseInfo.setCompany("Space Flowers");
        purchaseInfo.setCountry("Germany");
        purchaseInfo.setAddress1("1 Willi Brandt Avenue Tiergarten");
        purchaseInfo.setAddress2("Lotzowplatz 17");
        purchaseInfo.setCity("Berlin");
        purchaseInfo.setZip("10115");
        purchaseInfo.setPhone("+00498888999281");

        purchaseFacade.verifyItemPurchase("Saturn V", "happybirthday", 3, "355.00€",
purchaseInfo);
    }
}
```

As you can see, they became shorter, and we could hide some of the low-level details. This may be a good or a bad thing. Some engineers may say this made the readability worse which may be right. To see the exact workflow, now you need to open the facade class file. However, we improved the maintainability significantly since we can do it in a single place if we need to change the workflow. Another improvement is that the creation of new tests is more straightforward.

Combining Facade with Template Method Design Pattern

In the previous section, we saw how we could reuse the test workflows. However, there might be cases where this solution may not be sufficient. Imagine that we have the current shopping cart for our rockets. However, after a year or two, we decide to redesign it. The workflow will stay the same, but since it is possible to use another back-end system, we can slightly change the way we apply coupons or add products.

We may need to support both shopping carts to decide which design suits our users better for a while. If you recall the code of the purchase facade, you will notice it depends on specific page objects, and they will be different for the new shopping cart. When we deprecate the old shopping cart, we want to change the existing tests as little as possible. How can we prepare for such events? We can combine the two design patterns we discussed in this chapter - **Template Method** and **Facade**.

Purchase Facade with Template Methods

Instead of having a facade with specific dependent pages, we can create an abstract one which defines the workflow using template methods. Later we can create concrete implementations of the facade - one with the new and one with the old page objects.

```
public abstract class PurchaseFacade {
    public void verifyItemPurchase(String rocketName, String couponName, int quantity,
String expectedPrice, PurchaseInfo purchaseInfo) {
        addItemToShoppingCart(rocketName);
        applyCoupon(couponName);
        assertCouponAppliedSuccessfully();
        increaseProductQuantity(quantity);
        assertTotalPrice(expectedPrice);
        proceedToCheckout();
        fillBillingInfo(purchaseInfo);
        assertOrderReceived();
    }

    protected abstract void addItemToShoppingCart(String itemName);

    protected abstract void applyCoupon(String couponName);

    protected abstract void assertCouponAppliedSuccessfully();

    protected abstract void increaseProductQuantity(int quantity);

    protected abstract void assertTotalPrice(String expectedPrice);

    protected abstract void proceedToCheckout();

    protected abstract void fillBillingInfo(PurchaseInfo purchaseInfo);

    protected abstract void assertOrderReceived();
}
```

Just like in the Facade, the workflow is defined in the public method `verifyItemPurchase`, but instead of calling the page objects' methods, we call the abstract template methods.

Concrete Facade Implementation

For the old shopping cart and for the new one, we will have separate implementations of the above abstract `PurchaseFacade`. Let's name the old shopping cart implementation `PurchaseFirstVersionFacade`.

```
public class NewPurchaseFacade extends PurchaseFacade {
```

```
    private final MainPage mainPage;
    private final CartPage cartPage;
    private final CheckoutPage checkoutPage;

    public NewPurchaseFacade(MainPage mainPage, CartPage cartPage, CheckoutPage
checkoutPage) {
        this.mainPage = mainPage;
        this.cartPage = cartPage;
        this.checkoutPage = checkoutPage;
    }

    @Override
    protected void addItemToShoppingCart(String itemName) {
        mainPage.open();
        mainPage.addRocketToShoppingCart(itemName);
    }

    @Override
    protected void applyCoupon(String couponName) {
        cartPage.applyCoupon(couponName);
    }

    @Override
    protected void assertCouponAppliedSuccessfully() {
        cartPage.assertions().assertCouponAppliedSuccessfully();
    }

    @Override
    protected void increaseProductQuantity(int quantity) {
        cartPage.increaseProductQuantity(quantity);
    }

    @Override
    protected void assertTotalPrice(String expectedPrice) {
        cartPage.assertions().assertTotalPrice(expectedPrice);
    }

    @Override
    protected void proceedToCheckout() {
        cartPage.clickProceedToCheckout();
    }

    @Override
    protected void fillBillingInfo(PurchaseInfo purchaseInfo) {
        checkoutPage.fillBillingInfo(purchaseInfo);
    }

    @Override
    protected void assertOrderReceived() {
        checkoutPage.assertions().assertOrderReceived();
    }
}
```

As with the initial design of the pattern, the page objects were initialized in the constructor, and we used **composition** to store the pages needed for implementing our method. However, we don't define the workflow method `verifyItemPurchase` since we inherit it from the base class. Instead, we only need to override and implement all protected abstract methods, and this is where we call the logic from the dependent page objects. We can create a similar facade for the new shopping cart with its own page objects used in the same workflow.

The usage in tests remains identical, we just use the concrete facade - `NewPurchaseFacade` instead of `PurchaseFacade`.

```
public class ProductPurchaseTestsWithPageObjects {
    private Driver driver;
    private static MainPage mainPage;
    private static CartPage cartPage;
    private static CheckoutPage checkoutPage;
    private static NewPurchaseFacade purchaseFacade;

    @BeforeMethod
    public void testInit() {
        driver = new LoggingDriver(new WebCoreDriver());
        driver.start(Browser.CHROME);
        mainPage = new MainPage(driver);
        cartPage = new CartPage(driver);
        checkoutPage = new CheckoutPage(driver);
        purchaseFacade = new NewPurchaseFacade(mainPage, cartPage, checkoutPage);
    }

    @AfterMethod
    public void testCleanup() {
        driver.quit();
    }

    @Test
    public void purchaseFalcon9WithFacade() {
        var purchaseInfo = new PurchaseInfo();
        purchaseInfo.setEmail("info@berlinspaceflowers.com");
        purchaseInfo.setFirstName("Anton");
        purchaseInfo.setLastName("Angelov");
        purchaseInfo.setCompany("Space Flowers");
        purchaseInfo.setCountry("Germany");
        purchaseInfo.setAddress1("1 Willi Brandt Avenue Tiergarten");
        purchaseInfo.setAddress2("Lotzowplatz 17");
        purchaseInfo.setCity("Berlin");
        purchaseInfo.setZip("10115");
        purchaseInfo.setPhone("+00498888999281");

        purchaseFacade.verifyItemPurchase("Falcon 9", "happybirthday", 2, "114.00€",
purchaseInfo);
    }

    @Test
    public void purchaseSaturnVWithFacade() {
```

```
        var purchaseInfo = new PurchaseInfo();
        purchaseInfo.setEmail("info@berlinspaceflowers.com");
        purchaseInfo.setFirstName("Anton");
        purchaseInfo.setLastName("Angelov");
        purchaseInfo.setCompany("Space Flowers");
        purchaseInfo.setCountry("Germany");
        purchaseInfo.setAddress1("1 Willi Brandt Avenue Tiergarten");
        purchaseInfo.setAddress2("Lotzowplatz 17");
        purchaseInfo.setCity("Berlin");
        purchaseInfo.setZip("10115");
        purchaseInfo.setPhone("+00498888999281");

        purchaseFacade.verifyItemPurchase("Saturn V", "happybirthday", 3, "355.00€",
purchaseInfo);
    }
}
```

Summary

In this chapter, we discussed various techniques to increase maintainability and reusability in our tests. Now our page objects follow more precisely the **Single Responsibility Principle**. To get there first, we divided our base page class into two base classes - one for pages that can be navigated to and another for those that cannot. We integrated the **Template Method design pattern** to allow navigatable pages to wait for a unique element to appear before performing any actions, making the tests more stable. Later, we moved all elements and assertions to separate classes and used them through composition, so our pages have a single reason to change. After that, we discussed how we could further optimize the code and follow the DRY principle more closely by moving these methods to base pages using generics and Reflection API. In the second part of the chapter, we discussed how we could reuse test workflows through the **Facade design pattern**. We combined both patterns, which allowed us to reuse the test workflow for different versions of the web pages.

In the next chapter, we will talk about API usability or how we can ease all these library classes as part of our framework. We will look into a couple of new design patterns - **Singleton**, **Factory**, **Adapter**, and **Fluent API**. Also, we will discuss the pros and cons of exposing the page's elements as public properties.

Questions

1. Can you explain what test maintainability is?
2. What metric do we use to measure maintainability?
3. What is the difference between composition and inheritance?
4. What are the participants in the Template Method design pattern?
5. What is the Facade design pattern used for?

Chapter 6. API Usability

In the previous chapter, we talked about how to increase maintainability and reusability in our tests. Now we will investigate how we can ease the use of all these library classes as part of our framework. We will learn how to make the test library API easy to use, learn, and understand. Initially, we will apply the **Interface Segregation principle** by splitting the driver API into smaller, but more focused parts.

After that, we will talk about different approaches using the already developed page objects through **Singleton design pattern** or **App design pattern**. We will also look at another interesting approach called **Fluent API** or **chaining methods**. At the end of the section, we will talk about whether to expose the page objects elements to the users of your test library.

These topics will be covered in this chapter:

- Interface Segregation Principle for WebCoreDriver Decorator
- Use Page Objects Through Singleton Design Pattern
- App Design Pattern for Creating Page Objects
- Fluent API Page Objects
- Page Objects Elements Access Styles

Interface Segregation principle for WebDriver Decorator

In the previous chapters, we created helper classes related to WebDriver to stabilize and optimize our tests. We used the **Decorator design pattern** for that. Why not revise what the current class contains?

WebDriver Decorator Current Implementation

If we check the names of the methods, we will see several groups of methods for finding elements and controlling browser actions. However, we have missed implementing several other functionalities. For example, we will need methods for working with cookies and dialogs. The usage of the class will become harder and harder with the increasing number of methods.

```
public class DriverDecorator extends Driver {
    protected final Driver driver;
```

```
    public DriverDecorator(Driver driver) {
        this.driver = driver;
    }

    @Override
    public void start(Browser browser) {
        driver.start(browser);
    }

    @Override
    public void quit() {
        driver.quit();
    }

    @Override
    public void goToUrl(String url) {
        driver.goToUrl(url);
    }

    @Override
    public Element findElement(By locator) {
        return driver.findElement(locator);
    }

    @Override
    public List<Element> findElements(By locator) {
        return driver.findElements(locator);
    }

    @Override
    public void waitForAjax() {
        driver.waitForAjax();
    }

    @Override
    public void waitUntilPageLoadsCompletely() {
        driver.waitUntilPageLoadsCompletely();
    }
}
```

The following code block shows how we have been using the `Driver` decorator in our page objects.

```
public class CartPage extends NavigatableEShopPage {
    public CartPage(Driver driver) {
        super(driver);
    }

    @Override
    protected String getUrl() {
        return "http://demos.bellatrix.solutions/cart/";
```

```
    }

    public CartPageElements elements() {
        return new CartPageElements(driver);
    }

    public BreadcrumbSection breadcrumbSection() {
        return new BreadcrumbSection(driver);
    }
    public void applyCoupon(String coupon) {
        elements().couponCodeTextField().typeText(coupon);
        elements().applyCouponButton().click();
        driver.waitForAjax();
    }
   // rest of the code
}
```

As you can see, we pass a single instance to the `Driver` class, and we use it for multiple purposes - navigating to the page, finding elements, or controlling the browser. However, not on all pages do we need to navigate to the page or to control the browser.

How about recalling the **Interface Segregation principle**? - "*clients should not be forced to implement interfaces they don't use. Instead of one fat interface, many small interfaces are preferred based on groups of methods, each one serving one sub-module.*"

If we want to apply the principle in our case, we need to split the driver interface into a couple of smaller interfaces.

Splitting Driver Interface into Smaller Interfaces

Each of the mentioned groups of methods can be moved to a separate interface. So, we will end up with five smaller interfaces:

- One for controlling the browser
- One for navigating
- One for finding elements
- One for working with cookies
- One for handling dialogs

All can be combined into one bigger interface through inheritance, and the implementation will still be in a single place. Let's create these interfaces.

Here is how the one for browser actions looks like:

```
public interface BrowserService {
    void start(Browser browser);
    void quit();
```

```
    void waitForAjax();
    void waitUntilPageLoadsCompletely();
}
```

For navigation, we only need the `goToUrl` method and the `getUrl` getter.

```
public interface NavigationService {
    void goToUrl(String url);
    String getUrl();
}
```

There are two methods for finding elements.

```
public interface ElementFindService {
    Element findElement(By locator);
    List<Element> findElements(By locator);
}
```

For the new functionality for working with cookies, we need to add, delete and get cookies.

```
public interface CookiesService {
    void addCookie(String cookieName, String cookieValue, String path);
    void deleteAllCookies();
    void deleteCookie(String cookieName);
    List<Cookie> getAllCookies();
    String getCookie(String cookieName);
}
```

The dialog service contains a single method responsible for closing dialogs.

```
public interface DialogService {
    void handle(Function<Object, Alert> function, DialogButton dialogButton);
}
```

The abstract decorator class `Driver` implements all mentioned interfaces, meaning that all concrete decorators should implement all the smaller interfaces because of the inheritance.

```
public abstract class Driver implements NavigationService, BrowserService, CookiesService,
ElementFindService, DialogService {
}
```

Smaller Interfaces Usage in Page Objects

At the beginning of the section, we saw how the `Driver` class was used before separating the interfaces. Let's investigate how the usage changed? Instead of passing the whole `Driver` object, we pass only the interface we need as a parameter to the page.

```
public class CartPage extends NavigatableEShopPage {
    private final BrowserService browserService;
```

```java
    public CartPage(ElementFindService elementFindService, NavigationService
navigationService, BrowserService browserService) {
        super(elementFindService, navigationService);
        this.browserService = browserService;
    }

    @Override
    protected String getUrl() {
        return "http://demos.bellatrix.solutions/cart/";
    }

    public CartPageElements elements() {
        return new CartPageElements(elementFindService);
    }

    public BreadcrumbSection breadcrumbSection() {
        return new BreadcrumbSection(elementFindService);
    }

    public void applyCoupon(String coupon) {
        elements().couponCodeTextField().typeText(coupon);
        elements().applyCouponButton().click();
        browserService.waitForAjax();
    }
    // rest of the code
}
```

The base class `NavigatableEShopPage` requires `ElementFindService` and `NavigationService` interfaces. They are used for finding the elements on the page and for navigation to the pages, respectively. However, if our page inherits from the `EShopPage` base class, you must pass only the ElementFindService interface as a parameter since we cannot navigate to such pages. Also, in most pages, we won't need to control the browser, so we won't need to supply an instance to `BrowserService`. But here we need it because we call the `waitForAjax` method.

> **NOTE**
>
> Strive to apply the **Interface Segregation principle** to all your most complex classes. This will make not only the usage of your classes easier but will make your tests much more readable.

Use Page Objects Through Singleton Design Pattern

In the rest of the chapter, we will investigate different approaches for using our page objects. How about recalling how we used them till now in our tests?

```
public class ProductPurchaseTestsWithPageObjects {
    private Driver driver;
    private static MainPage mainPage;
    private static CartPage cartPage;

    @BeforeMethod
    public void testInit() {
        driver = new LoggingDriver(new WebCoreDriver());
        driver.start(Browser.CHROME);
        mainPage = new MainPage(driver);
        cartPage = new CartPage(driver);

        mainPage.open();
    }

    @AfterMethod
    public void testCleanup() {
        driver.quit();
    }

    @Test
    public void falcon9LinkAddsCorrectProduct() {
        mainPage.open();

        mainPage.assertions().assertProductBoxLink("Falcon 9",
"http://demos.bellatrix.solutions/product/falcon-9/");
    }

    @Test
    public void saturnVLinkAddsCorrectProduct() {
        mainPage.open();

        mainPage.assertions().assertProductBoxLink("Saturn V",
"http://demos.bellatrix.solutions/product/saturn-v/");
    }
}
```

In the testInit method, we always start a new browser and create all pages. The page objects are shared and used through local variables in the test class.

Now, we will discuss an alternative approach using the **Singleton design pattern**.

Singleton Design Pattern

Definition: Singleton Design Pattern
The class has only one instance and provides access to it.

Abstract UML Class Diagram

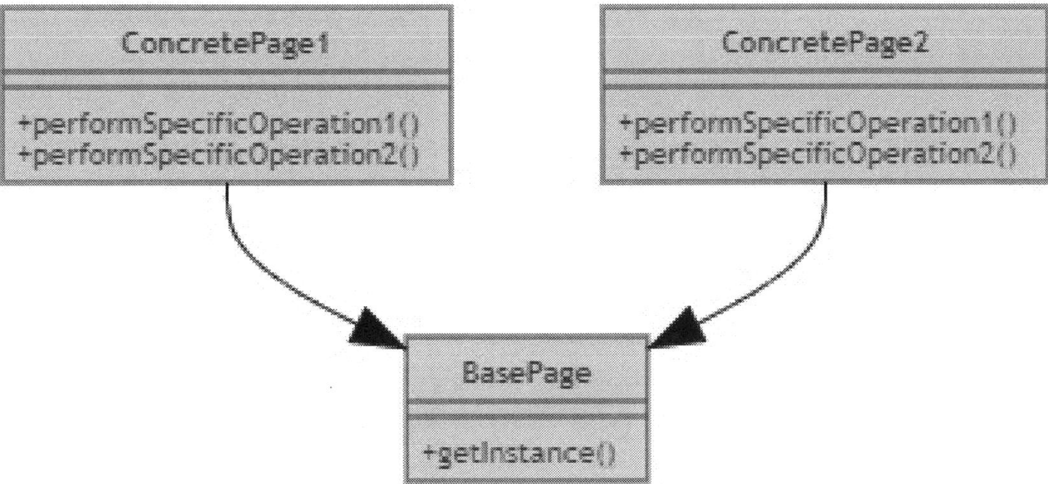

Participants

The classes and objects participating in this pattern are:

- **Base Page** - holds a static getter method returning the instance of the class. It is created on the first call to the class. The class cannot be created through the usage of the keyword `new`.
- **Concrete Page** - inherits the base page. It can be used in tests through the `getInstance` getter but cannot be created by using the keyword `new`.

Singleton Design Pattern Implementation

The basic implementation of the pattern requires a static variable and a static property. Also, to ensure that the class cannot be initialized through the keyword **new**, the constructor access modifier is set to **private.**

Basic Singleton Implementation

You use the `getInstance` getter to access the page, which will be shared across all tests since it is static. Because of the null check, the instance variable will be initialized only the first time. The following code block will show how it is done:

```
public class CartPage extends NavigatableEShopPage {
    private static CartPage instance;

    public static CartPage getInstance() {
        if (instance == null) {
            instance = new CartPage();
        }

        return instance;
    }
    // rest of the code
}
```

However, this basic implementation won't work out of the box for us for two reasons:

- First, we have dependencies to the `Driver` decorator interfaces, which are not static.
- Second, there is too much code duplication to add this static code to each page.

To handle the first issue, we can make our `Driver` class singleton too. To resolve the second, we can move the singleton code to our base classes.

Making Driver Decorator Singleton

How about making our `LoggingDriver` singleton? To do so, we need to introduce a static variable and a property as in the following example:

```
public class LoggingSingletonDriver extends DriverDecorator {
    private static LoggingSingletonDriver instance;

    private LoggingSingletonDriver(core.Driver driver) {
        super(driver);
    }

    public static LoggingSingletonDriver getInstance() {
        if (instance == null) {
            instance = new LoggingSingletonDriver(new WebCoreDriver());
        }

        return instance;
    }
```

```
    @Override
    public void start(Browser browser) {
        System.out.printf("start browser = %s", browser.name());
        driver.start(browser);
    }
    // rest of the code
}
```

Making Pages Singleton

We initialize the section page objects by passing the singleton `Driver` in the protected constructor. This way, we don't need to pass it as a parameter to the constructor.

```
public abstract class EShopPage {
    protected final ElementFindService elementFindService;

    protected EShopPage() {
        this.elementFindService = LoggingSingletonDriver.getInstance();
    }

    public MainMenuSection mainMenuSection() {
        return new MainMenuSection(elementFindService);
    }

    public CartInfoSection cartInfoSection() {
        return new CartInfoSection(elementFindService);
    }

    public SearchSection searchSection() {
        return new SearchSection(elementFindService);
    }
}

public abstract class NavigatableEShopPage extends EShopPage {
    protected final NavigationService navigationService;

    protected NavigatableEShopPage() {
        this.navigationService = LoggingSingletonDriver.getInstance();
    }

    protected abstract String getUrl();

    public void open()
    {
        navigationService.goToUrl(getUrl());
        waitForPageLoad();
    }

    protected abstract void waitForPageLoad();
}
```

This is how our page objects need to change.

```
public class MainPage extends NavigatableEShopPage {
    private static MainPage instance;

    private MainPage() {
    }

    public static MainPage getInstance() {
        if (instance == null) {
            instance = new MainPage();
        }

        return instance;
    }

    public MainPageElements elements() {
        return new MainPageElements(elementFindService);
    }

    public MainPageAssertions assertions() {
        return new MainPageAssertions(elements());
    }
    // rest of the code
}
```

Because we use the singleton version of the `Driver` decorator, so we don't need to pass any parameters to the constructor. We have a new static private variable holding the page itself. The page is initialized only once using lazy loading in the method getInstance, which we will use later to access the page. The constructor is also marked as `private`, so we cannot create new class instances via the `new` keyword.

> **NOTE**
>
> Lazy initialization is a technique that defers the creation of an object until the first time it is needed. The initialization of the object happens only on demand. Note that lazy initialization and lazy instantiation mean the same thing - they can be used interchangeably.

Singleton Implementation via SingletonFactory

We can spare some of the boilerplate code by moving some of the heavy liftings in a separate class called `SingletonFactory`, responsible for keeping track of the classes' instances.

```
public class SingletonFactory {
    private static final SingletonFactory singletonFactory = new SingletonFactory();
```

```
    private final Map<String, Object> mapHolder = new HashMap<>();

    private SingletonFactory() {
    }

    public static <T> T getInstance(Class<T> classOf, Object ... initargs) {
        try {
            if (!singletonFactory.mapHolder.containsKey(classOf.getName())) {
                T obj = (T) classOf.getConstructors()[0].newInstance(initargs);
                singletonFactory.mapHolder.put(classOf.getName(), obj);
            }

            return (T) singletonFactory.mapHolder.get(classOf.getName());
        } catch (Exception e) {
            // not the best practice to return null. But probably we will never end here so
it is OK.
            return null;
        }
    }
}
```

> **NOTE**
>
> Boilerplate is the term used to describe code sections that have to be included in many places with little or no alteration. It is often used when referring to languages considered verbose, i.e., the programmer must write a lot of code to do minimal jobs.

We keep a static HashMap that holds all created instances and uses the class's name as a key. If it was already there, we return it. Otherwise, we create it via the Java Reflection API. If any exceptions occur, we return null. As a second parameter, we pass an arbitrary number of arguments that some of our objects might require.
The usage in pages is straightforward.

```
public class MainPage extends NavigatableEShopPage {
    private MainPage() {
    }

    public static MainPage getInstance() {
        return SingletonFactory.getInstance(MainPage.class);
    }

    public MainPageElements elements() {
        return new MainPageElements(elementFindService);
    }

    public MainPageAssertions assertions() {
        return new MainPageAssertions(elements());
```

```
    }
    // rest of the code
}
```

The `getInstance` method calls the `SingletonFactory` providing the page's class. The private page's variable and lazy loading check are no longer needed.

Thread-safe Singleton Implementation

The previous examples are not thread-safe, meaning there might be deadlocks if you execute your tests in parallel. After our latest refactoring, we can change just a few lines in the `SingletonFactory` class.

```
public class SingletonFactory {
    private static final SingletonFactory instance = new SingletonFactory();
    private final Map<String, Object> mapHolder = new HashMap<>();

    private SingletonFactory() {
    }

    public static <T> T getInstance(Class<T> classOf, Object ... initargs) {
        synchronized (SingletonFactory.class) {
            if (!instance.mapHolder.containsKey(classOf.getName())) {
                T obj = null;
                try {
                    obj = (T)classOf.getConstructors()[0].newInstance(initargs);
                } catch (Exception e) {
                    return obj;
                }
                instance.mapHolder.put(classOf.getName(), obj);
            }
            return (T)instance.mapHolder.get(classOf.getName());
        }
    }
}
```

The change I did was that I wrapped the code in a `synchronized` block, guaranteeing the thread-safety.

NOTE

Using `synchronized` across multiple processing cores is often far more expensive than you expect because synchronization forces code to execute sequentially, which works against the goal of parallelism. Multicore CPUs have separate caches (fast memory) attached to each processor core. Locking requires these to be synchronized, requiring relatively slow cache-coherency-protocol inter-core communication. [Kia 18]

Singleton Design Pattern Usage in Tests

The usage of singleton page object models in tests is straightforward. As you can see, the code in the `testInit` method is much shorter, and our tests became more concise.

```
public class ProductPurchaseTestsWithPageObjects {
    @BeforeMethod
    public void testInit() {
        LoggingSingletonDriver.getInstance().start(Browser.CHROME);
        MainPage.getInstance().open();
    }

    @AfterMethod
    public void testCleanup() {
        LoggingSingletonDriver.getInstance().quit();
    }

    @Test
    public void falcon9LinkAddsCorrectProduct() {
        MainPage.getInstance().open();
        MainPage.getInstance().assertions().assertProductBoxLink("Falcon 9",
"http://demos.bellatrix.solutions/product/falcon-9/");
    }

    @Test
    public void saturnVLinkAddsCorrectProduct() {
        MainPage.getInstance().open();
        MainPage.getInstance().assertions().assertProductBoxLink("Saturn V",
"http://demos.bellatrix.solutions/product/saturn-v/");
    }
}
```

We access the pages through their getInstance method. For all tests in our project, we will create a single static instance for every page object.

App Design Pattern for Creating Page Objects

Now let's discuss another approach for accessing our page objects called **App design pattern**. The `App` is something between a facade and a factory class. It provides an easier way of using the `Driver` decorator and its interfaces. Also, it creates or navigates to the requested pages. The `App` class will create regular page objects, not the singleton ones we created in the previous section.

App Design Pattern Implementation

Here is its implementation:

```java
public class App implements AutoCloseable {
    private Boolean disposed = false;

    public App(Browser browserType)  {
        LoggingSingletonDriver.getInstance().start(browserType);
    }

    public NavigationService getNavigationService() {
        return SingletonFactory.getInstance(NavigationService.class);
    }

    public BrowserService getBrowserService() {
        return SingletonFactory.getInstance(BrowserService.class);
    }

    public CookiesService getCookiesService() {
        return SingletonFactory.getInstance(CookiesService.class);
    }

    public DialogService getDialogService() {
        return SingletonFactory.getInstance(DialogService.class);
    }

    public <TPage extends NavigatableEShopPage> TPage goTo(Class<TPage> pageOf)  {
        var page = SingletonFactory.getInstance(pageOf,
LoggingSingletonDriver.getInstance());
        page.open();

        return page;
    }

    public <TPage extends EShopPage> TPage create(Class<TPage> pageOf)  {
        return SingletonFactory.getInstance(pageOf, LoggingSingletonDriver.getInstance());
    }

    @Override
    public void close() {
        if (disposed)  {
            return;
        }

        LoggingSingletonDriver.getInstance().quit();

        disposed = true;
    }
}
```

There are a couple of interesting parts of the code above. First, we get a singleton instance to the `Driver` decorator through the `LoggingSingletonDriver` class, which we use in the constructor to start the browser. We expose through public getters the `BrowserService`, `CookiesService`, `DialogService`, and `NavigationService` interfaces. The service for finding elements is not exposed since it is up to the page objects to locate the web elements.

We implement the Java `AutoCloseable` interface through the `close` method to properly close the browser. This allows us to use the `App` class in `try` statements, at the end of which the browser will be automatically closed. Here is how the code looks if we use a `try` statement. Here, the `close` method is called automatically at the end of the using scope:

```
try (var app = new App(Browser.CHROME)) {
    var mainPage = app.goTo(MainPage.class);
    app.create(MainPage.class).assertions().assertProductBoxLink("Saturn V",
"http://demos.bellatrix.solutions/product/saturn-v/");
}
```

NOTE

The try-with-resources statement is a try statement that declares one or more resources. A resource is an object that must be closed after the program is finished with it. The try-with-resources ensures that each resource is closed at the end of the statement. Any object that implements `java.lang.AutoCloseable`, which includes all objects which implement `java.io.Closeable`, can be used as a resource. The `try-with-resources` statement was introduced in Java 7.

NOTE

The pattern for disposing of an object, referred to as a dispose pattern, imposes order on the lifetime of an object. The dispose pattern is used only for objects that access unmanaged resources, such as file and pipe handles, registry handles, wait handles, or pointers to unmanaged memory blocks. This is because the garbage collector is very efficient at reclaiming unused managed objects, but it cannot reclaim unmanaged objects. To help ensure that resources are always cleaned up appropriately, a close method should be callable multiple times without throwing an exception.

The `create` and `goTo` methods are implemented as generic ones. The only difference between the `create` and `goTo` methods is that the former is just creating and returning an instance of the page. The latter is doing the same but navigating to the page. To ease the creation of pages and use them as singleton objects, we use the developed `SingletonFactory` class. As a second parameter, we pass the already initialized instance of the `Driver` through the `LoggingSingletonDriver`.

NOTE

Reflection API in Java and C# allows you to examine the objects at runtime, manipulate internal properties, dynamically create an instance of a type, invoke its methods, or access its fields or properties no matter their access modifiers.

In the `SingletonFactory` class, we use Reflection API to create the instances, invoking the first public constructor. However, the usage of Reflection API for such cases is a bit "hacky" and slower than using the `new` keyword. The better way to handle it is to use an inversion of the control container (IoC Container). However, I will not refactor it further to avoid complicating the examples.

App Usage in Tests

As with the singleton driver decorator and page objects, the `beforeClass` method is a single line of code. The other methods are more concise.

```
public class ProductPurchaseTestsWithPageObjects {
    private static App app;

    @BeforeClass
    public void beforeClass() {
        app = new App(Browser.CHROME);
    }

    @AfterClass
    public void afterClass() {
        app.close();
    }

    @Test
    public void falcon9LinkAddsCorrectProduct() {
        var mainPage = app.goTo(MainPage.class);

        mainPage.assertions().assertProductBoxLink("Falcon 9",
"http://demos.bellatrix.solutions/product/falcon-9/");
    }

    @Test
    public void saturnVLinkAddsCorrectProduct() {
        var mainPage - app.goTo(MainPage.class);

        app.create(MainPage.class).assertions().assertProductBoxLink("Saturn V",
"http://demos.bellatrix.solutions/product/saturn-v/");
    }
}
```

Since the `App` is created in the `beforeClass`, which means that the browser will be reused for all tests in the class. You can always create the `App` in each test, but you can benefit from implementing the `AutoClosable` interface. You can create the object wrapped in a try-with-resources statement without worrying about calling the `close` method each time (it will be called at the end of the statement).

```
@Test
public void saturnVLinkAddsCorrectProduct() {
    try (var app = new App(Browser.CHROME)) {
        var mainPage = app.goTo(MainPage.class);
        app.create(MainPage.class).assertions().assertProductBoxLink("Saturn V",
"http://demos.bellatrix.solutions/product/saturn-v/");
    }
}
```

Fluent API Page Objects

Would you like to discuss the third strategy for using page object models in tests? It is also known as **Fluent Interface**. The fluent API is usually implemented through method chaining (method cascading).

> **NOTE**
>
> Eric Evans and Martin Fowler first defined the Fluent Interface as an implementation of an OOP API that gives the user a more concise and readable code.

Fluent API Implementation

We will make a couple of changes to our page objects to implement the **Fluent API**. First, each method will return the page itself. Next, we will make the `elements` get method private, available only for the page itself. Last, we will move the assertions methods to the page itself. We will make this sacrifice to the **Single Responsibility principle** for following the pattern and making our code eventually more concise and more readable.

```
public class CartPage extends NavigatableEShopPage {
    private final BrowserService browserService;

    public CartPage(Driver driver) {
        super(driver, driver);
        this.browserService = driver;
```

```
}

private CartPageElements elements() {
    return new CartPageElements(elementFindService);
}

@Override
protected String getUrl() {
    return "http://demos.bellatrix.solutions/cart/";
}

@Override
protected void waitForPageLoad() {
    elements().couponCodeTextField().waitToExists();
}

public BreadcrumbSection breadcrumbSection() {
    return new BreadcrumbSection(elementFindService);
}

public CartPage applyCoupon(String coupon) {
    elements().couponCodeTextField().typeText(coupon);
    elements().applyCouponButton().click();
    browserService.waitForAjax();
    return this;
}

public CartPage increaseProductQuantity(int newQuantity) {
    elements().quantityBox().typeText(String.valueOf(newQuantity));
    elements().updateCart().click();
    browserService.waitForAjax();
    return this;
}

public CartPage clickProceedToCheckout() {
    elements().proceedToCheckout().click();
    browserService.waitUntilPageLoadsCompletely();
    return this;
}

public String getTotal() {
    return elements().totalSpan().getText();
}

public String getMessageNotification() {
    return elements().messageAlert().getText();
}

public CartPage assertCouponAppliedSuccessfully() {
    Assert.assertEquals(getMessageNotification(), "Coupon code applied successfully.");
    return this;
}

public CartPage assertTotalPrice(String expectedPrice) {
```

```
        Assert.assertEquals(elements().totalSpan().getText(), expectedPrice);
        return this;
    }
}
```

Also, remember that you can combine the **Fluent API** with the **Singleton** and **App design patterns**.

Using Fluent API in Tests

This is how our tests will look like using a combination of **Fluent API** and **App design pattern**.

```
public class ProductPurchaseTestsWithPageObjects {
    private static App app;

    @BeforeClass
    public void beforeClass() {
        app = new App(Browser.CHROME);
    }

    @AfterClass
    public void afterClass() {
        app.close();
    }

    @Test
    public void completePurchaseSuccessfully_WhenNewClient() {
        var mainPage = app.goTo(MainPage.class);

        mainPage.addRocketToShoppingCart();
        var cartPage = app.goTo(CartPage.class);
        cartPage.applyCoupon("happybirthday")
                .assertCouponAppliedSuccessfully()
                .increaseProductQuantity(2)
                .assertTotalPrice("114.00€")
                .clickProceedToCheckout();
    }
}
```

As you can see, the interesting part here is how you call the page methods one after another. This is the so-called **Method Chaining**, which is achieved by returning the page itself as a return type for each function.

Page Objects Elements Access Styles

The API usability is all about how easy it is for the users of your test library to write and configure the automated tests. We have investigated various ways for how you can create and use page objects in the tests. Another API usability aspect is whether you can use the page object elements directly in tests or not. This is a theological question, and it is a matter of preference, the same way you decide whether to use the **Page Object Model design pattern** or not. Sometimes, when you must write only a couple of tests without recurring elements, it may be OK to use vanilla WebDriver syntax.

> **NOTE**
>
> The term "vanilla" means using pure WebDriver library code directly in tests with no abstraction on top. The term comes from Vanilla JavaScript, which differentiates pure JS code from libraries such as jQuery.

Now let us investigate a couple of variations on how you can access web elements in tests.

Exposing Elements Through Public Get Methods

We looked into the most straightforward approach for accessing elements in previous chapters when we first discussed the **Page Object Model design pattern**. All the web elements are exposed directly as public get methods - part of the page object class.

```
public class MainPage extends BaseEShopPage {
    public Element addToCartFalcon9() {
        return driver.findElement(By.cssSelector("[data-product_id*='28']"));
    }

    public Element viewCartButton() {
        return driver.findElement(By.cssSelector("[class*='added_to_cart wc-forward']"));
    }

    public void addRocketToShoppingCart() {
        open();
        addToCartFalcon9().click();
        viewCartButton().click();
    }
    // rest of the code
}
```

To use the elements in the tests, use the mentioned public getters.

```
@Test(priority = 1)
public void completePurchaseSuccessfully_whenNewClient() {
    mainPage.open();
    mainPage.addToCartFalcon9().click();
```

```
    mainPage.assertProductBoxLink("Falcon 9",
"http://demos.bellatrix.solutions/product/falcon-9/");
}
```

Accessing Elements Through Elements Public Get Method

Some of the book's examples use the approach to expose the page object elements through the method `elements`. Let us review it again.

```
public class MainPage extends NavigatableEShopPage {
    public MainPage(Driver driver) {
        super(driver);
    }

    public MainPageElements elements() {
        return new MainPageElements(driver);
    }

    public MainPageAssertions assertions() {
        return new MainPageAssertions(elements());
    }

    @Override
    protected String getUrl() {
        return "http://demos.bellatrix.solutions/";
    }

    @Override
    protected void waitForPageLoad() {
        elements().addToCartFalcon9().waitToExists();
    }

    public void addRocketToShoppingCart() {
        open();
        elements().addToCartFalcon9().click();
        elements().viewCartButton().click();
    }
}
```

To use some of the elements directly in the tests, you can do it through the `Elements` public property of the page.

```
@Test(priority = 1)
public void completePurchaseSuccessfully_whenNewClient() {
    mainPage.open();
    mainPage.elements().addToCartFalcon9().click();
    mainPage.assertions().assertProductBoxLink("Falcon 9",
"http://demos.bellatrix.solutions/product/falcon-9/");
}
```

Hiding Elements in Tests

Sometimes, we may hide the elements from outside tests by marking the `elements` get method private, as we did when we implemented the Fluent API page objects.

```
public class MainPage extends NavigatableEShopPage {
    public MainPage(Driver driver) {
        super(driver, driver);
    }

    private MainPageElements elements() {
        return new MainPageElements(elementFindService);
    }

    public MainPage addRocketToShoppingCart() {
        open();
        elements().addToCartFalcon9().click();
        elements().viewCartButton().click();
        return this;
    }
    // rest of the code
}
```

In the tests, you don't have access to the elements. Instead, you need to use only the publicly available page object methods.

Hiding Element Unnecessary Details

Finally, I want to discuss another aspect of the elements' usage - no matter which of the above access variations you choose. If you locate some web element only to get its getText getter or type into it, you can hide all other unnecessary details.

Let me give you an example. This is how normally we expose a web element as a public get method.

```
public Element viewCartButton() {
    return driver.findElement(By.cssSelector("[class*='added_to_cart wc-forward']"));
}
```

As you can see, we return the entire `Element` object, not just some of its properties.

If you need to get only the text of the element, then change the element getter's return type to String and return the result of the call to the `getText` method.

```
public String viewCartButtonText() {
    return driver.findElement(By.cssSelector("[class*='added_to_cart wc-
forward']")).getText();
}
```

```
public String addToCartFalcon9Href() {
    return
driver.findElement(By.cssSelector("[dataproduct_id*='28']")).getAttribute("href");
}
```

As you can see, the `viewCartButtonText` property returns only the text of the button, whereas the `addToCartFalcon9Href` returns the HREF of the anchor.

If you need to set the text of some element, you can declare a setter and use the `typeText` method to set the element's text.

```
public String getFirstName() {
    return driver.findElement(By.id("firstName")).getText();
}

public void setFirstName(String newName) {
    driver.findElement(By.id("firstName")).typeText(newName);
}
```

With this variant, there is some code duplication in the searching for the element. We can refactor the code by creating a private variable of the element and then wrap it through the getter.

```
private Element firstName = elementFindService.findElement(By.id("firstName"));

public String getFirstName() {
    return firstName.getText();
}

public void setFirstName(String newName) {
    firstName.typeText(newName);
}
```

Summary

In this chapter, we defined what API usability is, how to make the test code more readable, and at the same time - how it can allow our library users to write tests more quickly. We applied the **Interface Segregation principle** by splitting the driver API into smaller functional parts. After that, we talked about different approaches to using the already developed page objects through the **Singleton design pattern** or the **App design pattern**. After that, we investigated another interesting approach called **Fluent API**. We covered whether it is a good idea to expose the page objects' elements to the users of your test library instead of returning the concrete value you need in the test.

In the next chapter, we will discuss various techniques to make your test library more extensible and customizable. We will design an API that allows our users to create custom WebDriver locators using the **Strategy design pattern**. Also, we will look into the native WebDriver support for behavior adding. We will use the `EventFiringWebDriver` class.

Questions

1. What is the benefit of splitting the WebDriver interface into smaller interfaces?
2. How can you make a class to be a singleton?
3. What is the primary purpose of the App design pattern?
4. What changes should you make to a regular page object to make it use the Fluent API?
5. Define three approaches for accessing elements in tests?

Chapter 7. Building Extensibility in Your Test Library

In the previous chapter, we talked about how we can ease the use of all these framework library classes. We applied the **Interface Segregation principle** to split the fat `WebDriver` interface into smaller, easier-to-use components. We also used **Singleton** and **App design patterns** to improve the framework's API usability.

This chapter will discuss maybe an even more important topic - how to make the framework's code easier to modify and customize while following the **Open/Closed principle**. We will look at how the **Strategy design pattern** can help us build such extensibility for locating and waiting for elements. At the end of the chapter, you will read about the existing Vanilla WebDriver functionality that allows you to add and execute custom code at various points of the WebDriver execution flow.

These topics will be covered in this chapter:

- Building extensibility for elements finding through Strategy design pattern
- Building extensibility for elements waiting through Strategy design pattern
- Adding extensibility points through `EventFiringWebDriver`

Building Extensibility for Finding Elements through Strategy Design Pattern

We will investigate how we can make the finding of web elements more extensible by following the **Open/Closed principle**. First, we will look into the standard localization of elements in Vanilla WebDriver and discuss its source code. After that, we will use the **Strategy design pattern** to build such extensibility in our test automation framework.

Vanilla WebDriver Finding of Elements

Below, you can see the standard approach for finding elements in Vanilla WebDriver.

```
WebDriver webDriver = new ChromeDriver();
WebElement button = webDriver.findElement(By.id("buttonId"));
```

To find an element, we need to call the `findElement` method and pass as an argument some of the static methods of the `By` class. Here, we use the `Id` method, which accepts one parameter - the id of the web element. There are several of these methods, such as - `xpath`, `tagName`, `className`, etc. Let's see the full source code of the `By` class.

> **NOTE**
>
> You can find the WebDriver Java source code in the official GitHub repository of the project. It is located under the java folder of Selenium repository.

```
public abstract class By {
  public static By id(String id) {
    return new ById(id);
  }

  public static By linkText(String linkText) {
    return new ByLinkText(linkText);
  }

  public static By partialLinkText(String partialLinkText) {
    return new ByPartialLinkText(partialLinkText);
  }

  public static By name(String name) {
    return new ByName(name);
  }

  public static By tagName(String tagName) {
    return new ByTagName(tagName);
  }

  public static By xpath(String xpathExpression) {
    return new ByXPath(xpathExpression);
  }

  public static By className(String className) {
    return new ByClassName(className);
  }

  public static By cssSelector(String cssSelector) {
    return new ByCssSelector(cssSelector);
  }
  // rest of the code
}
```

Imagine that you want to add a custom locator not part of the initial version of the `By` class.

The only way is to edit the source code and add a new static method. Since the methods are static, you cannot create a child class or use other OOP strategies.

Since the project maintainers are conservative about making such updates, this will mean you cannot add a new locator, or you won't be able to add it easily. Before we can enable our framework to support such extensibility points, we need to discuss the **Strategy design pattern**.

Strategy Design Pattern

> **Definition: Strategy Design Pattern**
>
> Enables an algorithm's behavior to be selected at runtime. This pattern defines a family of algorithms, encapsulates each algorithm. Also, it makes the algorithms interchangeable within that family.

Abstract UML Class Diagram

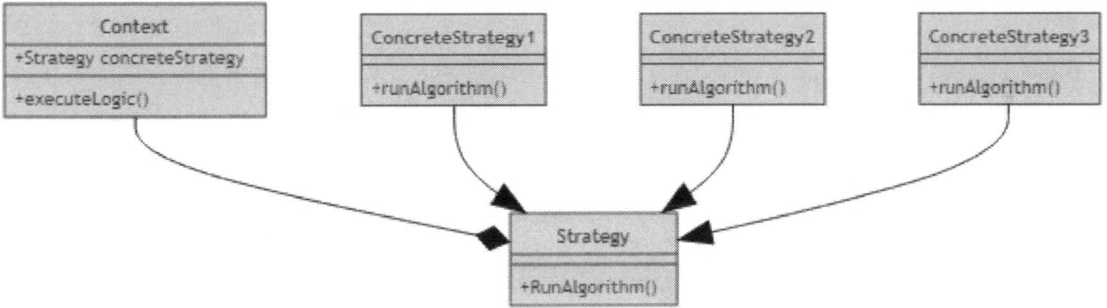

Participants

The classes and objects participating in this pattern are:

- **Strategy** - defines the interface of the algorithm. The clients use it to call the interface methods.
- **Concrete Strategy** - hold the specific implementation of the algorithm.
- **Context** - uses the concrete strategies through an instance of the Strategy and gives the possibility to clients to change the algorithm setting Concrete strategy.

Reviewing Current Version for Finding Elements

Before refactoring our test library, why not make a quick recap of how we currently find and use elements? In the previous chapter, we defined a new interface called `ElementFindService`. The `WebCoreDriver` decorator implements its two methods - `find` and `findElements`. They accept the Vanilla WebDriver `By` class for specifying the locator type.

```
public class WebCoreDriver extends Driver {
    @Override
    public Element findElement(By locator) {
        var nativeWebElement =
                webDriverWait.until(ExpectedConditions.presenceOfElementLocated(locator));
        Element element = new WebCoreElement(webDriver, nativeWebElement, locator);

        // If we use log decorator.
        Element logElement = new LogElement(element);

        return logElement;
    }

    @Override
    public List<Element> findElements(By locator) {
        List<WebElement> nativeWebElements =

webDriverWait.until(ExpectedConditions.presenceOfAllElementsLocatedBy(locator));
        var elements = new ArrayList<Element>();
        for (WebElement nativeWebElement : nativeWebElements) {
            Element element = new WebCoreElement(webDriver, nativeWebElement, locator);
            Element logElement = new LogElement(element);
            elements.add(logElement);
        }

        return elements;
    }
    // rest of the code
}
```

We use the interface through composition rather than inheritance. Later, the two methods and some of the static methods of the `By` class are called.

```
public class CartPageElements {
    private final ElementFindService elementFindService;

    public CartPageElements(ElementFindService elementFindService) {
        this.elementFindService = elementFindService;
    }

    public Element couponCodeTextField() {
        return elementFindService.findElement(By.id("coupon_code"));
    }
```

```
    public Element applyCouponButton() {
        return elementFindService.findElement(By.cssSelector("[value*='Apply coupon']"));
    }

    public Element quantityBox() {
        return elementFindService.findElement(By.cssSelector("[class*='input-text qty
text']"));
    }
  // rest of the code
}
```

As we discussed at the beginning of the section, the problem with this code is that it is hard for you to add custom locators. For example, let us create a locator for finding an element by Id containing particular text.

Creating Elements Find Strategies

Now let's refactor the above code to support the locators' extensibility:

1. We need to define the base strategy algorithm interface.

```
public abstract class FindStrategy {
    private final String value;

    protected FindStrategy(String value) {
        this.value = value;
    }

    public String getValue() {
        return value;
    }

    public abstract By convert();
}
```

The strategy abstract class contains the `getValue` get method, which returns the actual locator value. Our engine will call the `convert` method to generate the Vanilla WebDriver `By` locator, which the native WebDriver find method requires.

2. Next, we need to create concrete implementations. We will start with the `By.id` locator strategy. In the `convert` method, we call the native `By.id` method.

```
public class IdFindStrategy extends FindStrategy {
    public IdFindStrategy(String value) {
        super(value);
    }
```

```
    @Override
    public By convert() {
        return By.id(getValue());
    }
}
```

3. Now shall we review how our new Id containing strategy will look like:

```
public class IdContainingFindStrategy extends FindStrategy {
    public IdContainingFindStrategy(String value) {
        super(value);
    }

    @Override
    public By convert() {
        return By.cssSelector(String.format("[id*='%s']", getValue()));
    }
}
```

Since there isn't a native method for finding web elements by Id containing, we use the `cssSelector` method to build a CSS locator expression.

You need to locate an element by inner text containing a particular string? No problem - this time instead of CSS we will use XPath.

```
public class InnerTextContainsFindStrategy extends FindStrategy {
    public InnerTextContainsFindStrategy(String value) {
        super(value);
    }

    @Override
    public By convert() {
        return By.xpath(String.format("//*[contains(text(), '%s')]", getValue()));
    }
}
```

Refactoring ElementFindService

In our case, the context class from the diagram is the `WebCoreDriver` decorator. We need to change it and in the `ElementFindService` interface to start using the new find strategies.

```
public interface ElementFindService {
    Element findElement(By locator);
    List<Element> findElements(By locator);
}
```

We added a parameter holding the find strategy.

```
public interface ElementFindService {
    List<Element> findAll(FindStrategy findStrategy);
```

```
    Element find(FindStrategy findStrategy);
}
```

Here are the changes made to the `WebCoreDriver` decorator.

```
public class WebCoreDriver extends Driver {
    @Override
    public Element find(FindStrategy findStrategy) {
        var nativeWebElement =

webDriverWait.until(ExpectedConditions.presenceOfElementLocated(findStrategy.convert()));
        Element element = new WebCoreElement(webDriver, nativeWebElement,
findStrategy.convert());
        Element logElement = new LogElement(element);
        return logElement;
    }

    @Override
    public List<Element> findAll(FindStrategy findStrategy) {
        List<WebElement> nativeWebElements =

webDriverWait.until(ExpectedConditions.presenceOfAllElementsLocatedBy(findStrategy.convert()
));
        var elements = new ArrayList<Element>();
        for (WebElement nativeWebElement:nativeWebElements) {
            Element element = new WebCoreElement(webDriver, nativeWebElement,
findStrategy.convert());
            Element logElement = new LogElement(element);
            elements.add(logElement);
        }
        return elements;
    }
    // rest of the code
}
```

We pass the find strategy as a parameter to the `find` and `findAll` methods of the `WebCoreDriver` decorator. After that, we use the strategy to return the locator to find the native web elements. When the element is found, we wrap it in the element decorators and return it.

> **NOTE**
>
> Maybe you have noticed that our wait for elements to exist logic disappeared. We will add it to the `ElementFinderService` in the next section.

How about examining the usage of the methods after the refactoring?

```
public class CartPageElements {
    private final ElementFindService elementFindService;
```

```
    public CartPageElements(ElementFindService elementFindService) {
        this.elementFindService = elementFindService;
    }

    public Element couponCodeTextField() {
        return elementFindService.findElement(new ByIdStrategy("coupon_code"));
    }

    public Element applyCouponButton() {
        return elementFindService.findElement(new ByCssStrategy("[value*='Apply coupon']"));
    }

    public Element quantityBox() {
        return elementFindService.findElement(new ByCssStrategy("[class*='input-text qty
text']"));
    }
  // rest of the code
}
```

As you probably noticed, the code is verbose and hard to use with all these find parameters. How about investigating how we can improve the API usability?

Improving Elements Find Strategies API Usability

I propose changing the `ElementFindService`. Instead of having two general find methods, let us have a separate method for each locator strategy. Perhaps we go back to the initial state; I will show you how to preserve the extensibility which we fight to deliver.

```
public interface ElementFindService {
    Element findById(String id);
    Element findByXPath(String xpath);
    Element findByTag(String tag);
    Element findByClass(String cssClass);
    Element findByCss(String css);
    Element findByLinkText(String linkText);
    List<Element> findAllById(String id);
    List<Element> findAllByXPath(String xpath);
    List<Element> findAllByTag(String tag);
    List<Element> findAllByClass(String cssClass);
    List<Element> findAllByCss(String css);
    List<Element> findAllByLinkText(String linkText);

    List<Element> findAll(FindStrategy findStrategy);
    Element find(FindStrategy findStrategy);
}
```

In the `WebCoreDriver` decorator we need to create all these methods. To spare some code we can preserve the general find implementation and call it internally.

```java
public class WebCoreDriver extends Driver {
    @Override
    public Element findById(String id) {
        return find(new IdFindStrategy(id));
    }

    @Override
    public Element findByXPath(String xpath) {
        return find(new XPathFindStrategy(xpath));
    }

    @Override
    public Element findByTag(String tag) {
        return find(new TagFindStrategy(tag));
    }

    @Override
    public Element findByClass(String cssClass) {
        return find(new ClassFindStrategy(cssClass));
    }

    @Override
    public Element findByCss(String css) {
        return find(new CssFindStrategy(css));
    }

    @Override
    public Element findByLinkText(String linkText) {
        return find(new LinkTextFindStrategy(linkText));
    }

    @Override
    public List<Element> findAllById(String id) {
        return findAll(new IdFindStrategy(id));
    }

    @Override
    public List<Element> findAllByXPath(String xpath) {
        return findAll(new XPathFindStrategy(xpath));
    }

    @Override
    public List<Element> findAllByTag(String tag) {
        return findAll(new TagFindStrategy(tag));
    }

    @Override
    public List<Element> findAllByClass(String cssClass) {
        return findAll(new ClassFindStrategy(cssClass));
    }

    @Override
    public List<Element> findAllByCss(String css) {
        return findAll(new CssFindStrategy(css));
```

```
    }

    @Override
    public List<Element> findAllByLinkText(String linkText) {
        return findAll(new LinkTextFindStrategy(linkText));
    }

    @Override
    public List<Element> findAll(FindStrategy findStrategy) {
        List<WebElement> nativeWebElements =
webDriverWait.until(ExpectedConditions.presenceOfAllElementsLocatedBy(findStrategy.convert()
));
        var elements = new ArrayList<Element>();
        for (WebElement nativeWebElement:nativeWebElements) {
            Element element = new WebCoreElement(webDriver, nativeWebElement,
findStrategy.convert());
            Element logElement = new LogElement(element);
            elements.add(logElement);
        }

        return elements;
    }

    @Override
    public Element find(FindStrategy findStrategy) {
        var nativeWebElement =
webDriverWait.until(ExpectedConditions.presenceOfElementLocated(findStrategy.convert()));
        Element element = new WebCoreElement(webDriver, nativeWebElement,
findStrategy.convert());
        Element logElement = new LogElement(element);
        return logElement;
    }
    // rest of the code
}
```

After these changes, the usage of the find API has been improved significantly. Let's see how:

```
public class CartPageElements {
    private final ElementFindService elementFindService;

    public CartPageElements(ElementFindService elementFindService) {
        this.elementFindService = elementFindService;
    }

    public Element couponCodeTextField() {
        return elementFindService.findById("coupon_code");
    }

    public Element applyCouponButton() {
        return elementFindService.findByCss("[value*='Apply coupon']");
    }
```

```
    public Element quantityBox() {
        return elementFindService.findByCss("[class*='input-text qty text']");
    }
  // rest of the code
}
```

Adding New Find Strategies via Extension Methods

However, now the `WebCoreDriver` decorator started to look like the `By` class with its static methods. We can make the code more user-friendly by creating extension methods for the `IElementFindService`. The change will allow our library users to add additional functions for their custom locators without adding them directly to the core services.

> **NOTE**
>
> The extension methods are special methods that allow adding logic to an existing type without the need to derive a type or to recompile the code. They are static methods that can be called as they were instance methods of the type. Natively Java doesn't support extension methods. However, there are alternatives, such as the Manifold project. To use it, you need to install a plug-in for IntelliJ and add dependencies to Maven's pom.xml. Remember that their plug-in is paid.
>
> An extension class does not physically alter its extended class. The methods defined in an extension are not inserted into the extended class. Instead, the Java compiler and Manifold cooperate in calling the extension's static method to look like a call to an instance method on the extended class. As a consequence, extension calls dispatch statically.

```
@Extension
public class ElementFindServiceExtensions  {
    public static Element findByIdContaining(@This ElementFindService elementFindService,
string idContaining)  {
        return driver.find(new IdContainingFindStrategy(idContaining));
    }
}
```

To create such an extension method for locating elements, we created a class called `ElementFindServiceExtensions` and added the new method. There are two important notes here. First, the method should be `static`. Second, you need to use the annotation `@This` to specify the class you want to extend, and it must be the first parameter, in our case, the `ElementFindService` interface (later, when you use the method, you don't need to supply this argument).

To use the extension methods in your code, you need to include the package of the extension class: `import core.locators.extensions;`

```
public class CartPageElements {
    private final ElementFindService elementFindService;

    public CartPageElements(ElementFindService elementFindService) {
        this.elementFindService = elementFindService;
    }

    public Element couponCodeTextField() {
        return elementFindService.findByIdContaining("coupon_code");
    }

    public Element applyCouponButton() {
        return elementFindService.findByCss("[value*='Apply coupon']");
    }

    public Element quantityBox() {
        return elementFindService.findByCss("[class*='input-text qty text']");
    }
  // rest of the code
}
```

NOTE

Remember that some of Lombok's features are marked as experimental. Thus, you may not use them. At the moment of writing the book, the extension methods are still in this stage. There is some ongoing effort to allow IntelliJ Lombok's plug-in to support experimental features.

NOTE

Another **free** alternative to Manifold is project Lombok. In their experimental features, they support extension methods too. I believe their version is even simpler. The Lombok plug-in is installed by default to the latest version of IntelliJ.

Let's quickly review the Lombok version. The declaration of the extension method is even simpler since you don't need to use any annotations.

```
public class ElementFindServiceExtensions  {
    public static Element findByIdContaining(ElementFindService elementFindService, string
idContaining)  {
        return driver.find(new IdContainingFindStrategy(idContaining));
    }
}
```

To use the extension method as part of the `ElementFindService`, you need to annotate the class with the `@ExtensionMethod(ElementFindServiceExtensions.class)` annotation.

```
@ExtensionMethod(ElementFindServiceExtensions.class)
public class CartPageElements {
    private final ElementFindService elementFindService;

    public CartPageElements(ElementFindService elementFindService) {
        this.elementFindService = elementFindService;
    }

    public Element couponCodeTextField() {
        return elementFindService.findByIdContaining("coupon_code");
    }

    public Element applyCouponButton() {
        return elementFindService.findByCss("[value*='Apply coupon']");
    }

    public Element quantityBox() {
        return elementFindService.findByCss("[class*='input-text qty text']");
    }
  // rest of the code
}
```

NOTE

To make these Lombok annotations work, you need to enable the annotations processing. You need to go to the **Preferences | Build, Execution, Deployment | Compiler | Annotation Processors** and make sure of the following:

- Enable annotation processing box is checked
- Obtain processors from project classpath option is selected

Building Extensibility for Waiting for Elements through Strategy Design Pattern

Waiting for web elements' workable state is essential for every stable automated test. In the previous versions of our framework, we already used the WebDriver wait API to wait for elements to be present on the page, but sometimes we need more methods to wait for other attributes to reach a specific state. Such as whether the element is clickable, visible or contains text.

Vanilla WebDriver Waiting for Elements

Below, you can see the standard approach for elements waiting in Vanilla WebDriver.

```
WebDriver webDriver = new ChromeDriver();
WebDriverWait webDriverWait = new WebDriverWait(webDriver, 30);
WebElement button =
webDriverWait.until(ExpectedConditions.presenceOfElementLocated(By.id("buttonId")));
```

Why not review the code of the `ExpectedConditions` class which is similar to the `By` class part of the find API? I left only the parts of the code I want us to discuss.

```
public class ExpectedConditions {
  public static ExpectedCondition<Boolean> titleIs(final String title) {
    // rest of the method's code
  }

  public static ExpectedCondition<WebElement> visibilityOf(final WebElement element) {
  // rest of the method's code
  }

  public static ExpectedCondition<List<WebElement>> presenceOfAllElementsLocatedBy(final By
locator) {
    // rest of the method's code
  }

  public static ExpectedCondition<Boolean> textToBePresentInElement(final WebElement
element, final String text) {
  // rest of the method's code
  }

  public static ExpectedCondition<Boolean> invisibilityOfElementLocated(final By locator) {
    // rest of the method's code
  }

  public static ExpectedCondition<Boolean> invisibilityOfElementWithText(final By locator,
final String text) {
    // rest of the method's code
  }

  public static ExpectedCondition<WebElement> elementToBeClickable(final By locator) {
   // rest of the method's code
  }

  public static ExpectedCondition<WebElement> elementToBeClickable(final WebElement element)
{
    // rest of the method's code
  }
  // rest of the code
}
```

As with the By class, there are tons of methods besides the ones I deleted - a large class. But to create a new wait condition method, you need to add a new static method and make this class even larger (if the maintainers allow you to).
As in the case of the Find API, we can use the **Strategy design pattern** to build such extensibility in our test automation framework.

Reviewing Current Version of Elements Waiting

We don't have an interface in the framework for elements waiting. Each time, we wait for elements to exist before returning them. Also, we use the native WebDriverWait API for waiting for asynchronous operations.

```
public class WebCoreDriver extends Driver {
    @Override
    public Element findElement(By locator) {
        var nativeWebElement =
                webDriverWait.until(ExpectedConditions.presenceOfElementLocated(locator));
        Element element = new WebCoreElement(webDriver, nativeWebElement, locator);
        Element logElement = new LogElement(element);
        return logElement;
    }

    @Override
    public List<Element> findElements(By locator) {
        List<WebElement> nativeWebElements =
           webDriverWait.until(ExpectedConditions.presenceOfAllElementsLocatedBy(locator));
        var elements = new ArrayList<Element>();
        for (WebElement nativeWebElement : nativeWebElements) {
            Element element = new WebCoreElement(webDriver, nativeWebElement, locator);
            Element logElement = new LogElement(element);
            elements.add(logElement);
        }
        return elements;
    }
    // rest of the code
}
```

Creating Elements Wait Strategies

To create an extensible wait API, we first need to create the Strategy API interface.

```
public abstract class WaitStrategy {
    private final int timeoutIntervalSeconds;
    private final int sleepIntervalSeconds;

    public WaitStrategy(int timeoutIntervalSeconds, int sleepIntervalSeconds) {
        this.timeoutIntervalSeconds = timeoutIntervalSeconds;
        this.sleepIntervalSeconds = sleepIntervalSeconds;
```

```
    }

    public int getTimeoutIntervalSeconds() {
        return timeoutIntervalSeconds;
    }

    public int getSleepIntervalSeconds() {
        return sleepIntervalSeconds;
    }

    public abstract void waitUntil(SearchContext searchContext, WebDriver driver, By by);

    protected void waitUntil(Function<SearchContext, Boolean> waitCondition, WebDriver
driver)  {
        var webDriverWait = new WebDriverWait(driver, timeoutIntervalSeconds,
sleepIntervalSeconds);
        webDriverWait.until(waitCondition);
    }

    protected WebElement findElement(SearchContext searchContext, By by)  {
        var element = searchContext.findElement(by);
        return element;
    }
}
```

I implemented the base strategy as an abstract class, instead of a Java interface, since I wanted to share some code between all wait strategies. The only public method available to the clients is the following one: `public abstract void waitUntil(SearchContext searchContext, WebDriver driver, By by);`
The concrete strategies need to implement it helped by the protected functions of the abstract class. In the helper protected `waitUntil` methods, we create a new instance of the `WebDriverWait` class by passing a delegate function that returns `bool`. Also, we give the flexibility to overwrite the default timeouts.
Now let us see what the concrete wait strategy will look like in the case of waiting for the web element to exist.

```
public class ToExistsWaitStrategy extends WaitStrategy {
    public ToExistsWaitStrategy(int timeoutIntervalSeconds, int sleepIntervalSeconds) {
       super(timeoutIntervalSeconds, sleepIntervalSeconds);
    }

    @Override
    public void waitUntil(SearchContext searchContext, WebDriver driver, By by) {
        waitUntil((x) -> elementExists(searchContext, by), driver);
    }

    private Boolean elementExists(SearchContext searchContext, By by)
    {
        try
        {
            var element = findElement(searchContext, by);
```

```
            return element != null;
        }
        catch (NoSuchElementException e)
        {
            return false;
        }
    }
}
```

The class needs to derive from the base strategy `WaitStrategy`. The core functionality is held in the private `elementExists` method. There we return true or false depending on whether the element exists. Then we pass it as an argument via lambda expression to the derived `waitUntil` method, which will internally call this function several times until it returns true or the specified timeout is reached.

> **NOTE**
>
> Lambda Expressions were added in Java 8. A lambda expression is a short block of code that takes in parameters and returns a value. Lambda expressions are similar to methods, but they do not need a name, and they can be implemented right in the body of a method.

Shall we develop one more concrete wait strategy, for example, the one for waiting for the element to be clickable?

```
public class ToBeClickableWaitStrategy extends WaitStrategy {
    public ToBeClickableWaitStrategy(int timeoutIntervalSeconds, int sleepIntervalSeconds) {
       super(timeoutIntervalSeconds, sleepIntervalSeconds);
    }

    @Override
    public void waitUntil(SearchContext searchContext, WebDriver driver, By by) {
        waitUntil((x) -> elementIsClickable(searchContext, by), driver);
    }

    private Boolean elementIsClickable(SearchContext searchContext, By by)  {
        var element = findElement(searchContext, by);
        try  {
            return element != null && element.isEnabled();
        }  catch (StaleElementReferenceException e)  {
            return false;
        }  catch (NoSuchElementException e)  {
            return false;
        }
    }
}
```

For an element to be counted as clickable, we check it is found and enabled.

Creating ElementWaitService

As mentioned till now, we had no API for allowing users to wait for elements explicitly. How about encapsulating all our wait logic in a service only responsible for elements waiting? To do that, we need to follow a few steps:

1. Define such an interface that needs to be later implemented by the `WebCoreDriver` decorator.

```
public interface ElementWaitService {
    void wait(Element element, WaitStrategy waitStrategy);
}
```

2. In the decorator we can add the implementation.

```
public void wait(Element element, WaitStrategy waitStrategy) {
      waitStrategy.waitUntil(webDriver, webDriver, element.getBy());
}
```

We pass the concrete initialized wait strategy as an argument.

3. To ease the usage, we can create a wait strategy factory. In the class, we have a method for each concrete strategy. If we need to add new wait strategies, we can use the extension methods approach.

```
public class WaitStrategyFactory {
    public ToExistsWaitStrategy exists() {
        return new ToExistsWaitStrategy(30, 2);
    }

    public ToExistsWaitStrategy exists(int timeoutInterval, int sleepInterval) {
        return new ToExistsWaitStrategy(timeoutInterval, sleepInterval);
    }

    public ToBeVisibleWaitStrategy beVisible(int timeoutInterval, int sleepInterval) {
        return new ToBeVisibleWaitStrategy(timeoutInterval, sleepInterval);
    }

    public ToBeVisibleWaitStrategy beVisible() {
        return new ToBeVisibleWaitStrategy(30, 2);
    }

    public ToBeClickableWaitStrategy beClickable(int timeoutInterval, int sleepInterval) {
        return new ToBeClickableWaitStrategy(timeoutInterval, sleepInterval);
    }
```

```
    public ToBeClickableWaitStrategy beClickable() {
        return new ToBeClickableWaitStrategy(30, 2);
    }
}
```

> **NOTE**
>
> We have overloads without timeout parameters. Inside the methods' body, we use the default timeouts in *Chapter 10. Test Data Preparation and Test Environments* will review how to set/read these default values from configuration files based on the environment against which we execute the automated tests.

4. The factory works with a static class used for syntax sugar for easier usage and making the code more readable.

```
public class Wait {
    public static WaitStrategyFactory to() {
        return new WaitStrategyFactory();
    }
}
```

5. Here is how we use it. You can see why we didn't follow the best practices for naming methods and classes from the code.

```
public class CartPage extends NavigatableEShopPage {
    private final BrowserService browserService;
    private final ElementWaitService elementWaitService;

    public CartPage(Driver driver) {
        super(driver, driver);
        this.browserService = driver;
        this.elementWaitService = driver;
    }

    public CartPage applyCoupon(String coupon) {
        elementWaitService.wait(elements().couponCodeTextField(), Wait.to().exists());
        elements().couponCodeTextField().typeText(coupon);
        elements().applyCouponButton().click();
        browserService.waitForAjax();
        return this;
    }
    // rest of the code
}
```

We initialize `ElementWaitService` in the page's constructor. To use it, we call its `wait` method and pass the element which will be waited. The second parameter is generated by our `WaitStrategyFactory` class - from the static `to` method of the `Wait` class. We created a 'sentence' of more meaningful code through the sequence of a class name, property name, and method name.

> **NOTE**
>
> If we want to enable our framework users to add their custom wait strategies, they can create an extension method for the `WaitStrategyFactory` and `Wait` classes. Lombok or Manifold projects can be used for the job as we developed find element extensions.

Adding Extensibility Points through EventFiringWebDriver

We looked in the previous chapters at how we could add up a behavior to the web element's or the driver's methods. We did it by using the **Decorator design pattern**. We added a logging functionality to our framework without adding a single line of code to our tests. WebDriver gives us a native way for adding behavior to some of its actions by exposing delegates. To use this functionality, you need to initialize the `EventFiringWebDriver` class.

Integrating EventFiringWebDriver

We can add the `EventFiringWebDriver` logic to our `WebCoreDriver` decorator. The first version will look like this:

```
public class WebCoreDriver extends Driver {
    private WebDriver webDriver;
    private WebDriverWait webDriverWait;
    private EventFiringWebDriver eventFiringWebDriver;

    @Override
    public void start(Browser browser) {
        switch (browser)
        {
            case CHROME:
                WebDriverManager.chromedriver().setup();
                webDriver = new ChromeDriver();
                break;
```

```
            case FIREFOX:
                WebDriverManager.firefoxdriver().setup();
                webDriver = new FirefoxDriver();
                break;
            case EDGE:
               WebDriverManager.edgedriver().setup();
                webDriver = new EdgeDriver();
                break;
            case OPERA:
               WebDriverManager.operadriver().setup();
                webDriver = new OperaDriver();
                break;
            case SAFARI:
                WebDriverManager.safaridriver().setup();
                webDriver = new SafariDriver();
                break;
            case INTERNET_EXPLORER:
               WebDriverManager.iedriver().setup();
                webDriver = new InternetExplorerDriver();
                break;
            default:
                throw new IllegalArgumentException(browser.name());
        }

        webDriverWait = new WebDriverWait(webDriver, 30);
        eventFiringWebDriver = new EventFiringWebDriver(webDriver);
        eventFiringWebDriver.register(new LoggingListener());
    }
    // rest of the code
}
```

When we initialize WebDriver in the `start` method, we create an instance of the `EventFiringWebDriver`, and we register our listener classes. `LoggingListener` prints to the console a message when a particular action happens. The `LoggingListener` class needs to implement the interface `WebDriverEventListener`.

```
public class LoggingListener implements WebDriverEventListener {
    @Override
    public void beforeNavigateRefresh(WebDriver driver) {
        System.out.print("before navigate refresh");
    }

    @Override
    public void afterNavigateRefresh(WebDriver driver) {
        System.out.print("after navigate refresh");
    }

    @Override
    public void beforeFindBy(By by, WebElement element, WebDriver driver) {
        System.out.print("before find by");
    }

    @Override
```

```
    public void afterFindBy(By by, WebElement element, WebDriver driver) {
        System.out.print("after find by");
    }

    @Override
    public void beforeClickOn(WebElement element, WebDriver driver) {
        System.out.print("before click on");
    }

    @Override
    public void afterClickOn(WebElement element, WebDriver driver) {
        System.out.print("after click on");
    }
    // rest of the code
}
```

Summary

In this chapter, we discussed topics related to framework extensibility. How to make the test code easier to extend and customize following the **Open/Closed principle**. We used the **Strategy design pattern** to build extensibility for locating and waiting for elements. At the end of the chapter, we talked about the existing Vanilla WebDriver support for adding execution of custom code at various points of the WebDriver execution flow.

This chapter ended up the second part of the book, where we discussed the attributes of the high-quality tests - test readability, test maintainability/reusability, API usability, and extensibility. In the next part, we will learn a systematic method of evaluating and deciding which is the best approach for test writing - having in mind the attributes of the designs. Also, we will talk about how to use the most appropriate test data and create the right environment for test execution.

Questions

1. Can you define the main participants in the Strategy design pattern?
2. Why is the vanilla WebDriver `By` class difficult to extend?
3. How can you wait for a specific element to be clickable?
4. What is the primary role of the `EventFiringWebDriver` class?

Chapter 8. Assessment System for Test Architecture Design

In the previous chapter, we discussed topics related to the framework's extensibility and made the framework's code easier to extend and customize, following the **Open/Closed principle**. We used the **Strategy design pattern** to build such extensibility for locating and waiting for elements. At the end of the chapter, we talked about the existing Vanilla WebDriver support for allowing you to add and execute custom code at various points of the WebDriver execution flow. With this, we ended up the second part of the book, where we discussed the high-quality attributes - test readability, test maintainability/reusability, API usability, and extensibility.

In the next part, we will learn a systematic method of evaluating and deciding which is the best approach for test writing - having various attributes of the designs in mind. Also, we will talk about how to use the most appropriate test data and create the right environment for test execution. First, we will discuss the test's design assessment system, defining its criteria, explaining how to apply it in practice. In the second section, we will evaluate three of the designs we already used in the book - tests without page objects, the ones that used the pattern, and the end tests that use the **Facade design pattern**.

These topics will be covered in this chapter:

- Assessment System Introduction Assessment
- System Usage Examples

Assessment System Introduction

What Problem Are We Trying to Solve?

If you need to write just one or two automated tests, it rarely matters how you write them. You can place the whole code inside the tests' body, and that may be just fine. However, if you plan to have hundreds or thousands of sophisticated system tests, you need to plan how to maintain this test suite. If you think before having all these tests, then good for you. Usually, you create a spike project with 2-3 types of tests' architectures and pick one of them. The same can be valid if, after a year or two, you realize that something needs to be changed and your test suite needs to be refactored. But how do you choose between the different tests' designs? The assessment system we discuss in the chapter will help you make a systematic decision based on numbers and not feelings or moods.

Criteria Definitions

What is the automated test designs' assessment system? It contains 7 criteria that will be used later to evaluate each design. For each, we assign ratings based on our judgment. Most are not tool evaluated, but rather they depend on our understanding of the terms and architecture know-how. Don't worry, reading previous chapters should give you enough knowledge to include proper ratings. We will discuss later more thoroughly the exact steps to incorporate the system into your team. The whole second section is dedicated to sample usages of it. Let us start with defining the assessment criteria. We already reviewed some definitions in chapter one, but I will go through them again with some additions. Additionally, we had whole chapters discussing some of the criteria, so till now, you should have a good feel for what the terms mean.

1. Readability

By reading the code, you should be able to discover what the code does easily. A code that is not readable usually requires more time to read, maintain, understand, and increase the chance to introduce bugs. Some programmers use huge comments instead of writing more simple and readable code. It is much easier to name your variables, methods, classes correctly instead of relying on these comments. With time passing, the comments tend not to be maintained, and they can mislead the readers.

2. Maintainability

"The ease with which we can customize or change our software solution to accommodate new requirements, fix problems, improve performance."

Imagine there is a problem with your tests. How much time do you need to figure out where the problem is? Is it an automation bug or an issue in the system under test? It is tightly related to the design of your tests - how the tests are grouped, what design patterns are used, where your elements' locators are placed. It depends on the extensibility and reusability of your code, but as a whole, it should measure the ease with which you analyze the test failures and keep the tests running. The better the maintainability is, the easier it is for us to support our existing code, accommodate new requirements, or fix bugs.

3. Reusability

It is tightly connected to maintainability. A related principle is the so-called DRY- Don't Repeat Yourself. The most basic idea behind the DRY principle is to reduce long-term maintenance costs by removing all unnecessary duplication. But if at the beginning you haven't designed your code in such a way, the changes may need to be applied to multiple places, which can lead to missing some and thus resulting in more bugs. This can slow down the new tests' development, analysis of test failures, and existing tests' maintenance.

4. API Usability

The API is the specification of what you can do with a software library. API usability means how easy it is for you to discover what the methods do and figure out how to use them. If we are talking about a test library - how much time is needed for a new user to create a new test? It is related to the learning curve.

In the programming community, we sometimes use another term for the same thing called **syntactic sugar**. It describes how easy it is to use or read some expressions. It sweetens the programming languages for humans. The programming statements become more concise and clearer.

5. Extensibility

One of the hardest things to develop is to allow these **generic frameworks to be extensible and customizable**. The whole point of creating a shared library is to be used by multiple teams across the company. However, the different teams work in different contexts. They may have to test a little bit different thing. So, the library code may not be working out of the box for them. Thus, the engineers should be able to customize some parts to fit them to their needs.

With automated tests, we already looked into a test suite used for testing an online shopping cart. The testing workflow consists of multiple steps- choosing the product, changing the quantity, adding more products, applying discount coupons, filling billing info, providing payment info, etc. If a new requirement comes that the system should prefill the billing info for logged users- how easy would it be for you to change the existing tests? Did you write your tests so that if you add this new functionality, it will not affect your existing tests?

6. Code Complexity Index

The code complexity index is the only tool calculated metric. The four components can be calculated through IntelliJ + a plug-in called **MetricsReloaded**. Later on, we can evaluate the ratings based on the table you will see below.

Code Complexity Index Rating = (Depth of Inheritance Rating + Class Coupling Rating + Maintainability Index Rating + Cyclomatic Complexity Rating)/4

- **Depth of Inheritance** - we measure how many classes you inherited in your tests. Usually, the deeper the inheritance is, the more difficult it is to understand the code and maintain it.
- **Class Coupling** - calculated based on the number of classes that your code depends on. The more independent your tests are- the better. More dependencies bring more changes to your code if they are refactored, or their API differs with new versions.
- **Maintainability Index** - represents a number between 0 and 100. High numbers mean that your tests are more maintainable. Below you can see a sample formula that can calculate the index. We will use tools to calculate it for us, so don't worry.

Maintainability Index = MAX(0, (171 – 5.2 * ln(Halstead Volume) – 0.23 * (Cyclomatic Complexity) – 16.2 * ln(Lines of Code))*100 / 171)

> **NOTE**
>
> The Halstead complexity measures were introduced in 1977 by Maurice Halstead. They are software metrics part of the empirical science of software development. He observed that the metrics should reflect the expression or implementation of algorithms in different languages but be independent of their execution on a specific platform.

Cyclomatic Complexity - Below, you can find the formula for Cyclomatic complexity.

- **Cyclomatic Complexity = CC=E-N + 2**
- E = the number of edges of the graph
- N = the number of nodes of the graph

The Cyclomatic complexity calculation is based on the number of decisions in a program. We get each component of the Code Complexity Index formula, and based on the table below, we get their specific rating.

Ratings	Maintainability Index	**Cyclomatic Complexity**	**Class Coupling**	**Depth of Inheritance**
(5) Excellent	> 70	< 10	< 10	=< 3
(4) Very Good	> 60	10-12	< 15	4
(3) Good	40-60	12-15	< 20	5
(2) Poor	20-40	15-20	< 30	6-8
(1) Very Poor	< 20	> 20	> 30	>8

In the second section, you will see examples of how to calculate all these numbers.

NOTE

The numbers in the table are an example. We used them in my teams to measure the code complexity index. They are based on research in books that developers have used to evaluate the Cyclomatic complexity. However, the numbers varied significantly, so modify them as you please or do your own research.

NOTE

The Cyclomatic Complexity was invented by Thomas J. McCabe, Sr. in 1976 in his paper where he explained the idea. He borrowed concepts from graph theory to represent the programs' code as a graph. The goal is to capture the complexity of a module in a single number.

7. Learning Curve

I also like to call this attribute "**Easy Knowledge Transfer**". The attribute answers the question- "How easy is it for someone to learn by himself?". The learning curve is tightly connected to API usability, but it means something different. If a new member joins your team, is he able to learn by himself how to use your test automation framework, or he needs to read the documentation if it exists? Or you have a mentoring program where you need to teach these new members yourself every time to use your code?

8. KISS*

The last criterion is not something that we will calculate; rather, it is a principle- "**Keep It Simple Stupid**". The below quote from Martin Fowler best describes the principle.
"Any fool can write code that a computer can understand. Good programmers write code that humans can understand."

We can use it if all other numbers/ratings/index are equal, which in my practice haven't happened. But if in some rare case happens, the rule of thumb is that you chose the simplest design. Later we will assess a design that uses page objects and the more sophisticated one that uses facades. If they have equal ratings, and we apply the KISS rule, we will most probably pick the page objects design since it is simpler than the facade one.

> **NOTE**
>
> Martin Fowler is a British software developer. He is an international speaker and author of several popular software development books. Two of his most famous pieces are Refactoring: Improving the Design of Existing Code and Patterns of Enterprise Application Architecture.

Assessment Ratings

For each of the above criteria, we assign a rating, which is a number. To calculate the final **TDI (Test Design Index)**, we sum all the criteria ratings. The design with a better TDI score wins the competition.

(1) Very Poor

(2) Poor

(3) Good

(4) Very Good

(5) Excellent

Steps to Apply

The test architecture design assessment is a team effort. You can do it on your own, but this way, you may not be too objective. When you have the TDI ratings from a couple of experienced colleagues, it will decrease the preferences during the final decision. Here is the recommended assessment flow.

1. Create a research & development branch different from the one where your tests are right now
2. Create separate projects for each test design
3. Develop a few tests using the proposed design
4. Implement the same set of test cases for each design
5. Present the solutions to the team members that will be part of the assessment
6. Every participant uses the system and assigns ratings
7. Create a final assessment meeting

Assessment System Usage Examples

Now it is time to put the assessment system into practice. If you see a couple of examples of how we define the ratings, you can do the same for your test designs. We will evaluate the three designs we covered in previous chapters. The first one is with Vanilla WebDriver without page objects. The second one will be the last version of the Page Object Model design pattern we discussed. The last one will be tests that use the second variation of the facade design pattern. Don't worry - there will be code snippets to remind you how each of these designs looks. For each, we will first remember what the tests looked like. Then we will go through each criterion from the previous section and place rating based on our personal judgment. In the end, we will have the TDI index calculated for each design. The design with the highest score will win. If some have equal ratings, we will use the KISS rule - the simplest of them will win.

Tests without Page Objects Assessment

Architecture Design Overview

Here is what our tests without page objects looked like.

```
public class ProductPurchaseTests {
    private WebDriver driver;
    private static String purchaseEmail;
    private static String purchaseOrderNumber;

    @BeforeMethod
```

```
    public void testInit() {
        WebDriverManager.chromedriver().setup();
        driver = new ChromeDriver();
        driver.manage().timeouts().implicitlyWait(10, TimeUnit.SECONDS);
    }

    @AfterMethod
    public void testCleanup() {
        driver.quit();
    }

    @Test(priority=1)
    public void completePurchaseSuccessfully_whenNewClient() {
        driver.navigate().to("http://demos.bellatrix.solutions/");
        var addToCartFalcon9 = waitAndFindElement(By.cssSelector("[data-
product_id*='28']"));
        addToCartFalcon9.click();
        var viewCartButton = waitAndFindElement(By.cssSelector("[class*='added_to_cart wc-
forward']"));
        viewCartButton.click();

        var couponCodeTextField = waitAndFindElement(By.id("coupon_code"));
        couponCodeTextField.clear();
        couponCodeTextField.sendKeys("happybirthday");
        var applyCouponButton = waitAndFindElement(By.cssSelector("[value*='Apply
coupon']"));
        applyCouponButton.click();
        Thread.sleep(4000);
        var messageAlert = waitAndFindElement(By.cssSelector("[class*='woocommerce-
message']"));
        Assert.assertEquals(messageAlert.getText(), "Coupon code applied successfully.");

        var quantityBox = waitAndFindElement(By.cssSelector("[class*='input-text qty
text']"));
        quantityBox.clear();
        quantityBox.sendKeys("2");

        var updateCart = waitAndFindElement(By.cssSelector("[value*='Update cart']"));
        updateCart.click();
        Thread.sleep(4000);
        var totalSpan = waitAndFindElement(By.xpath("//*[@class='order-total']//span"));
        Assert.assertEquals("114.00€", totalSpan.getText());

        var proceedToCheckout = waitAndFindElement(By.cssSelector("[class*='checkout-button
button alt wc-forward']"));
        proceedToCheckout.click();

        var billingFirstName = waitAndFindElement(By.id("billing_first_name"));
        billingFirstName.sendKeys("Anton");
        var billingLastName = waitAndFindElement(By.id("billing_last_name"));
        billingLastName.sendKeys("Angelov");
        var billingCompany = waitAndFindElement(By.id("billing_company"));
        billingCompany.sendKeys("Space Flowers");
```

```
        var billingCountryWrapper = waitAndFindElement(By.id("select2-billing_country-
container"));
        billingCountryWrapper.click();
        var billingCountryFilter = waitAndFindElement(By.className("select2-
search__field"));
        billingCountryFilter.sendKeys("Germany");
        var germanyOption = waitAndFindElement(By.xpath("//*[contains(text(),'Germany')]"));
        germanyOption.click();
        var billingAddress1 = waitAndFindElement(By.id("billing_address_1"));
        billingAddress1.sendKeys("1 Willi Brandt Avenue Tiergarten");
        var billingAddress2 = waitAndFindElement(By.id("billing_address_2"));
        billingAddress2.sendKeys("Lotzowplatz 17");
        var billingCity = waitAndFindElement(By.id("billing_city"));
        billingCity.sendKeys("Berlin");
        var billingZip = waitAndFindElement(By.id("billing_postcode"));
        billingZip.clear();
        billingZip.sendKeys("10115");
        var billingPhone = waitAndFindElement(By.id("billing_phone"));
        billingPhone.sendKeys("+00498888999281");
        var billingEmail = waitAndFindElement(By.id("billing_email"));
        billingEmail.sendKeys("info@berlinspaceflowers.com");
        purchaseEmail = "info@berlinspaceflowers.com";

        // This pause will be removed when we introduce a logic for waiting for AJAX
requests.
        Thread.sleep(5000);
        var placeOrderButton = waitAndFindElement(By.id("place_order"));
        placeOrderButton.click();

        Thread.sleep(10000);
        var receivedMessage =
waitAndFindElement(By.xpath("/html/body/div[1]/div/div/div/main/div/header/h1"));
        Assert.assertEquals(receivedMessage.getText(), "Order received");
    }

    @Test(priority=2)
    public void completePurchaseSuccessfully_whenExistingClient() {
        driver.navigate().to("http://demos.bellatrix.solutions/");

        var addToCartFalcon9 = waitAndFindElement(By.cssSelector("[data-
product_id*='28']"));
        addToCartFalcon9.click();
        var viewCartButton = waitAndFindElement(By.cssSelector("[class*='added_to_cart wc-
forward']"));
        viewCartButton.click();

        var couponCodeTextField = waitAndFindElement(By.id("coupon_code"));
        couponCodeTextField.clear();
        couponCodeTextField.sendKeys("happybirthday");
        var applyCouponButton = waitAndFindElement(By.cssSelector("[value*='Apply
coupon']"));
        applyCouponButton.click();
        var messageAlert = waitAndFindElement(By.cssSelector("[class*='woocommerce-
message']"));
```

```
        Thread.sleep(4000);
        Assert.assertEquals(messageAlert.getText(), "Coupon code applied successfully.");

        var quantityBox = waitAndFindElement(By.cssSelector("[class*='input-text qty
text']"));
        quantityBox.clear();
        quantityBox.sendKeys("2");
        var updateCart = waitAndFindElement(By.cssSelector("[value*='Update cart']"));
        updateCart.click();
        Thread.sleep(4000);
        var totalSpan = waitAndFindElement(By.xpath("//*[@class='order-total']//span"));
        Assert.assertEquals(totalSpan.getText(), "114.00€");

        var proceedToCheckout = waitAndFindElement(By.cssSelector("[class*='checkout-button
button alt wc-forward']"));
        proceedToCheckout.click();

        var loginHereLink = waitAndFindElement(By.linkText("Click here to login"));
        loginHereLink.click();
        var userName = waitAndFindElement(By.id("username"));
        userName.sendKeys(purchaseEmail);
        var password = waitAndFindElement(By.id("password"));
        password.sendKeys(GetUserPasswordFromDb(purchaseEmail));
        var loginButton = waitAndFindElement(By.xpath("//button[@name='login']"));
        loginButton.click();

        // This pause will be removed when we introduce a logic for waiting for AJAX
requests.
        Thread.sleep(5000);
        var placeOrderButton = waitAndFindElement(By.id("place_order"));
        placeOrderButton.click();

        var receivedMessage = waitAndFindElement(By.xpath("//h1[text() = 'Order
received']"));
        Assert.assertEquals(receivedMessage.getText(), "Order received");

        var orderNumber = waitAndFindElement(By.xpath("//*[@id='post-7']//li[1]/strong"));
        purchaseOrderNumber = orderNumber.getText();
    }

    @Test(priority=3)
    public void correctOrderDataDisplayed_whenNavigateToMyAccountOrderSection() {
        driver.navigate().to("http://demos.bellatrix.solutions/");

        var myAccountLink = waitAndFindElement(By.linkText("My account"));
        myAccountLink.click();
        var userName = waitAndFindElement(By.id("username"));
        Thread.sleep(4000);
        userName.sendKeys(purchaseEmail);
        var password = waitAndFindElement(By.id("password"));
        password.sendKeys(GetUserPasswordFromDb(GetUserPasswordFromDb(purchaseEmail)));
        var loginButton = waitAndFindElement(By.xpath("//button[@name='login']"));
        loginButton.click();
```

```
        var orders = waitAndFindElement(By.linkText("Orders"));
        orders.click();

        var viewButtons = waitAndFindElements(By.linkText("View"));
        viewButtons.get(0).click();

        var orderName = waitAndFindElement(By.xpath("//h1"));
        String expectedMessage = String.format("Order #%s", purchaseOrderNumber);
        Assert.assertEquals(expectedMessage, orderName.getText());
    }

    private String GetUserPasswordFromDb(String userName)  {
        return "@purISQzt%%DYBnLCIhaoG6$";
    }

    private void waitToBeClickable(By by)  {
        var webDriverWait = new WebDriverWait(driver, 30);
        webDriverWait.until(ExpectedConditions.elementToBeClickable(by));
    }

    private WebElement waitAndFindElement(By by) {
        var webDriverWait = new WebDriverWait(driver, 30);
        return webDriverWait.until(ExpectedConditions.presenceOfElementLocated(by));
    }

    private List<WebElement> waitAndFindElements(By by)  {
        var webDriverWait = new WebDriverWait(driver, 30);
        return webDriverWait.until(ExpectedConditions.presenceOfAllElementsLocatedBy(by));
    }
}
```

Let's summarize the design approach. We define the web elements in each test separately. We reuse some of the logic in private methods placed in the test class. The data used in tests is passed directly to WebDriver methods with no model classes like `PurchaseInfo`. If we want to add more cases, we will add them here in this particular class. If we split the test cases into more classes, we will need to duplicate the private methods or require refactoring.

Here are the ratings for each of the assessment criteria.

1. Readability

I will rate the readability here as Poor. Why? Well, the whole workflow is visible from the test- that is true. However, we use lots of low-level vanilla WebDriver code, which makes the tests long and obscure. Usually, we want to see only the test case details with no low-level details like waits, or how the elements are located.

Criteria	**Rating**
Readability	2

Maintainability	
Reusability	
API Usability	
Extensibility	
Code Complexity Index	
Learning Curve	
Test Design Index	

2. Maintainability

As far as we have only a single class, it may not be so much work to maintain the tests. However, it will get harder and harder to fix the logic with the increase of added tests. We can use find and replace to change locators but imagine that we haven't moved some of the logic in a private method and it is duplicated in all tests- then you will need to change it everywhere. Also, since the tests are copy-pasted in most parts but with small modifications, when you have lots of failed tests, you cannot be sure of the reasons for the failures in the workflow- you will need to debug and investigate each failure separately. If you have only a few tests, then the maintainability won't be as bad as described, but it won't be great. I gave a Poor rating of 2.

Criteria	**Rating**
Readability	2
Maintainability	2
Reusability	
API Usability	
Extensibility	
Code Complexity Index	
Learning Curve	
Test Design Index	

3. Reusability

As you can see from the example, our code reuse is limited to a couple of private methods, which will be copy-pasted in new test classes as mentioned in the quick fix scenario. No further review of the design will make the tests even harder to maintain. My rating here is very poor (1).

Criteria	Rating
Readability	2
Maintainability	2
Reusability	1
API Usability	
Extensibility	
Code Complexity Index	
Learning Curve	
Test Design Index	

4. API Usability

How easy is it to use the design API? Well, in this particular case, I cannot say we have an API at all. We have a few private methods, but that is all. It is not fair to rate how easy it is to use the vanilla WebDriver API since the whole idea of the exercise is to create our abstraction layer for more robust and stable tests. Again, I gave a rating of very poor (1).

Criteria	Rating
Readability	2
Maintainability	2
Reusability	1
API Usability	1
Extensibility	
Code Complexity Index	
Learning Curve	
Test Design Index	

5. Extensibility

Imagine that we want to add a new step to the online shopping cart purchase workflow. What will we do with non-page-object tests? If the logic is a private method, we can add it in a single place, but this would be true only if it is not copy-pasted among other test classes. If it is not reused, the code for extending may appear in multiple tests. Then we will need to analyze which of them to refactor and copy-paste the new logic, which again, with each addition, will worsen the maintenance. I gave a rating of poor (2).

Criteria	Rating
Readability	2
Maintainability	2
Reusability	1
API Usability	1
Extensibility	2
Code Complexity Index	
Learning Curve	
Test Design Index	

6. Code Complexity Index

Now the time comes to see how we can calculate all the indexes we reviewed.
Code Complexity Index Rating = (Depth of Inheritance Rating + Class Coupling Rating + Maintainability Index Rating + Cyclomatic Complexity Rating)/4

To calculate the metrics in IntelliJ, you need to install a free plug-in called **MetricsReloaded**. After that, in IntelliJ, you can go to the **Analyze** menu item and click on the **Calculate Metrics**.

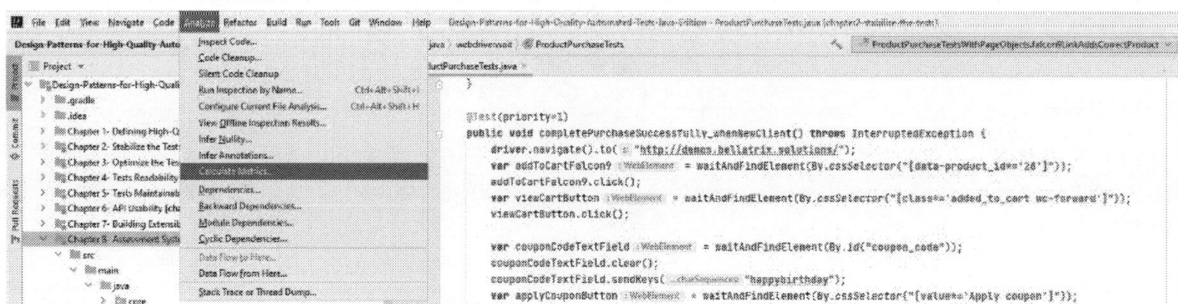

There are too many metrics when analyzing the whole project, so we need only a few that we will use. To do so, click on the "..." buttons under the Metrics profile.

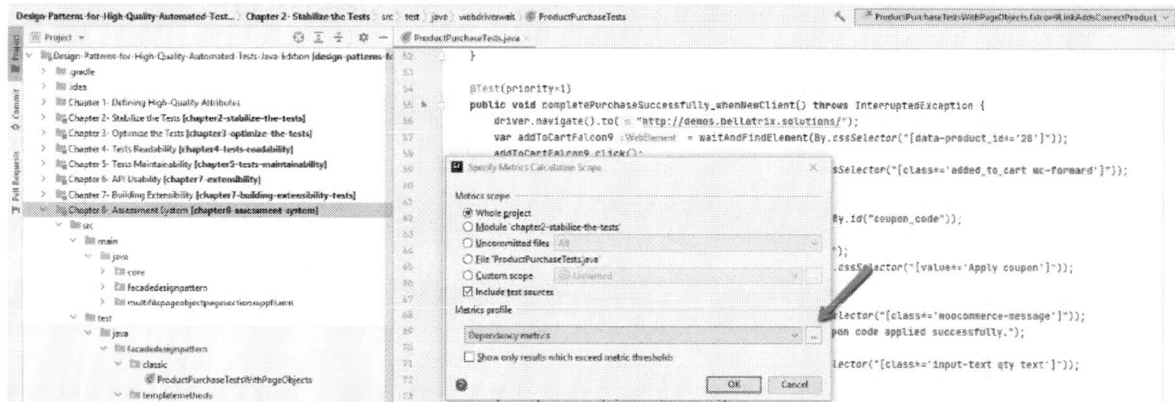

We will use only the **Class metrics** so you can uncheck the rest. From the Class metrics section, choose Coupling between Objects, Depth of Inheritance tree, Weighted method complexity (Total methods' Cyclomatic Complexity), Lines of code, and Halstead volume.

Then, in the **Class Metrics Results** window, you can find the code metrics for each class part of your solution.

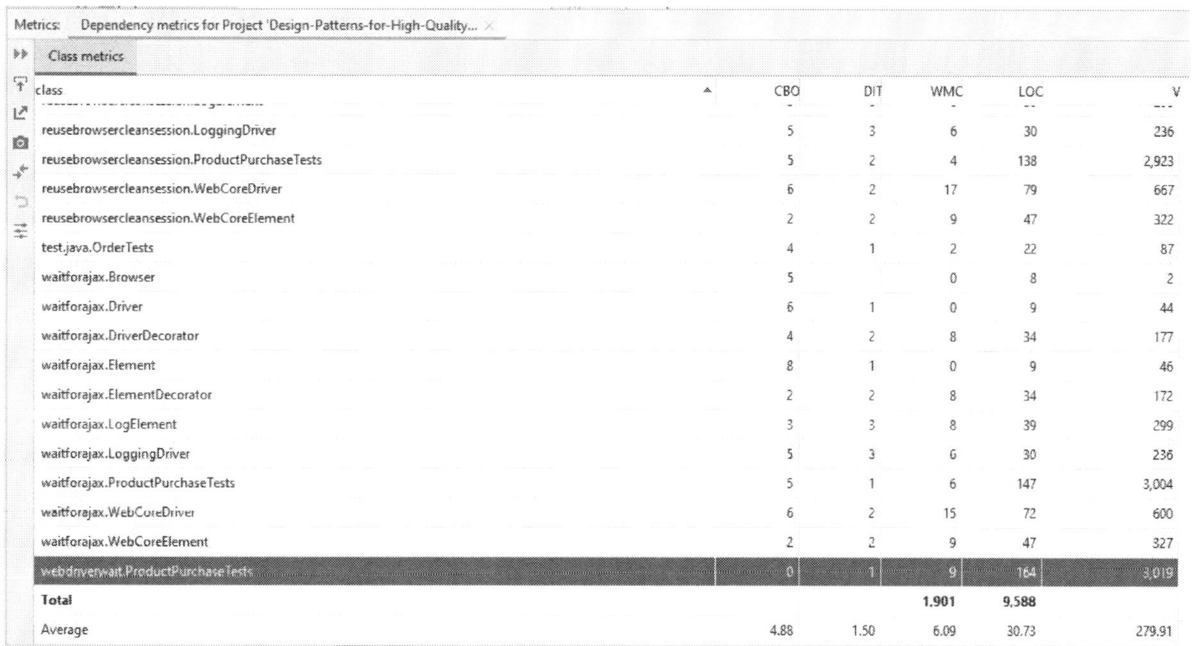

Metrics: Dependency metrics for Project 'Design-Patterns-for-High-Quality...

Class metrics

class	CBO	DIT	WMC	LOC	V
reusebrowsercleansession.LoggingDriver	5	3	6	30	236
reusebrowsercleansession.ProductPurchaseTests	5	2	4	138	2,923
reusebrowsercleansession.WebCoreDriver	6	2	17	79	667
reusebrowsercleansession.WebCoreElement	2	2	9	47	322
test.java.OrderTests	4	1	2	22	87
waitforajax.Browser	5		0	8	2
waitforajax.Driver	6	1	0	9	44
waitforajax.DriverDecorator	4	2	8	34	177
waitforajax.Element	8	1	0	9	46
waitforajax.ElementDecorator	2	2	8	34	172
waitforajax.LogElement	3	3	8	39	299
waitforajax.LoggingDriver	5	3	6	30	236
waitforajax.ProductPurchaseTests	5	1	6	147	3,004
waitforajax.WebCoreDriver	6	2	15	72	600
waitforajax.WebCoreElement	2	2	9	47	327
webdriverwait.ProductPurchaseTests	0	1	9	164	3,019
Total			**1,901**	**9,588**	
Average	4.88	1.50	6.09	30.73	279.91

If your design contains more than one class - we get the numbers for each class part and get the average rating. To ease these calculations, we can copy the data to an Excel sheet. There, created a new column for calculating the maintainability index based on the formula **Maintainability Index = MAX(0, (171 – 5.2 * ln(Halstead Volume) – 0.23 * (Cyclomatic Complexity) – 16.2 * ln(Lines of Code))*100 / 171)**

G2 =MAX(0,(171-5.2*LN(F2)-0.23*D2-16.2*LN(E2))*100/171)

Class Names	Coupling	Depth of Inheritance	Cyclomatic Complexity	Lines of Code	Halstead Volume	Maintainability Index
facadedesignpattern.classic.CartPage.CartPage	10	3	11	45	343.4823417	44.70091346
facadedesignpattern.classic.CartPage.CartPageAssertions	5	1	3	14	83.76180829	61.12970179
facadedesignpattern.classic.CartPage.CartPageElements	5	1	8	27	212.3963757	51.40554433
facadedesignpattern.classic.CheckoutPage.CheckoutAssertions	5	1	2	10	53.77443751	65.79951507
facadedesignpattern.classic.CheckoutPage.CheckoutElements	5	1	17	55	525.1448089	40.70181131
facadedesignpattern.classic.CheckoutPage.CheckoutPage	9	2	6	36	504.6426222	46.31752667
facadedesignpattern.classic.EShopPage	8	1	4	15	69.76048999	60.89779776
facadedesignpattern.classic.MainPage.MainPage	8	3	6	27	140.1816079	52.93810591
facadedesignpattern.classic.MainPage.MainPageAssertions	3	1	2	11	70.32403072	64.08064679
facadedesignpattern.classic.MainPage.MainPageElements	5	1	5	21	147.1486623	55.30598299
facadedesignpattern.classic.NavigatableEShopPage	7	2	2	12	68.11428751	63.35341515
facadedesignpattern.classic.ProductPurchaseTestsWithPageObjects	13	1	6	96	1422.801956	33.87343014
facadedesignpattern.classic.PurchaseFacade	8	1	2	22	235.5307486	53.8383256
facadedesignpattern.classic.PurchaseInfo	3	1	24	86	554.8699868	35.35798707
facadedesignpattern.classic.Sections.BreadcrumbSection	4	1	3	13	85.83671967	61.75736644
facadedesignpattern.classic.Sections.CartInfoSection	4	1	5	20	114.4489596	56.53243661
facadedesignpattern.classic.Sections.MainMenuSection	4	1	11	40	267.5658971	46.5762867
facadedesignpattern.classic.Sections.SearchSection	4	1	3	12	80	62.72980922
AVG	6.111111111	1.333333333	6.666666667	31.22222222	276.6547634	53.18314461
Ratings	5	5	5		3	4.5

Let us review the table again. It helps us to determine the index of each component used in the formula.

Ratings	Maintainability Index	**Cyclomatic Complexity**	**Class Coupling**	**Depth of Inheritance**
(5) Excellent	> 70	< 10	< 10	=< 3
(4) Very Good	> 60	10-12	< 15	4
(3) Good	40-60	12-15	< 20	5
(2) Poor	20-40	15-20	< 30	6-8
(1) Very Poor	< 20	> 20	> 30	>8

The maintainability index is equal to 26.1, so we put an index poor (2). For Cyclomatic Complexity = 9 - excellent (5). Class Coupling = 0 - excellent (5). Depth of Inheritance = 1 excellent (5). After we have each separate component index, we replace them in the formula to get the Code Complexity Index Rating.

Code Complexity Index Rating = (2 + 5 + 5 + 5)/4 = 4

Criteria	Rating
Readability	2
Maintainability	2
Reusability	1
API Usability	1
Extensibility	2
Code Complexity Index	4
Learning Curve	
Test Design Index	

7. Learning Curve

This design is the easiest to start with since it requires no previous knowledge besides how to use WebDriver. However, the tests' bodies tend to be much longer when they contain low-level WebDriver API details, making understanding the test cases harder. Since some of the code is copy-pasted, another part is reused as private methods, which can get confusing for newcomers. Therefore, I give only a good (3) rating.

Criteria	Rating
Readability	2
Maintainability	2
Reusability	1
API Usability	1
Extensibility	2
Code Complexity Index	4
Learning Curve	3
Test Design Index	

Test Design Index

Criteria	Rating
Readability	2
Maintainability	2
Reusability	1
API Usability	1
Extensibility	2
Code Complexity Index	4
Learning Curve	3
Test Design Index	2.43

Test Design Index = (2 + 2 + 1 + 1 + 2 + 4 + 3) / 7 = 2.43

Tests with Page Objects Assessment

Architecture Design Overview

Why not review a design that uses page objects directly without facades?

We have two base page objects - one for pages that can be navigated to and one for those that cannot.

```
public abstract class EShopPage {
    protected final ElementFindService elementFindService;

    public EShopPage(ElementFindService elementFindService) {
        this.elementFindService = elementFindService;
    }

    public MainMenuSection mainMenuSection() {
        return new MainMenuSection(elementFindService);
    }

    public CartInfoSection cartInfoSection() {
        return new CartInfoSection(elementFindService);
    }

    public SearchSection searchSection() {
        return new SearchSection(elementFindService);
    }
```

```java
}

public abstract class NavigatableEShopPage extends EShopPage {
    protected final NavigationService navigationService;

    public NavigatableEShopPage(ElementFindService elementFindService, NavigationService
navigationService) {
        super(elementFindService);
        this.navigationService = navigationService;
    }

    protected abstract String getUrl();

    public void open()  {
        navigationService.goToUrl(getUrl());
        waitForPageLoad();
    }

    protected abstract void waitForPageLoad();
}
```

In these base pages, we define abstract methods that each separate page objects need to implement, and we reuse common logic such as navigation and page sections.

We have one class for the page object itself and one more that contains the element locators.

```java
public class MainPage extends NavigatableEShopPage {
    public MainPage(Driver driver) {
        super(driver, driver);
    }

    private MainPageElements elements() {
        return new MainPageElements(elementFindService);
    }

    @Override
    protected String getUrl() {
        return "http://demos.bellatrix.solutions/";
    }

    public MainPage addRocketToShoppingCart()  {
        open();
        elements().addToCartFalcon9().click();
        elements().viewCartButton().click();
        return this;
    }

    @Override
    protected void waitForPageLoad() {
        elements().addToCartFalcon9().waitToExists();
    }

    public MainPage assertProductBoxLink(String name, String expectedLink)  {
```

```
        var actualLink = elements().getProductBoxByName(name).getAttribute("href");
        Assert.assertEquals(actualLink, expectedLink);
        return this;
    }
}
```

Here is how we reuse the elements locators.

```
public class MainPageElements {
    private final ElementFindService elementFindService;

    public MainPageElements(ElementFindService elementFindService) {
        this.elementFindService = elementFindService;
    }

    public Element addToCartFalcon9() {
        return elementFindService.findElement(By.cssSelector("[data-product_id*='28']"));
    }

    public Element viewCartButton() {
        return elementFindService.findElement(By.cssSelector("[class*='added_to_cart wc-
forward']"));
    }

    public Element getProductBoxByName(String name)  {
        return
elementFindService.findElement(By.xpath(String.format("//h2[text()='%s']/parent::a[1]",
name)));
    }
}
```

The pages in tests are used through the **App design pattern** based on the **Factory design pattern**.

```
public class App implements AutoCloseable {
    private Boolean disposed = false;

    public App(Browser browserType)  {
        LoggingSingletonDriver.getInstance().start(browserType);
    }

    public NavigationService getNavigationService() {
        return SingletonFactory.getInstance(NavigationService.class);
    }

    public BrowserService getBrowserService() {
        return SingletonFactory.getInstance(BrowserService.class);
    }

    public CookiesService getCookiesService() {
        return SingletonFactory.getInstance(CookiesService.class);
    }
```

```java
    public DialogService getDialogService() {
        return SingletonFactory.getInstance(DialogService.class);
    }

    public <TPage extends NavigatableEShopPage> TPage goTo(Class<TPage> pageOf)  {
        var page = SingletonFactory.getInstance(pageOf,
LoggingSingletonDriver.getInstance());
        page.open();

        return page;
    }

    public <TPage extends EShopPage> TPage create(Class<TPage> pageOf)  {
        return SingletonFactory.getInstance(pageOf, LoggingSingletonDriver.getInstance());
    }

    @Override
    public void close() {
        if (disposed)  {
            return;
        }

        LoggingSingletonDriver.getInstance().quit();

        disposed = true;
    }
}
```

Finally, here is what our code looks like.

```java
public class ProductPurchaseTestsWithPageObjects {
    private static App app;

    @BeforeMethod
    public void testInit() {
        app = new App(Browser.CHROME);
    }

    @AfterMethod
    public void testCleanup() {
        app.close();
    }

    @Test
    public void completePurchaseSuccessfully_WhenNewClient() {
        var mainPage = app.goTo(MainPage.class);

        mainPage.addRocketToShoppingCart();
        var cartPage = app.goTo(CartPage.class);
        cartPage.applyCoupon("happybirthday")
                .assertCouponAppliedSuccessfully()
                .increaseProductQuantity(2)
                .assertTotalPrice("114.00€")
                .clickProceedToCheckout();
```

```
    }
}
```

This implementation of page objects uses the **Fluent API**, which we discussed in *Chapter 6. API Usability*. Here the `App` class is declared as a private static variable, meaning it cannot be shared among test classes. If there are changes in the workflow, we will need to go through each test separately. The usage of **Fluent API** makes the usage of find-and-replace harder.

1. Readability

The readability here is excellent (5). If you name your methods and page objects right, you can understand the whole business use case from the code. At the same time, the page objects hide the low-level details of the vanilla WebDriver API.

Criteria	**Rating**
Readability	5
Maintainability	
Reusability	
API Usability	
Extensibility	
Code Complexity Index	
Learning Curve	
Test Design Index	

2. Maintainability

Debugging and fixing tests using the page objects is relatively easy since we reuse most of the code, and the fixes happen in a single place. The only drawback I stated is that if there are changes in the test workflow (changes in the purchase workflow), we need to change that in every single test. The same is valid if you add or remove method parameters to the page objects' actions. Therefore, I give here the rating of (4) very good.

Criteria	**Rating**
Readability	5
Maintainability	4

Reusability	
API Usability	
Extensibility	
Code Complexity Index	
Learning Curve	
Test Design Index	

3. Reusability

I rate the reusability as very good (4). Most of the stated arguments are valid for it too.

Criteria	Rating
Readability	5
Maintainability	4
Reusability	4
API Usability	
Extensibility	
Code Complexity Index	
Learning Curve	
Test Design Index	

4. API Usability

Fluent API is intuitive to use. The page object design has one drawback compared to facade ones - you must know the order of the pages inside the user workflow. You need to write much more code and, as in this case, call much more methods to describe the purchase workflow. Therefore I rate the API Usability as only very good (4).

Criteria	Rating
Readability	5
Maintainability	4

Reusability	4
API Usability	4
Extensibility	
Code Complexity Index	
Learning Curve	
Test Design Index	

5. Extensibility

If you need to add a new section for all pages, you will add it to the pages' base classes. If you need to add a behavior to page creation, you will do it in the `App` class. If you need to add something to a particular page specific action, you will do it in the page object itself. I repeat myself, but again, the drawback here is that if you need to add new behavior to the existing tests workflow, you need to go through each test. This is why, again, I put a rating of (4) very good.

Criteria	**Rating**
Readability	5
Maintainability	4
Reusability	4
API Usability	4
Extensibility	4
Code Complexity Index	
Learning Curve	
Test Design Index	

6. Code Complexity Index

Here are the code metrics for this test design.

Metrics: Dependency metrics for Project 'Design-Patterns-for-High-Quality...

Class metrics

class	CBO	DIT	WMC	LOC	V
pages.v10.multifilepageobjectpagesectionsappfluent.CartPage.CartPageElements	3	1	8	27	179
pages.v10.multifilepageobjectpagesectionsappfluent.EShopPage	8	1	4	15	69
pages.v10.multifilepageobjectpagesectionsappfluent.LoggingSingletonDriver	9	3	8	37	320
pages.v10.multifilepageobjectpagesectionsappfluent.MainPage.MainPage	7	3	6	29	201
pages.v10.multifilepageobjectpagesectionsappfluent.MainPage.MainPageElements	3	1	4	16	97
pages.v10.multifilepageobjectpagesectionsappfluent.NavigatableEShopPage	6	2	2	14	96
pages.v10.multifilepageobjectpagesectionsappfluent.ProductPurchaseTestsWithPageObjects	4	1	3	22	162
pages.v10.multifilepageobjectpagesectionsappfluent.Sections.BreadcrumbSection	3	1	3	13	74
pages.v10.multifilepageobjectpagesectionsappfluent.Sections.CartInfoSection	3	1	5	20	104
pages.v10.multifilepageobjectpagesectionsappfluent.Sections.MainMenuSection	3	1	11	40	237
pages.v10.multifilepageobjectpagesectionsappfluent.Sections.SearchSection	3	1	3	12	74
pages.v10.multifilepageobjectpagesectionsappfluent.SingletonFactory	1	1	3	20	176

G2 =MAX(0,(171-5.2*LN(F2)-0.23*D2-16.2*LN(E2))*100/171)

Class Names	Coupling	Depth of Inheritance	Cyclomatic Complexity	Lines of Code	Halstead Volume	Maintainability Index	
facadedesignpattern.classic.CartPage.CartPage	10	3	11	45	343.4823417	44.70091346	
pages.v10.multifilepageobjectpagesectionsappfluent.CartPage.CartPageElements	3	1	8	27	179.3067751	51.92054521	
pages.v10.multifilepageobjectpagesectionsappfluent.EShopPage	8	1	4	15	69.76048999	60.89779776	
pages.v10.multifilepageobjectpagesectionsappfluent.LoggingSingletonDriver	9	3	8	37	320	47.17418751	
pages.v10.multifilepageobjectpagesectionsappfluent.MainPage.MainPage	7	3	6	29	201.9089067	51.15155616	
pages.v10.multifilepageobjectpagesectionsappfluent.MainPage.MainPageElements	3	1	4	16	97.67226489	59.26296379	
pages.v10.multifilepageobjectpagesectionsappfluent.NavigatableEShopPage	6	2	2	14	96	60.84950916	
pages.v10.multifilepageobjectpagesectionsappfluent.ProductPurchaseTestsWithPageObjects	4	1	3	22	162.8482304	54.82599719	
pages.v10.multifilepageobjectpagesectionsappfluent.Sections.BreadcrumbSection	3	1	3	13	74.23092132	62.19911128	
pages.v10.multifilepageobjectpagesectionsappfluent.Sections.CartInfoSection	3	1	5	20	104	56.82366988	
pages.v10.multifilepageobjectpagesectionsappfluent.Sections.MainMenuSection	3	1	11	40	237.1851408	46.94279505	
pages.v10.multifilepageobjectpagesectionsappfluent.Sections.SearchSection	3	1	3	12	74.23092132	62.95741061	
pages.v10.multifilepageobjectpagesectionsappfluent.SingletonFactory	1	1	3	20	176.4189163	55.48553101	
AVG	4.84615385	1.538461538	5.461538462	23.84615385	164.3880699	55.01475985	
Ratings	5	5	5			3	4.5

Maintainability Index AVG = 55.01 - Good (3)
Cyclomatic Complexity AVG = 5.46 - Excellent (5)
Class Coupling AVG = 4.84 - Excellent (5)
Depth of Inheritance AVG = 1.54 - Excellent (5)

Code Complexity Index Rating = (3 + 5 + 5 + 5)/4 = 4.5 = 5

Criteria	Rating
Readability	5
Maintainability	4
Reusability	4
API Usability	4
Extensibility	4
Code Complexity Index	5

Learning Curve	
Test Design Index	

7. Learning Curve

The tests are relatively understandable - this is true. However, this design has lots of moving parts - base page objects, page objects classes, the `App` factory, and the test class. As pointed out before, you need to learn the sequence of the pages and how to call their methods. This is why I give a rating of (4) very good.

Criteria	**Rating**
Readability	5
Maintainability	4
Reusability	4
API Usability	4
Extensibility	4
Code Complexity Index	5
Learning Curve	4
Test Design Index	

Test Design Index

Criteria	**Rating**
Readability	5
Maintainability	4
Reusability	4
API Usability	4
Extensibility	4
Code Complexity Index	5
Learning Curve	4
Test Design Index	4.29

Test Design Index = (5 + 4 + 4 + 4 + 4 + 5 + 4) / 7 = 4.29

Tests with Facades Assessment

Architecture Design Overview

In this design, we use almost identical page objects. The difference is that they don't expose a **Fluent API**. The purchase workflow is kept in the main facade class.

```
public class PurchaseFacade {
    private final MainPage mainPage;
    private final CartPage cartPage;
    private final CheckoutPage checkoutPage;

    public PurchaseFacade(MainPage mainPage, CartPage cartPage, CheckoutPage checkoutPage)
{
        this.mainPage = mainPage;
        this.cartPage = cartPage;
        this.checkoutPage = checkoutPage;
    }

    public void verifyItemPurchase(String rocketName, String couponName, int quantity,
String expectedPrice, PurchaseInfo purchaseInfo) {
        mainPage.open();
        mainPage.addRocketToShoppingCart(rocketName);
        cartPage.applyCoupon(couponName);
        cartPage.assertions().assertCouponAppliedSuccessfully();
        cartPage.increaseProductQuantity(quantity);
        cartPage.assertions().assertTotalPrice(expectedPrice);
        cartPage.clickProceedToCheckout();
        checkoutPage.fillBillingInfo(purchaseInfo);
        checkoutPage.assertions().assertOrderReceived();
    }
}
```

Also, for this design, we don't use the **App design pattern**. We initialize the pages and the facades directly in the `beforeClass` method executed once for all tests in the class.

```
public class ProductPurchaseTestsWithPageObjects {
    private Driver driver;
    private static MainPage mainPage;
    private static CartPage cartPage;
    private static CheckoutPage checkoutPage;
    private static PurchaseFacade purchaseFacade;

    @BeforeClass
    public void beforeClass() {
        driver = new LoggingDriver(new WebCoreDriver());
```

```
        driver.start(Browser.CHROME);
        mainPage = new MainPage(driver);
        cartPage = new CartPage(driver);
        checkoutPage = new CheckoutPage(driver);
        purchaseFacade = new PurchaseFacade(mainPage, cartPage, checkoutPage);
    }

    @AfterClass
    public void afterClass() {
        driver.quit();
    }

    @Test
    public void purchaseFalcon9WithFacade() {
        var purchaseInfo = new PurchaseInfo();
        purchaseInfo.setEmail("info@berlinspaceflowers.com");
        purchaseInfo.setFirstName("Anton");
        purchaseInfo.setLastName("Angelov");
        purchaseInfo.setCompany("Space Flowers");
        purchaseInfo.setCountry("Germany");
        purchaseInfo.setAddress1("1 Willi Brandt Avenue Tiergarten");
        purchaseInfo.setAddress2("Lotzowplatz 17");
        purchaseInfo.setCity("Berlin");
        purchaseInfo.setZip("10115");
        purchaseInfo.setPhone("+00498888999281");

        purchaseFacade.verifyItemPurchase("Falcon 9", "happybirthday", 2, "114.00€",
purchaseInfo);
    }

    @Test
    public void purchaseSaturnVWithFacade() {
        var purchaseInfo = new PurchaseInfo();
        purchaseInfo.setEmail("info@berlinspaceflowers.com");
        purchaseInfo.setFirstName("Anton");
        purchaseInfo.setLastName("Angelov");
        purchaseInfo.setCompany("Space Flowers");
        purchaseInfo.setCountry("Germany");
        purchaseInfo.setAddress1("1 Willi Brandt Avenue Tiergarten");
        purchaseInfo.setAddress2("Lotzowplatz 17");
        purchaseInfo.setCity("Berlin");
        purchaseInfo.setZip("10115");
        purchaseInfo.setPhone("+00498888999281");

        purchaseFacade.verifyItemPurchase("Saturn V", "happybirthday", 3, "355.00€",
purchaseInfo);
    }
}
```

We have an additional level of abstraction, but we will make them in a single place if there are changes in the workflow. This can be both a good and a bad thing. From one side, we can fix many failing tests with less effort, but from another side, if we make a mistake, we can introduce a regression in many others. Looking at the test code directly, the workflow is hidden from the user who needs to navigate to the inner method to understand the use case.

1. Readability

Using facades, the automated tests are much shorter than the page objects ones, making them easier to understand. You can view the data used in the test. However, to know the exact workflow, you will need to go inside the workflow method of the facade - you cannot view it from the test itself. But this is usually a one-time effort. Here I give a rating of (5) excellent.

Criteria	**Rating**
Readability	5
Maintainability	
Reusability	
API Usability	
Extensibility	
Code Complexity Index	
Learning Curve	
Test Design Index	

2. Maintainability

With this design, you have all the benefits of using page objects. It solves the only maintainability problem I see with page objects - extending and fixing the overall test workflow. If you need to add something to the workflow or fix something in it, you can do it in a single place - inside the facade's action methods. There are no perfect solutions. You need to be careful not to cause regression. But still, this is not enough of a reason to decrease the rating. I give a rating excellent (5).

Criteria	**Rating**
Readability	5
Maintainability	5

Reusability	
API Usability	
Extensibility	
Code Complexity Index	
Learning Curve	
Test Design Index	

3. Reusability

Everything said till now is valid for the reusability too. My rating, again, here is 5. We reuse everything to the optimal maximum.

Criteria	**Rating**
Readability	5
Maintainability	5
Reusability	5
API Usability	
Extensibility	
Code Complexity Index	
Learning Curve	
Test Design Index	

4. API Usability

The facades provide much fewer methods compared to the many page objects. You need not know the exact order of page object calls. It is now a hidden detail in the facade itself. The only thing you need to know is the minimum of initializing the data correctly for the facade's methods. API Usability is excellent (5).

Criteria	**Rating**
Readability	5

Maintainability	5
Reusability	5
API Usability	5
Extensibility	
Code Complexity Index	
Learning Curve	
Test Design Index	

5. Extensibility

Everything we said about the page objects solution is valid for this design. With the addition, we can extend the tests' workflow. Therefore, the rating is increased to 5 (excellent).

Criteria	**Rating**
Readability	5
Maintainability	5
Reusability	5
API Usability	5
Extensibility	5
Code Complexity Index	
Learning Curve	
Test Design Index	

6. Code Complexity Index

Here are the code metrics for this test design.

Metrics: Dependency metrics for Project 'Design-Patterns-for-High-Quality...

Class metrics

class	CBO	DIT	WMC	LOC	V
facadedesignpattern.classic.CartPage.CartPageAssertions	5	1	3	14	83
facadedesignpattern.classic.CartPage.CartPageElements	5	1	8	27	212
facadedesignpattern.classic.CheckoutPage.CheckoutAssertions	5	1	2	10	53
facadedesignpattern.classic.CheckoutPage.CheckoutElements	5	1	17	55	525
facadedesignpattern.classic.CheckoutPage.CheckoutPage	9	2	6	36	504
facadedesignpattern.classic.EShopPage	8	1	4	15	69
facadedesignpattern.classic.MainPage.MainPage	8	3	6	27	140
facadedesignpattern.classic.MainPage.MainPageAssertions	3	1	2	11	70
facadedesignpattern.classic.MainPage.MainPageElements	5	1	5	21	147
facadedesignpattern.classic.NavigatableEShopPage	7	2	2	12	68
facadedesignpattern.classic.ProductPurchaseTestsWithPageObjects	13	1	6	96	1,422
facadedesignpattern.classic.PurchaseFacade	8	1	2	22	235
facadedesignpattern.classic.PurchaseInfo	3	1	24	86	554
facadedesignpattern.classic.Sections.BreadcrumbSection	4	1	3	13	85
facadedesignpattern.classic.Sections.CartInfoSection	4	1	5	20	114
facadedesignpattern.classic.Sections.MainMenuSection	4	1	11	40	267
facadedesignpattern.classic.Sections.SearchSection	4	1	3	12	80

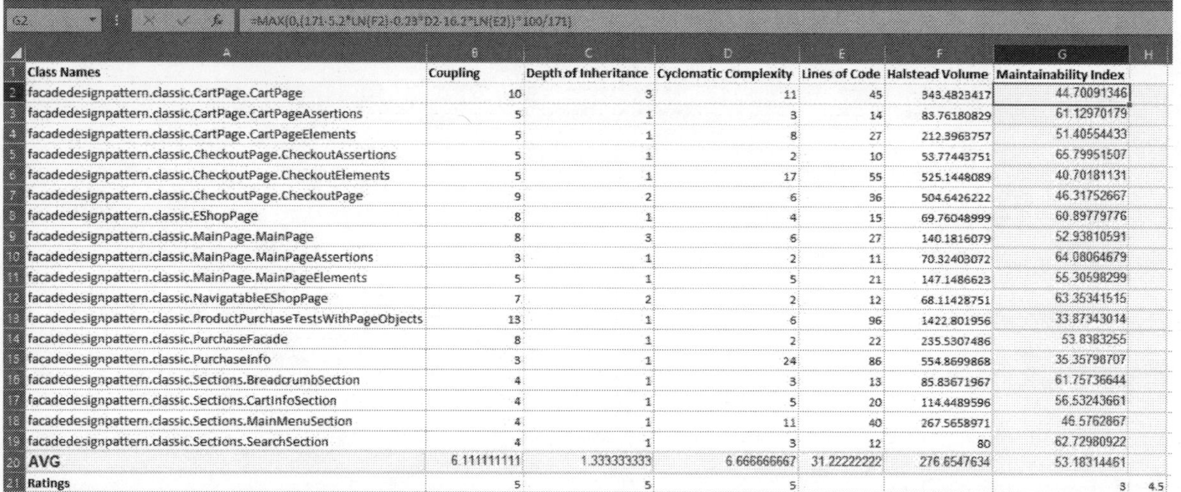
G2 =MAX(0,(171-5.2*LN(F2)-0.23*D2-16.2*LN(E2))*100/171)

Class Names	Coupling	Depth of Inheritance	Cyclomatic Complexity	Lines of Code	Halstead Volume	Maintainability Index	
facadedesignpattern.classic.CartPage.CartPage	10	3	11	45	343.4823417	44.70091346	
facadedesignpattern.classic.CartPage.CartPageAssertions	5	1	3	14	83.76180829	61.12970179	
facadedesignpattern.classic.CartPage.CartPageElements	5	1	8	27	212.3963757	51.40554433	
facadedesignpattern.classic.CheckoutPage.CheckoutAssertions	5	1	2	10	53.77443751	65.79951507	
facadedesignpattern.classic.CheckoutPage.CheckoutElements	5	1	17	55	525.1448089	40.70181131	
facadedesignpattern.classic.CheckoutPage.CheckoutPage	9	2	6	36	504.6426222	46.31752667	
facadedesignpattern.classic.EShopPage	8	1	4	15	69.76048999	60.89779776	
facadedesignpattern.classic.MainPage.MainPage	8	3	6	27	140.1816079	52.93810591	
facadedesignpattern.classic.MainPage.MainPageAssertions	3	1	2	11	70.32403072	64.08064679	
facadedesignpattern.classic.MainPage.MainPageElements	5	1	5	21	147.1486623	55.30598299	
facadedesignpattern.classic.NavigatableEShopPage	7	2	2	12	68.11428751	63.35341515	
facadedesignpattern.classic.ProductPurchaseTestsWithPageObjects	13	1	6	96	1422.801956	33.87343014	
facadedesignpattern.classic.PurchaseFacade	8	1	2	22	235.5307486	53.8383255	
facadedesignpattern.classic.PurchaseInfo	3	1	24	86	554.8699868	35.35798707	
facadedesignpattern.classic.Sections.BreadcrumbSection	4	1	3	13	85.83671967	61.75736644	
facadedesignpattern.classic.Sections.CartInfoSection	4	1	5	20	114.4489596	56.53243661	
facadedesignpattern.classic.Sections.MainMenuSection	4	1	11	40	267.5658971	46.5762867	
facadedesignpattern.classic.Sections.SearchSection	4	1	3	12	80	62.72980922	
AVG	6.111111111	1.333333333	6.666666667	31.22222222	276.6547634	53.18314461	
Ratings	5	5	5			3	4.5

I made an average for each of the metrics.
Maintainability Index AVG = 53.18 - Good (3)
Cyclomatic Complexity AVG = 6.67 - Excellent (5)
Class Coupling AVG = 6.11 - Excellent (5)
Depth of Inheritance AVG = 1.33 - Excellent (5)

Code Complexity Index Rating = (3 + 5 + 5 + 5)/4 = 4.5 = 5

Criteria	**Rating**
Readability	5

Maintainability	5
Reusability	5
API Usability	5
Extensibility	5
Code Complexity Index	5
Learning Curve	
Test Design Index	

7. Learning Curve

It is even easier to learn how to write tests with facades than page objects because you use a single API to write tests. You don't need to know how many pages you have or all their methods. You need to learn how to initialize the data objects supplied to the facade's methods and which method you should call first. However, the number of methods is much smaller compared to other solutions. This is why I give a rating of (5) excellent.

Criteria	**Rating**
Readability	5
Maintainability	5
Reusability	5
API Usability	5
Extensibility	5
Code Complexity Index	5
Learning Curve	5
Test Design Index	

Test Design Index

Criteria	**Rating**
Readability	5
Maintainability	5

Reusability	5
API Usability	5
Extensibility	5
Code Complexity Index	5
Learning Curve	5
Test Design Index	5

Test Design Index = (5 + 5 + 5 + 5 + 5 + 5 + 5) / 7 = 5

Final Assessment

Proposed Design Architecture	**TDI Rating**
Tests without Page Objects	2.43
Tests with Page Objects	4.29
Tests with Facades	5

Summary

In the chapter, we discussed a test design assessment system, defined its criteria, and explained how to apply it in practice. In the second section, we evaluated three of the designs we already used in the book - tests without page objects, ones that used the pattern, and at the end - tests that use the **Facade design pattern**. The ratings we assigned pointed out that the best choice of a design uses the Facade design pattern in our use case.

In the next chapter, we will talk about benchmarking and how to measure the performance of various automated test components.

Questions

1. Can you list the seven criteria of the assessment system?
2. What aspects of the code do you evaluate for the Reusability criterion?
3. Why is the learning curve a critical evaluation point?
4. What is the Test Design Index?
5. How do you calculate code metrics in IntelliJ?
6. What steps should you follow to apply the assessment system in your project?

Chapter 9. Benchmarking for Assessing Automated Test Components Performance

In the previous chapter, we looked into a system for evaluating different test architecture designs. However, evaluating core quality attributes is not enough to finally decide which implementation is better or not. The test execution time should be a key component too. For example, which method for searching in an HTML table is more performant - using vanilla WebDriver or a hybrid approach using in-memory calculations? Which button click approach is better - the Vanilla WebDriver one, or clicking through JavaScript?
This chapter will examine a library that can help us answer these and many more questions. Also, you will read about how to use the benchmarking tooling for exporting the results to various formats, profiling your test components' CPU, memory and hard drive utilization, and more. We will integrate this library with our existing solution for reusing the browser through the **Observer design pattern**.

These topics will be covered in this chapter:

- What is Benchmarking?
- Benchmarking Your Code with JMH - Java Microbenchmark Harness
- Benchmark Button Click Solutions
- JMH Profiling
- Optimized Browser Initialization with Benchmark Integration

What Is Benchmarking?

Before defining benchmarking, we need to answer the question - what is performance?

Our goal is to create benchmarking tooling to measure the performance of our components. Since there is more than one way to achieve the same result, we won't reinvent the wheel but use a standard solution instead.

Definition: Performance

In automated testing, it can mean two things- certain operations to take less time, e.g., run faster. A second interpretation is reducing resource usage and allocations. Or said with other words- *"doing more with less"*.

Here is the official definition for *"performance efficiency"* by ISTQB Glossary:

"The degree to which a component or system uses time, resources and capacity when accomplishing its designated functions."[Isg 19]

Benchmarking Your Code with JMH - Java Microbenchmark Harness

Benchmarking is hard. You can easily make a mistake during performance measurements. **JMH - Java Microbenchmark Harness** is a Java harness for building, running, and analysing micro benchmarks written in Java and other languages targeting the JVM. JMH is a toolkit that helps you implement Java microbenchmarks correctly. JMH is written by the people who developed the JVM Java virtual machine to know what they are doing.

Main Features

JMH has a lot of great features for in-depth performance investigations:

- **Standard benchmarking routine** - generating an isolation per each benchmark method; auto-selection of iteration amount; warmup; overhead evaluation; and so on.
- **Execution control** - JMH tries to choose the best way to evaluate performance, but you can also manually control the number of iterations, switch between cold start and warmed state, set the accuracy level, tune JMH parameters, change environment variables, and more.
- **Statistics** - by default, you will see the essential statistics like mean and standard deviation.
- **Memory diagnostics** - the library measures the performance of your code and prints information about memory, traffic, and the GC collections.
- **Parametrization** - performance can be evaluated for different sets of input parameters- like in popular unit test frameworks.

- **Command-line support** - you can run and configure micro benchmarks from the command line

JMH Example

It's straightforward to start using JMH. Let's look at an example:

```
@BenchmarkMode(Mode.Throughput)
@Warmup(iterations = 3)
@Measurement(iterations = 10, time = 5, timeUnit = TimeUnit.SECONDS)
@Threads(8)
@Fork(2)
@OutputTimeUnit(TimeUnit.MILLISECONDS)
public class StringBuilderBenchmark {
    @Benchmark
    public void testStringAdd() {
        String a = "";
        for (int i = 0; i < 10; i++) {
            a += i;
        }
        print(a);
    }

    @Benchmark
    public void testStringBuilderAdd() {
        StringBuilder sb = new StringBuilder();
        for (int i = 0; i < 10; i++) {
            sb.append(i);
        }
        print(sb.toString());
    }

    private void print(String a) {
      System.out.print(a);
    }
}
```

JMH allows designing a performance experiment in a user-friendly declarative way. At the end of the experiment, it will generate a summary which contains only essential data- in a compact and understandable form:

```
Warmup: 3 iterations, 1 s each
# Measurement: 10 iterations, 5 s each
# Timeout: 10 min per iteration
# Threads: 16 threads, will synchronize iterations
# Benchmark mode: Throughput, ops/time
# Benchmark: benchmark.string.StringBuilderBenchmark.testStringAdd
# Run progress: 0.00% complete, ETA 00:03:32
# Fork: 1 of 2
# Warmup Iteration   1: 7332.410 ops/ms
# Warmup Iteration   2: 8758.506 ops/ms
```

```
# Warmup Iteration   3: 9078.783 ops/ms
Iteration   1: 8824.713 ops/ms
Iteration   2: 9084.977 ops/ms
Iteration   3: 9412.712 ops/ms
Iteration   4: 8843.631 ops/ms
Iteration   5: 9030.556 ops/ms
Iteration   6: 9090.677 ops/ms
Iteration   7: 9493.148 ops/ms
Iteration   8: 8664.593 ops/ms
Iteration   9: 8835.227 ops/ms
Iteration  10: 8570.212 ops/ms

# Run progress: 25.00% complete, ETA 00:03:15
# Fork: 2 of 2
# Warmup Iteration   1: 5350.686 ops/ms
# Warmup Iteration   2: 8862.238 ops/ms
# Warmup Iteration   3: 8086.594 ops/ms
Iteration   1: 9105.306 ops/ms
Iteration   2: 8288.588 ops/ms
Iteration   3: 9307.902 ops/ms
Iteration   4: 9195.150 ops/ms
Iteration   5: 8715.555 ops/ms
Iteration   6: 9075.069 ops/ms
Iteration   7: 9041.037 ops/ms
Iteration   8: 9187.099 ops/ms
Iteration   9: 9145.134 ops/ms
Iteration  10: 9124.229 ops/ms

Result "benchmark.string.StringBuilderBenchmark.testStringAdd":
  9001.776 ±(99.9%) 253.496 ops/ms [Average]
  (min, avg, max) = (8288.588, 9001.776, 9493.148), stdev = 291.926
  CI (99.9%): [8748.280, 9255.272] (assumes normal distribution)

# Warmup: 3 iterations, 1 s each
# Measurement: 10 iterations, 5 s each
# Timeout: 10 min per iteration
# Threads: 16 threads, will synchronize iterations
# Benchmark mode: Throughput, ops/time
# Benchmark: benchmark.string.StringBuilderBenchmark.testStringBuilderAdd
# Run progress: 50.00% complete, ETA 00:02:07

# Fork: 1 of 2
# Warmup Iteration   1: 27202.528 ops/ms
# Warmup Iteration   2: 26500.586 ops/ms
# Warmup Iteration   3: 27190.346 ops/ms
Iteration   1: 27891.257 ops/ms
Iteration   2: 28704.541 ops/ms
Iteration   3: 27785.951 ops/ms
Iteration   4: 26841.454 ops/ms
Iteration   5: 26024.288 ops/ms
Iteration   6: 25592.494 ops/ms
Iteration   7: 25626.875 ops/ms
Iteration   8: 25302.248 ops/ms
Iteration   9: 25519.780 ops/ms
```

```
Iteration  10: 25275.334 ops/ms
# Run progress: 75.00% complete, ETA 00:01:02
# Fork: 2 of 2
# Warmup Iteration   1: 30376.008 ops/ms
# Warmup Iteration   2: 25131.064 ops/ms
# Warmup Iteration   3: 25622.342 ops/ms
Iteration   1: 25386.845 ops/ms
Iteration   2: 25825.139 ops/ms
Iteration   3: 26029.607 ops/ms
Iteration   4: 25531.748 ops/ms
Iteration   5: 25374.934 ops/ms
Iteration   6: 25204.530 ops/ms
Iteration   7: 22934.211 ops/ms
Iteration   8: 23907.677 ops/ms
Iteration   9: 24337.963 ops/ms
Iteration  10: 24660.626 ops/ms

Result "benchmark.string.StringBuilderBenchmark.testStringBuilderAdd":
  25687.875 ±(99.9%) 1167.955 ops/ms [Average]
  (min, avg, max) = (22934.211, 25687.875, 28704.541), stdev = 1345.019
  CI (99.9%): [24519.920, 26855.830] (assumes normal distribution)
# Run complete. Total time: 00:04:08
Benchmark                                     Mode  Cnt      Score      Error   Units
StringBuilderBenchmark.testStringAdd         thrpt   20   9001.776 ±  253.496  ops/ms
StringBuilderBenchmark.testStringBuilderAdd  thrpt   20  25687.875 ± 1167.955  ops/ms
```

NOTE

The easiest way to get started with JMH is to generate a new JMH project using the JMH Maven archetype. The JMH Maven archetype will create a new Java project with a single benchmark Java class. The Maven pom.xml file contains the correct dependencies to compile and build your JMH microbenchmark suite.

```
mvn archetype:generate
          -DinteractiveMode=false
          -DarchetypeGroupId=org.openjdk.jmh
          -DarchetypeArtifactId=jmh-java-benchmark-archetype
          -DgroupId=com.jenkov
          -DartifactId=first-benchmark
          -Dversion=1.0
```

These are the Maven dependencies you need and will be installed automatically for you by the archetype:

```
<dependencies>
    <dependency>
        <groupId>org.openjdk.jmh</groupId>
        <artifactId>jmh-core</artifactId>
        <version>1.19</version>
    </dependency>
    <dependency>
        <groupId>org.openjdk.jmh</groupId>
        <artifactId>jmh-generator-annprocess</artifactId>
```

```
        <version>1.19</version>
    </dependency>
</dependencies>
```

Benchmark Button Click Solutions

There are various use cases where you can utilize benchmarking, so you make better choices about the speed of your tests. The simplest scenario we will look into is choosing between regular vanilla WebDriver `click` method calls against a JavaScript click.

Button Benchmark Experiment

I created a simple demo HTML page where you can find a couple of screens of HTML buttons. Our two experiments, or benchmarks, will compare the clicking on all these buttons through vanilla WebDriver and afterward through JavaScript.

```
@BenchmarkMode(Mode.AverageTime)
@OutputTimeUnit(TimeUnit.MILLISECONDS)
@State(Scope.Benchmark)
@Warmup(iterations = 3)
@Measurement(iterations = 8)
public class BenchmarkRunner {
    private final String testPage = "https://bit.ly/3rSaqTZ";
    private WebDriver driver;

    public static void main(String[] args) {

        Options opt = new OptionsBuilder()
                .include(BenchmarkRunner.class.getSimpleName())
                .forks(1)
                .build();

        new Runner(opt).run();
    }

    @Setup(Level.Iteration)
    public void setup() {
        WebDriverManager.chromedriver().setup();
        driver = new ChromeDriver();
        driver.manage().timeouts().implicitlyWait(10, TimeUnit.SECONDS);
        driver.navigate().to(testPage);
    }

    @TearDown(Level.Iteration)
    public void tearDown() {
        driver.close();
    }
```

```java
    @Benchmark
    public void benchmarkWebDriverClick() {
        var buttons = driver.findElements(By.xpath("//input[@value='Submit']"));
        for (var button:buttons) {
            button.click();
        }
    }

    @Benchmark
    public void benchmarkJavaScriptClick() {
        JavascriptExecutor javascriptExecutor = (JavascriptExecutor) driver;
        var buttons = driver.findElements(By.xpath("//input[@value='Submit']"));
        for (var button:buttons) {
            javascriptExecutor.executeScript("arguments[0].click();", button);
        }
    }
}
```

I created a simple console application containing the main method. Inside of it, we configure the benchmark runner through the `OptionsBuilder` class. Instead of using annotations on top of the class, you can use `OptionsBuilder` to configure the runner. In our case, I specified the number of parallel threads using the `forks` method. Through annotations, we set that 3 iterations will be used for warmup and 8 ones for measurement. We measure the average time in milliseconds. The method marked with the `@Setup` annotation will be called once for iterations since we configured it to do so via the argument `Level.Iteration`. The same happens for the `tearDown` where we close the browser. The two methods annotated with `@Benchmark` contain the code we want to compare. After you run the main program, the benchmarking process begins, and at the end, the final score results are printed on the console. Here are the results after the execution.

```
Result "core.BenchmarkRunner.benchmarkWebDriverClick":
  4960.266 ±(99.9%) 1088.594 ms/op [Average]
  (min, avg, max) = (4238.173, 4960.266, 6016.205), stdev = 569.355
  CI (99.9%): [3871.673, 6048.860] (assumes normal distribution)


# Run complete. Total time: 00:02:35

Benchmark                                  Mode  Cnt     Score      Error  Units
BenchmarkRunner.benchmarkJavaScriptClick  avgt    8  1001.427 ±  534.926  ms/op
BenchmarkRunner.benchmarkWebDriverClick   avgt    8  4960.266 ± 1088.594  ms/op

Process finished with exit code 0
```

Find Run TODO Problems CheckStyle Terminal Build

It looks like the vanilla WebDriver native `click` is much less performant than the JavaScript approach. Mean 4960 ms against 1001 ms, which is almost a 395% increase in time!

JMH Profiling

JMH has a few very helpful profilers that aid in understanding your benchmarks. While these profilers are not the substitute for full-fledged external profilers, they often quickly dig into the benchmark behavior. When doing many cycles of tuning up the benchmark code itself, it is vital to have a quick turnaround for the results. There are quite a few profilers, and this sample would expand on a handful of the most useful ones.

StackProfiler

Stack profiler is useful to see if the code we are stressing executes quickly. Like many other sampling profilers, it is susceptible to sampling bias: it can overlook quickly running methods, for example.

```
public static void main(String[] args) {
    Options opt = new OptionsBuilder()
            .include(BenchmarkRunner.class.getSimpleName())
            .addProfiler(WinPerfAsmProfiler.class)
            .addProfiler(StackProfiler.class)
           .addProfiler(GCProfiler.class)
            .forks(1)
            .build();

    new Runner(opt).run();
}
```

After the execution, you get similar results:

```
....[Thread state:
RUNNABLE]..............................................................
99.0%  99.0% org.openjdk.jmh.samples.JMHSample_35_Profilers$Maps.test
0.4%   0.4%
org.openjdk.jmh.samples.generated.JMHSample_35_Profilers_Maps_test.test_avgt_jmhStub
0.2%   0.2% sun.reflect.NativeMethodAccessorImpl.invoke0
0.2%   0.2% java.lang.Integer.valueOf
0.2%   0.2% sun.misc.Unsafe.compareAndSwapInt
....[Thread state:
RUNNABLE]..............................................................
78.0%  78.0% java.util.TreeMap.getEntry
21.2%  21.2% org.openjdk.jmh.samples.JMHSample_35_Profilers$Maps.test
0.4%   0.4% java.lang.Integer.valueOf
0.2%   0.2% sun.reflect.NativeMethodAccessorImpl.invoke0
0.2%   0.2%
org.openjdk.jmh.samples.generated.JMHSample_35_Profilers_Maps_test.test_avgt_jmhStub
```

GC Profiler

To view the disassembly of your code, use the `DisassemblyDiagnoser` attribute.

```
public static void main(String[] args) {
    Options opt = new OptionsBuilder()
            .include(BenchmarkRunner.class.getSimpleName())
            .addProfiler(WinPerfAsmProfiler.class)
            .addProfiler(StackProfiler.class)
            .addProfiler(GCProfiler.class)
            .forks(1)
            .build();

    new Runner(opt).run();
}
```

After the execution, you get similar results:

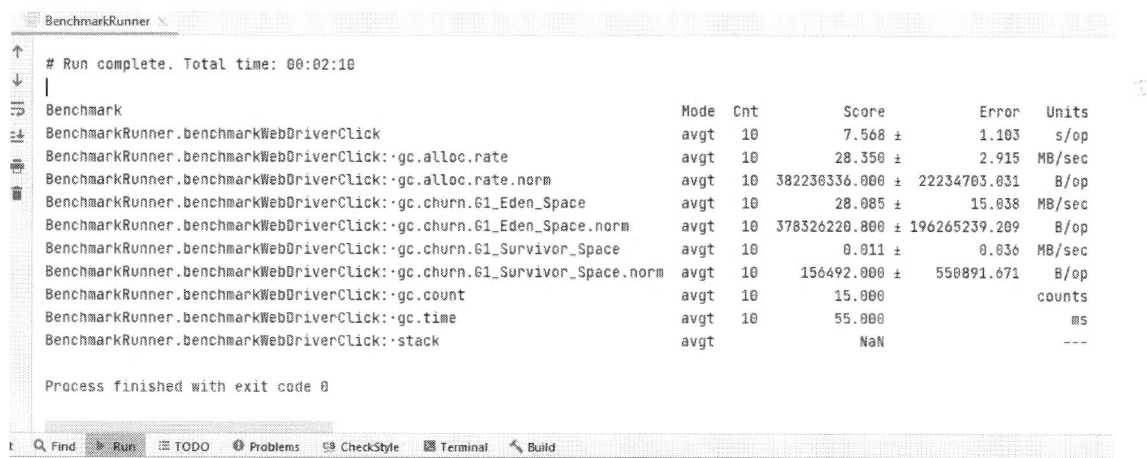

```
# Run complete. Total time: 00:02:10

Benchmark                                                             Mode  Cnt          Score           Error   Units
BenchmarkRunner.benchmarkWebDriverClick                               avgt   10          7.568 ±         1.103    s/op
BenchmarkRunner.benchmarkWebDriverClick:·gc.alloc.rate                avgt   10         28.350 ±         2.915  MB/sec
BenchmarkRunner.benchmarkWebDriverClick:·gc.alloc.rate.norm           avgt   10  382230336.000 ±  22234703.031    B/op
BenchmarkRunner.benchmarkWebDriverClick:·gc.churn.G1_Eden_Space       avgt   10         28.085 ±        15.038  MB/sec
BenchmarkRunner.benchmarkWebDriverClick:·gc.churn.G1_Eden_Space.norm  avgt   10  378326220.800 ± 196265239.209    B/op
BenchmarkRunner.benchmarkWebDriverClick:·gc.churn.G1_Survivor_Space   avgt   10          0.011 ±         0.036  MB/sec
BenchmarkRunner.benchmarkWebDriverClick:·gc.churn.G1_Survivor_Space.norm avgt 10    156492.000 ±    550891.671    B/op
BenchmarkRunner.benchmarkWebDriverClick:·gc.count                     avgt   10         15.000                  counts
BenchmarkRunner.benchmarkWebDriverClick:·gc.time                      avgt   10         55.000                      ms
BenchmarkRunner.benchmarkWebDriverClick:·stack                        avgt                 NaN                     ---

Process finished with exit code 0
```

There, we can see that the tests are producing some garbage. `gc.alloc` would say we are allocating 28 MB of objects per second. `gc.churn` would say that GC removes the same garbage from Eden space every second.

WinPerfAsmProfiler Profiler

Dealing with microbenchmarks like these requires looking into the abyss of runtime, hardware, and generated code. Luckily, JMH has a few handy tools that ease the pain. If you are running Linux, then `perf_events` are probably available as a standard package. This kernel facility taps into hardware counters and provides the data for user space programs like JMH. Windows has less sophisticated facilities but also usable.

```
public static void main(String[] args) {
    Options opt = new OptionsBuilder()
```

```
            .include(BenchmarkRunner.class.getSimpleName())
            .addProfiler(WinPerfAsmProfiler.class)
            .addProfiler(StackProfiler.class)
            .addProfiler(GCProfiler.class)
            .forks(1)
            .build();

    new Runner(opt).run();
}
```

After the execution, you get similar results:

```
Perf stats:
 --------------------------------------------------
    4172.776137 task-clock (msec)         #    0.411 CPUs utilized
            612 context-switches          #    0.147 K/sec
             31 cpu-migrations            #    0.007 K/sec
            195 page-faults               #    0.047 K/sec
 16,599,643,026 cycles                    #    3.978 GHz                      [30.80%]
<not supported> stalled-cycles-frontend
<not supported> stalled-cycles-backend
 17,815,084,879 instructions              #    1.07  insns per cycle          [38.49%]
  3,813,373,583 branches                  #  913.870 M/sec                    [38.56%]
      1,212,788 branch-misses             #    0.03% of all branches          [38.91%]
  7,582,256,427 L1-dcache-loads           # 1817.077 M/sec                    [39.07%]
        312,913 L1-dcache-load-misses     #    0.00% of all L1-dcache hits    [38.66%]
         35,688 LLC-loads                 #    0.009 M/sec                    [32.58%]
<not supported> LLC-load-misses:HG
<not supported> L1-icache-loads:HG
        161,436 L1-icache-load-misses:HG  #    0.00% of all L1-icache hits    [32.81%]
  7,200,981,198 dTLB-loads:HG             # 1725.705 M/sec                    [32.68%]
          3,360 dTLB-load-misses:HG       #    0.00% of all dTLB cache hits   [32.65%]
        193,874 iTLB-loads:HG             #    0.046 M/sec                    [32.56%]
          4,193 iTLB-load-misses:HG       #    2.16% of all iTLB cache hits   [32.44%]
<not supported> L1-dcache-prefetches:HG
              0 L1-dcache-prefetch-misses:HG #    0.000 K/sec                    [32.33%]
   10.159432892 seconds time elapsed
```

We can already see this benchmark goes with a good IPC, does lots of loads and lots of stores, all are more or less fulfilled without misses.

Optimized Browser Initialization Benchmark Integration

If you recall Chapter *3. Strategies for Speeding-up the Tests* we wrote a solution for reusing the browser through attributes using the **Observer design pattern**. Let us investigate how we can achieve the same in our benchmarks. Otherwise, you won't be able to benchmark your framework's code. We need to refactor our code since the first version of our solution used the TestNG framework to start the browser, but here we run the experiments without it in a console application.

Here is how our button experiment will change after the refactoring - producing the same results but controlling the browser through an attribute.

```
@BenchmarkMode(Mode.AverageTime)
@OutputTimeUnit(TimeUnit.SECONDS)
@State(Scope.Thread)
@Warmup(iterations = 0)
@Measurement(iterations = 10)
@ExecutionBrowser(browser = Browser.CHROME, browserBehavior =
BrowserBehavior.RESTART_EVERY_TIME)
public class BenchmarkRunner extends BaseBenchmark {
    private final String TEST_PAGE = "https://bit.ly/3rSaqTZ";

    public static void main(String[] args) {
        Options opt = new OptionsBuilder()
                .include(BenchmarkRunner.class.getSimpleName())
                .forks(1)
                .build();

        new Runner(opt).run();
    }

    @Override
    public void setup(PluginState pluginState) {
        setCurrentClass(BenchmarkRunner.class);
        super.setup(pluginState);
    }

    @Override
    public void init(Driver driver) {
        driver.goToUrl(TEST_PAGE);
    }

    @Benchmark
    public void benchmarkWebDriverClick(PluginState pluginState) {
        var buttons =
PluginState.getDriver().findElements(By.xpath("//input[@value='Submit']"));
        for (var button : buttons) {
            button.click();
        }
    }

    @Benchmark
    public void benchmarkJavaScriptClick(PluginState pluginState) {
        var buttons =
pluginState.getDriver().findElements(By.xpath("//input[@value='Submit']"));
        for (var button:buttons) {
            pluginState.getDriver().executeScript("arguments[0].click();", button);
        }
    }
}
```

The new things are that we derive from the `BaseBenchmark` class and the usage of the iteration setup and cleanup methods. We created the same plug-in architecture as for TestNG but now for JVM. Shall we examine all updates?

Updates in Observer Classes

The first update is in the base observer class `BaseTestBehaviorObserver`, where the dependency on TestNG is removed.

```
@State(Scope.Thread)
public class BaseBenchmark {
    private Class<?> currentClass;

    @State(Scope.Thread)
    public static class PluginState {
        private static TestExecutionSubject _currentTestExecutionSubject;
        private static Driver _driver;

        @Setup(Level.Trial)
        public void doSetup() {
            _currentTestExecutionSubject = new ExecutionSubject();
            _driver = new WebCoreDriver();
            new BrowserLaunchTestBehaviorObserver(_currentTestExecutionSubject, _driver);
        }

        @TearDown(Level.Trial)
        public void doTearDown() {
            if (getDriver() != null) {
                System.out.println("Do TearDown");
                getDriver().quit();
            }
        }

        public static TestExecutionSubject getCurrentTestExecutionSubject() {
            return _currentTestExecutionSubject;
        }

        public static Driver getDriver() {
            return _driver;
        }
    }

    public void setCurrentClass(Class<?> currentClass) {
        this.currentClass = currentClass;
    }

    @Setup(Level.Invocation)
    public void setup(PluginState pluginState) {
        PluginState.getCurrentTestExecutionSubject().preTestInit(currentClass);
        init(PluginState.getDriver());
        PluginState.getCurrentTestExecutionSubject().postTestInit(currentClass);
    }
```

```
    @TearDown(Level.Invocation)
    public void tearDown(PluginState pluginState) {
        PluginState.getCurrentTestExecutionSubject().preTestCleanup(currentClass);
        cleanup(PluginState.getDriver());
        PluginState.getCurrentTestExecutionSubject().postTestCleanup(currentClass);
    }

    public void init(Driver driver) {
    }

    public void cleanup(Driver driver) {
    }
}
```

In the method `doSetup`, we initialize all observers and the static `Driver` decorator. Then the next essential methods for the plug-in architecture are `setup` and `tearDown`. To execute your logic before or after the benchmark, you need to override the `init` and `cleanup` methods. Before and after the execution of the delegates, we trigger the pre- and post-plug-in events.

Summary

In the chapter, we talked about benchmarking and measuring the performance of various automated tests' components. We investigated how to **utilize JMH - Java Microbenchmark Harness** library for the job and how to use it to generate statistics and profile our tests' code. There was a discussion on how to refactor the reuse of the **Observer design pattern** plug-in architecture in our experiments.

In the last chapter, we will talk about using test data most appropriately and creating the right environment for test execution.

Questions

1. Why is it important to measure the performance of our code?
2. What is benchmarking?
3. How can you start using JMH?
4. What types of results can you generate in JMH?

Chapter 10. Test Data Preparation and Test Environments

Test data is a crucial part of automated tests. Building successful automation is not only about good programming knowledge, using best practices, and design patterns. It is not only about stable test locators or test environments you control. These are prerequisites, but the essential thing that many teams miss is the importance of proper test data preparation and its role in the success of any automated testing solution. Therefore, we end with this chapter - because, without this fundamental knowledge, you will be doomed to fix flaky tests until the rest of the days.
We will investigate strategies on how to handle test data in different test environments using configuration files. After that, we will check how to utilize code libraries for data generation. We will talk about using the DB and APIs for creating and managing the necessary data.

These topics will be covered in this chapter:

- Stop hard-coding input data
- Introducing test fixtures
- Using an API as a source of fixture data
- Using an API or DB for verification

Stop Hard-coding Input Data

Hardcoding test data is a quick and dirty fix and leads to flaky tests. In *Chapter 2- Optimizing and Refactoring Legacy Flaky Tests*, we refactored parts of the tests and mitigated some of the incorporated bad practices. We, however, have left the test data still hardcoded there.

Problematic Test Data

What are the different test data used in our automated tests?

- **URL of the website** - like any web project, we have several testing environments- DEV, STAGING, UAT (User Acceptance Testing), and so on. Our tests have the URL of the application hardcoded. So, without changing the test code, we cannot have the test run on both the staging and dev environments.

- **Hard-coded product** - different test environments do not share the same identical data such as products. Most environments will only have a subset of the products available in production. Test environments, in particular, will have products that never did and never will exist in production.
- **User data** - due to legal reasons, our test environment should never contain user data from the production environment. This is doubly true for sensitive user information, such as credit card numbers and emails.

Our tests should be able to run in any environment we have. But this is impossible if every piece of data we use is hard-coded for a specific test environment.

Configuration Transformations

How about implementing a code that reads data from a JSON configuration file and later using it in our test? There are three major places for which we can use such data: website URLs, WebDriver timeouts, and default billing information. The main goal will be to have separate data sets for different test environments such as LOCAL, DEV, or UAT.

First, we need to add a JSON config file to our project. Name it **testFrameworkSettings.json**. We will have separate JSON files for each environment, which will be changed by setting a particular environmental variable during execution called **environment**. For example, **dev** value will execute the tests against the local DEV environment. The **qa** value against the QA environment in CI. This means we will have two configuration files: one will be named **testFrameworkSettings.dev.json** and another **testFrameworkSettings.qa.json**.

> **NOTE**
>
> **Continuous Integration (CI)** is a development practice where developers **frequently integrate** code into a shared repository, preferably several times a day. An automated build and automated tests can then verify each integration. While automated testing is not strictly part of CI, it is typically implied. Popular **CI** tools are Jenkins, Azure DevOps, Bamboo, GitLab CI, TeamCity, etc.

```
{
  "webSettings": {
    "baseUrl": "http://demos.bellatrix.solutions/",
    "elementWaitTimeout": "30",
    "chrome": {
      "pageLoadTimeout": "120",
```

```
      "scriptTimeout": "5",
      "artificialDelayBeforeAction": "0"
    },
    "firefox": {
      "pageLoadTimeout": "30",
      "scriptTimeout": "1",
      "artificialDelayBeforeAction": "0"
    },
    "edge": {
      "pageLoadTimeout": "30",
      "scriptTimeout": "1",
      "artificialDelayBeforeAction": "0"
    },
    "internetExplorer": {
      "pageLoadTimeout": "30",
      "scriptTimeout": "1",
      "artificialDelayBeforeAction": "0"
    },
    "opera": {
      "pageLoadTimeout": "30",
      "scriptTimeout": "1",
      "artificialDelayBeforeAction": "0"
    },
    "safari": {
      "pageLoadTimeout": "30",
      "scriptTimeout": "1",
      "artificialDelayBeforeAction": "0"
    }
  },
  "urlSettings": {
    "shopUrl": "http://demos.bellatrix.solutions/cart/",
    "accountUrl": "http://demos.bellatrix.solutions/account/"
  },
  "billingInfoDefaultValues": {
    "email": "info@spaceFlowers.com",
    "company": "Space Flowers",
    "country": "Germany",
    "firstName": "Anton",
    "lastName": "Angelov",
    "phone": "+00498888999281",
    "zip": "10115",
    "city": "Berlin",
    "address1": "1 Willi Brandt Avenue Tiergarten",
    "address2": "2 Willi Brandt Avenue Tiergarten"
  }
}
```

This is the **dev** config that contains the values for the LOCAL environment. In the **qa** file, you can change the values for particular fields if there are differences.

There are two ways how you can set this environment variable. The first way to do it is to insert it through IntelliJ. You can set it from **Run | Edit Configurations**. As a key-value pair, set the desired environmental variables in the **Environment variables** text field. You can configure these variables from the other settings to be applied across the whole project, particular module, or only a few packages.

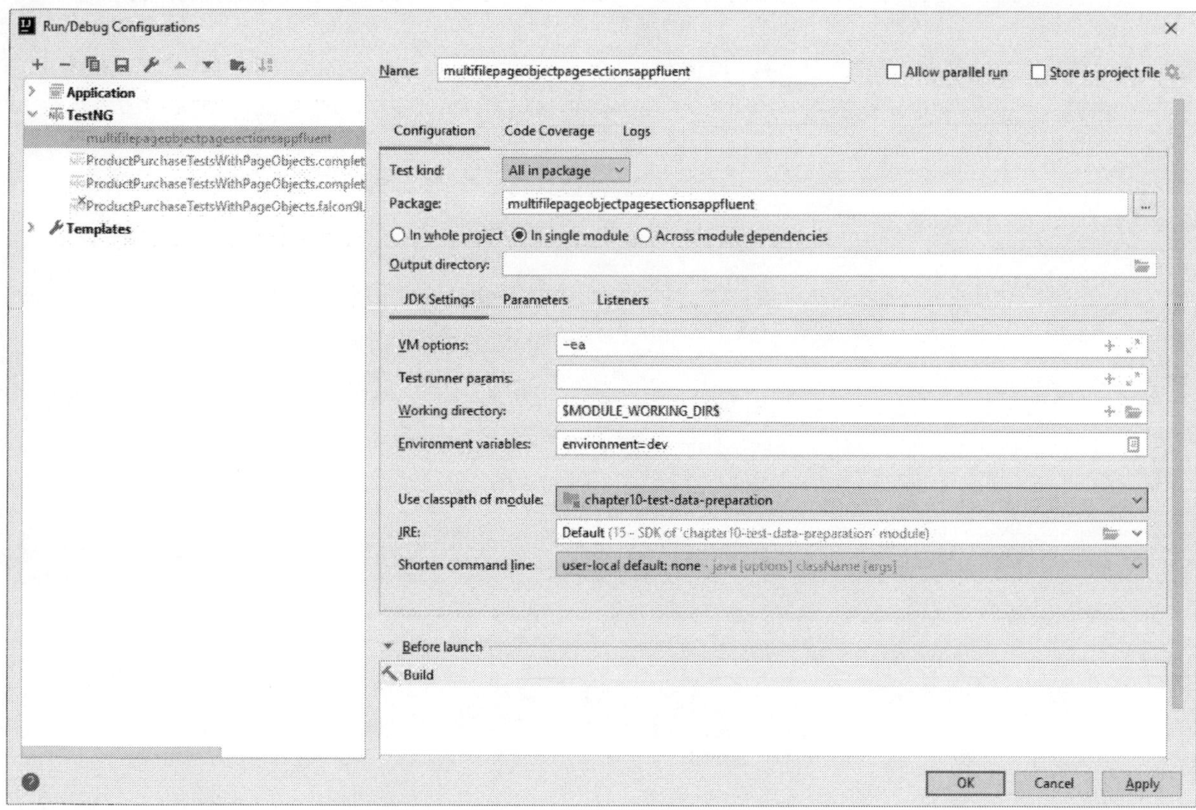

> **NOTE**
>
> The **project** can contain one or more related modules. A project is a convenient way to develop related, interdependent applications, libraries in concert.
>
> Each **module** is a separate library, application and can be a jar, ear, or war. The modules aren't just Java, either. You can have modules for ruby, scala, or something else. Module folders are subfolders of the project folder.
>
> An **artifact** is an assembly of the project assets you put together to test, deploy, or distribute your software solution or its part.

The second way is to set it from the command line if you run your tests in continuous integration.

```
java -cp "pathClassFilesOrTestngJarFilePath" yourPackageName testng.xml -Denvironment=qa
```

Through the `-D` argument, we can set the environment variable.

We won't use the native Java properties files support since it is too primitive for our purposes. So, we need to create a new service for accessing the configuration data. You need to add a new Maven dependency for working with JSON files called **com.google.code.gson**.

For each separate config section such as **urlSettings** or **webSettings**, we have a Java class representation.

This is the Java class representation for the web settings section.

```
public class WebSettings {
    private  String baseUrl;
    private  BrowserSettings chrome;
    private  BrowserSettings firefox;
    private  BrowserSettings edge;
    private  BrowserSettings opera;
    private  BrowserSettings internetExplorer;
    private  BrowserSettings safari;
    private  int elementWaitTimeout;

    public String getBaseUrl() {
        return baseUrl;
    }

    public BrowserSettings getChrome() {
        return chrome;
    }

    public BrowserSettings getFirefox() {
        return firefox;
    }

    public BrowserSettings getEdge() {
        return edge;
    }

    public BrowserSettings getOpera() {
        return opera;
    }

    public BrowserSettings getInternetExplorer() {
        return internetExplorer;
    }

    public BrowserSettings getSafari() {
```

```
        return safari;
    }

    public int getElementWaitTimeout() {
        return elementWaitTimeout;
    }
}
```

This is the code of the static utility class to help us access the data.

```
public class ConfigurationService {
    private static String environment;

    public static <T> T get(Class<T> configSection) {
        T mappedObject = null;
        if (environment == null) {
            String environmentOverride = System.getProperty("environment");
            if (environmentOverride == null) {
                InputStream input =
ConfigurationService.class.getResourceAsStream("/application.properties");
                var p = new Properties();
                try {
                    p.load(input);
                } catch (IOException e) {
                    return mappedObject;
                }

                environment = p.getProperty("environment");
            }
           else {
                environment = environmentOverride;
            }
        }

        String fileName = String.format("testFrameworkSettings.%s.json", environment);
        String jsonFileContent = getFileAsString(fileName);
        String sectionName = getSectionName(configSection);

        var jsonObject =
JsonParser.parseString(jsonFileContent).getAsJsonObject().get(sectionName).toString();

        var gson = new Gson();

        try {
            mappedObject= gson.fromJson(jsonObject, configSection);
        } catch (Exception e) {
            e.printStackTrace();
        }

        return mappedObject;
    }

    public static String getSectionName(Class<?> configSection)  {
        var sb = new StringBuilder(configSection.getSimpleName());
```

```java
        sb.setCharAt(0, Character.toLowerCase(sb.charAt(0)));
        return sb.toString();
    }

    public static String getFileAsString(String fileName) {
        try {
            InputStream input = ConfigurationService.class.getResourceAsStream("/" +
fileName);
            return IOUtils.toString(input, StandardCharsets.UTF_8);
        } catch (IOException e) {
            return null;
        }
    }
}
```

Many things are happening in the primary method `get`. Let's discuss them one by one. First, if we forgot to set the environment value, we have a default one put in the `application.properties` file. Based on the value read from the env variable, we build the name of the JSON config that we need to load and read. We use the method `getFileAsString` to get the JSON config file resource, convert it to stream and return it as a string. Via the method `parseString` part of the `JsonParser` class, which comes from Google's JSON dependency, we get only the specified JSON section as a string. After that, we initialize the special Google class `Gson` which we use later through the method `fromJson` to transform the JSON section's string to the corresponding mapping Java class.

Creating URL Settings

If you have a job to automate a single website, we don't need to over-engineer the solution. Let's use the **webSettings baseUrl** variable. This is especially useful if you test a single page app.

```java
public class MainPage extends NavigatableEShopPage {
    public MainPage(Driver driver) {
        super(driver);
    }

    @Override
    protected String getUrl() {
        return ConfigurationService.get(WebSettings.class).getBaseUrl();
    }

    @Override
    protected void waitForPageLoad() {
        elements().addToCartFalcon9().waitToExists();
    }

    public MainPage addRocketToShoppingCart()  {
        open();
        elements().addToCartFalcon9().click();
```

```
        elements().viewCartButton().click();
        return this;
    }

    public MainPage assertProductBoxLink(String name, String expectedLink)  {
        var actualLink = elements().getProductBoxByName(name).getAttribute("href");
        Assert.assertEquals(actualLink, expectedLink);
        return this;
    }

    private MainPageElements elements() {
        return new MainPageElements(elementFindService);
    }
}
```

The 'magic' happens in the `getUrl` method where we call `ConfigurationService.get(WebSettings.class).getBaseUrl();` to retrieve the current test environment URL. However, most of the time, we have multiple websites or web services to test. There are many pages which means you don't need only the base URLs but also a logic that will generate the correct full URL. To support this, we have a separate section in our JSON configuration file called `urlSettings`.

```
"urlSettings": {
  "shopUrl": "http://local.bellatrix.solutions/cart/",
  "accountUrl": "http://local.bellatrix.solutions/account/"
},
```

We also have a `UrlSettings` class that is 1 to 1 representation of the data.

```
public class UrlSettings {
    private String shopUrl;
    private String accountUrl;

    public String getShopUrl() {
        return shopUrl;
    }

    public String getAccountUrl() {
        return accountUrl;
    }
}
```

After that, let's create a service that will generate the correct full URLs for each website.

```
public class UrlDeterminer {
    public static String getShopUrl(String urlPart) {
        return contactUrls(ConfigurationService.get(UrlSettings.class).getShopUrl(),
urlPart);
    }

    public static String getAccountUrl(String urlPart) {
```

```
        return contactUrls(ConfigurationService.get(UrlSettings.class).getAccountUrl(),
urlPart);
    }

    private static String contactUrls(String url, String part) {
        try {
            var uriBuilder = new URIBuilder(url);
            URI uri = uriBuilder.setPath(uriBuilder.getPath() + part)
                    .build()
                    .normalize();
            return uri.toString();
        }
        catch (URISyntaxException ex) {
            return null;
        }
    }
}
```

As you can see, all methods are declared as static since this is a utility class that should be super easy to use. We have a method for each separate website part of the configuration section. We get the right test environment URL and combine it with the supplied partial URL. We use the `UriBuilder` method `setPath`, which knows how to properly combine them, no matter how many are out there.

This is how we will use the service in our page objects.

```
public class CartPage extends NavigatableEShopPage {
    private final BrowserService browserService;

    public CartPage(Driver driver) {
        super(driver);
        browserService = driver;
    }

    private CartPageElements elements() {
        return new CartPageElements(elementFindService);
    }

    public BreadcrumbSection breadcrumbSection() {
        return new BreadcrumbSection(elementFindService);
    }

    @Override
    protected String getUrl() {
        return UrlDeterminer.getShopUrl("cart");
    }
    // rest of the code
}
```

Creating WebDriver Timeouts Settings

Another critical aspect that needs to be configured is WebDriver timeouts. They can vary depending on the test environment since there may be differences in the website performance. Also, the timeouts may vary from browser to browser.

This is how we can change the `startBrowser` method, which is part of the `WebCoreDriver` decorator - to support this.

```
var webSettings = ConfigurationService.get(WebSettings.class);
WebDriverManager.chromedriver().setup();
webDriver = new ChromeDriver();
webDriver.manage().timeouts().pageLoadTimeout(webSettings.getChrome().getPageLoadTimeout(),
TimeUnit.SECONDS);
webDriver.manage().timeouts().setScriptTimeout(webSettings.getChrome().getScriptTimeout(),
TimeUnit.SECONDS);
webDriverWait = new WebDriverWait(webDriver, webSettings.getElementWaitTimeout());
```

Each browser settings are specified in the class `BrowserSettings`.

```
public class BrowserSettings {
    private int pageLoadTimeout;
    private int scriptTimeout;

    public int getPageLoadTimeout() {
        return pageLoadTimeout;
    }

    public int getScriptTimeout() {
        return scriptTimeout;
    }
}
```

Creating Default Billing Info Settings

Here are how our facade tests looked without using configuration for the billing information.

```
@Test
public void purchaseFalcon9WithFacade() {
    var purchaseInfo = new PurchaseInfo();
    purchaseInfo.setEmail("info@berlinspaceflowers.com");
    purchaseInfo.setFirstName("Anton");
    purchaseInfo.setLastName("Angelov");
    purchaseInfo.setCompany("Space Flowers");
    purchaseInfo.setCountry("Germany");
    purchaseInfo.setAddress1("1 Willi Brandt Avenue Tiergarten");
    purchaseInfo.setAddress2("Lotzowplatz 17");
    purchaseInfo.setCity("Berlin");
    purchaseInfo.setZip("10115");
    purchaseInfo.setPhone("+00498888999281");
```

```java
    purchaseFacade.verifyItemPurchase("Falcon 9", "happybirthday", 2, "114.00€", purchaseInfo);
}
```

It is possible that 90% of the `PurchaseInfo` to be the same most of the time. Also, the data can vary from environment to environment. This is why it is essential to move it to the configuration files. We have created a section called `billingDefaultValues`. Below, you can find the Java representation of it.

```java
public class BillingInfoDefaultValues {
    private String firstName;
    private String lastName;
    private String company;
    private String country;
    private String address1;
    private String address2;
    private String city;
    private String zip;
    private String phone;
    private String email;

    public String getFirstName() {
        return firstName;
    }

    public String getLastName() {
        return lastName;
    }

    public String getCompany() {
        return company;
    }

    public String getCountry() {
        return country;
    }

    public String getAddress1() {
        return address1;
    }

    public String getAddress2() {
        return address2;
    }

    public String getCity() {
        return city;
    }

    public String getZip() {
        return zip;
    }
```

```java
    public String getPhone() {
        return phone;
    }

    public String getEmail() {
        return email;
    }
}
```

The easiest way to use it is to set default values of the properties of the `PurchaseInfo` class.

```java
public class PurchaseInfo {
    private String firstName;
    private String lastName;
    private String company;
    private String country;
    private String address1;
    private String address2;
    private String city;
    private String zip;
    private String phone;
    private String email;
    private Boolean shouldCreateAccount = false;
    private Boolean shouldCheckPayment = false;

    public PurchaseInfo() {
        var billingInfoDefaultValues =
ConfigurationService.get(BillingInfoDefaultValues.class);
        this.firstName = billingInfoDefaultValues.getFirstName();
        this.lastName = billingInfoDefaultValues.getLastName();
        this.company = billingInfoDefaultValues.getCompany();
        this.country = billingInfoDefaultValues.getCountry();
        this.address1 = billingInfoDefaultValues.getAddress1();
        this.address2 = billingInfoDefaultValues.getAddress2();
        this.city = billingInfoDefaultValues.getCity();
        this.zip = billingInfoDefaultValues.getZip();
        this.phone = billingInfoDefaultValues.getPhone();
        this.email = billingInfoDefaultValues.getEmail();
        this.shouldCreateAccount = true;
        this.shouldCheckPayment = true;
    }
    // rest of the code
}
```

The usage in tests is straightforward.

```java
@Test
public void purchaseFalcon9WithFacade() {
    var purchaseInfo = new PurchaseInfo();
    purchaseFacade.verifyItemPurchase("Falcon 9", "happybirthday", 2, "114.00€",
purchaseInfo);
}
```

Refactoring Default Billing Info Settings

Java 14 added a new keyword to the language called `record`. Its usage will automatically add a constructor, getters, `equals`, `hashCode`, and `toString` methods for us. Records were introduced to reduce repetitive boilerplate code in data model POJOs. They simplify day-to-day development, improve efficiency and minimize the risk of human error. It's worth mentioning that records do have some restrictions. They are always final, cannot be declared abstract, and can't use native methods. Shall we see how the `PurchaseInfo` looks like utilizing the `record` keyword?

```
public record PurchaseInfo(
        String firstName,
        String lastName,
        String company,
        String country,
        String address1,
        String address2,
        String city,
        String zip,
        String phone,
        String email,
        Boolean shouldCreateAccount,
        Boolean shouldCheckPayment) {
    public PurchaseInfo() {
        this(ConfigurationService.get(BillingInfoDefaultValues.class).getFirstName(),
                ConfigurationService.get(BillingInfoDefaultValues.class).getLastName(),
                ConfigurationService.get(BillingInfoDefaultValues.class).getCompany(),
                ConfigurationService.get(BillingInfoDefaultValues.class).getCountry(),
                ConfigurationService.get(BillingInfoDefaultValues.class).getAddress1(),
                ConfigurationService.get(BillingInfoDefaultValues.class).getAddress2(),
                ConfigurationService.get(BillingInfoDefaultValues.class).getCity(),
                ConfigurationService.get(BillingInfoDefaultValues.class).getZip(),
                ConfigurationService.get(BillingInfoDefaultValues.class).getPhone(),
                ConfigurationService.get(BillingInfoDefaultValues.class).getEmail(),
                true,
                true);
    }
}
```

The header is where we store the details about the fields inside the `record`. The compiler can infer the header's internal fields, meaning we need not define specific member variables and accessors, as they are auto-generated by default. We also don't have to provide a constructor.

NOTE

POJO is an acronym for Plain Old Java Object. It is initially introduced to designate a simple, lightweight Java object implementing no javax.ejb interface, as opposed to heavyweight EJB 2.x (especially Entity Beans, Stateless Session Beans are not that bad IMO). Today, the term is used for any simple object with no extra stuff. Martin Fowler, Rebecca Parsons, and Josh MacKenzie first coined the term in September 2000.

Remember that the following code won't be valid anymore:

```
var purchaseInfo = new PurchaseInfo();
purchaseInfo.setEmail("info@berlinspaceflowers.com");
purchaseInfo.setFirstName("Anton");
purchaseInfo.setLastName("Angelov");
purchaseInfo.setCompany("Space Flowers");
purchaseInfo.setCountry("Germany");
purchaseInfo.setAddress1("1 Willi Brandt Avenue Tiergarten");
purchaseInfo.setAddress2("Lotzowplatz 17");
purchaseInfo.setCity("Berlin");
purchaseInfo.setZip("10115");
purchaseInfo.setPhone("+00498888999281");
```

To initialize a new purchase info object with custom data, we need to use the parameters constructor.

```
var purchaseInfo = new PurchaseInfo(
        "info@berlinspaceflowers.com",
        "Anton",
        "Angelov",
        "Space Flowers",
        "Germany",
        "1 Willi Brandt Avenue Tiergarten",
        "Lotzowplatz 17",
        "Berlin",
        "10115",
        "+00498888999281",
        false,
        false);
```

At first, it may look like it is unclear which field is which, but as depicted in the image, IntelliJ helps us and provides the required information.

```java
// Java 14 Records
var purchaseInfo = new PurchaseInfo(
        firstName: "info@berlinspaceflowers.com",
        lastName: "Anton",
        company: "Angelov",
        country: "Space Flowers",
        address1: "Germany",
        address2: "1 Willi Brandt Avenue Tiergarten",
        city: "Lotzowplatz 17",
        zip: "Berlin",
        phone: "10115",
        email: "+00498888999281",
        shouldCreateAccount: false,
        shouldCheckPayment: false);
```

Creating Default Browser Settings

We can upgrade the `Browser` enum if we want to add a default browser to the new configuration file. To do so, I added a string private variable value which we return in the `toString` method. For each enum option, we set a default text. Through complex Stream API syntax, we parse the supplied text to a `Browser` option.

```java
public enum Browser {
    CHROME("chrome"),
    CHROME_HEADLESS("chrome"),
    FIREFOX("firefox"),
    FIREFOX_HEADLESS("firefox"),
    EDGE("edge"),
    EDGE_HEADLESS("edge"),
    OPERA("opera"),
    SAFARI("safari"),
    INTERNET_EXPLORER("ie");

    private String value;

    Browser(String value){
        this.value = value;
    }

    @Override
    public String toString() {
        return value;
    }

    public static Browser fromText(String text) {
        return Arrays.stream(values())
                .filter(l -> l.value.equalsIgnoreCase(text))
                .findFirst().orElse(Browser.CHROME);
```

```
    }
}
```

NOTE

A significant new feature in JDK 8 is the stream functionality – `java.util.stream`. It contains classes for processing sequences of elements. A stream is not a data structure. Instead, it takes input from the Collections, Arrays, or I/O channels. Streams don't change the original data structure but rather only provide the result per the pipelined methods. Each intermediate operation is lazily executed and returns a stream. The various intermediate operations can be pipelined. Terminal operations mark the end of the stream and yield the outcome. Collections are mostly about storing and accessing data, whereas Streams are mostly about describing computations on data. Stream API simplifies multithreading by providing the parallelStream method that runs operations over the stream's elements in parallel mode.

For example, we can rewrite `preTestInit` method part of the `ExecutionSubject` class as follows:

```
@Override
public void preTestInit(ITestResult result, Method memberInfo) {
      testBehaviorObservers.forEach(o -> o.preTestInit(result, memberInfo));
}
```

Later we can use the new code in the browser launch observer as follows:

```
var defaultBrowser =
Browser.fromText(ConfigurationService.get(WebSettings.class).getDefaultBrowser());
```

Environmental Variables

Sometimes there is information such as credentials it is not appropriate to be persisted even in configuration files. Usually, such is the case for credentials for accessing Selenium Grid cloud providers. One way is to put such info in environment variables and later read them from the tests.

Here is an example for login into the website using environment variables.

```
private void loginWithEnvironmentalVariables(string userName) {
   var userNameTextField = driver.findElement(By.id("username"));
   userNameTextField.typeText(userName);
   var passwordField = driver.findElement(By.id("password"));
   string userNamePass = System.getenv(String.format("%s_pass", userName));
```

```
    passwordField.typeText(userNamePass );
    var loginButton = driver.findElement(By.xpath("//button[@name='login']"));
    loginButton.Click();
}
```

The environmental variable should be named `aangelov_pass` if it will hold the password for the user `aangelov`.

Introducing Test Fixtures

In software development, **test fixture** is a term used to describe any test data that lives outside of that test and is used to set the application to a known fixed state.

Fixtures work best in any highly available environment. If we are testing on the localhost or in the CI environment, we can start with an empty test database and fill it up with fixture data. When the tests are ready to run, the code will know the exact state of the application, how many registered users we have, the prices of every product, and so on.

Using Faker for Generating Data

We already investigated how you can use default values for filling the purchase information. However, sometimes we need to change a bit of it. Other times, we need to set random info if it is not empty. For cases where you don't care about specifics, you can use a library called **Faker** for handling the data generation. It will assign random values to the properties. It can handle complex setups such as whole object initialization and even doing recursive data generation.

```
Faker faker = new Faker();
String name = faker.name().fullName(); // Miss Samanta Schmidt
String firstName = faker.name().firstName(); // Emory
String lastName = faker.name().lastName(); // Barton
String streetAddress = faker.address().streetAddress(); // 60018 Sawayn Brooks Suite 449
```

Here we use the `Faker` class part of the **Faker** library to generate random names and addresses.

> **NOTE**
>
> Faker is a port of Ruby's faker gem (and Perl's Data::Faker library). To use the Faker logic, you need to add a dependency to **javafaker**.
>
> **NOTE**

Other popular Java fake data generators are **jFairy**, **JFixture** (based on the popular .NET library, AutoFixture), and **AutoFixtureGenerator**.

Using TestNG Data Driven Tests

Sometimes we want to run the same test but with different data sets. One way to do it is to copy-paste tests and change the data. The benefit here is that maybe you can give a more appropriate name to the test. However, when there is even a slight change in API usage, you will need to go to all methods and refactor them, making the tests' maintenance costs higher.

```
@Test
public void purchaseFalcon9WithFacade() {
    var purchaseInfo = new PurchaseInfo();
    purchaseFacade.verifyItemPurchase("Falcon 9", "happybirthday", 2, "114.00€",
purchaseInfo);
}

@Test
public void purchaseSaturnVWithFacade() {
    var purchaseInfo = new PurchaseInfo();
    purchaseFacade.verifyItemPurchase("Saturn V", "happybirthday", 3, "355.00€",
purchaseInfo);
}
```

Instead, we can use data-driven tests supported in most test frameworks. TestNG and JUnit support such features. You define the data in CSV or similar format, later for each row of information, the bound test will be run.

Why not review the second option in TestNG using the `DataProvider` annotation? I prefer to use it since the tests are much easier to debug compared to the CSV approach. The test code is also more understandable and readable since the data is visible directly in the test class instead of switching between various files.

This is how we create a data-driven TestNG test.

First, we need to create a method that returns a multidimensional array holding your data. You need to mark it with the `DataProvider` annotation. If so, you need to set the `dataProvider` argument of the `Test` annotation to the name of the method. You pass the data to the test as you list them as parameters with the appropriate data type.

```
@Test(dataProvider = "getPurchaseInfoData")
public void purchaseSaturnDataDrivenFacade(String product, String coupon, int quantity,
String expectedPrice) {
    var purchaseInfo = new PurchaseInfo();
    purchaseFacade.verifyItemPurchase(product, coupon, quantity, expectedPrice,
purchaseInfo);
```

```
}

@DataProvider
public Object[][] getPurchaseInfoData(){
    Object[][] data = new Object[2][4];
    data[0][0] = "Falcon 9";
    data[0][1] = "happybirthday";
    data[0][2] = 2;
    data[0][3] = "114.00€";

    data[1][0] = "Saturn V";
    data[1][1] = "happybirthday";
    data[1][2] = 3;
    data[1][3] = "355.00€";

    return data;
}
```

Using an API as a Source of Fixture Data

Using fixtures for test data is great for environments highly accessible. If we need to test something other than the localhost or CI environment, where we cannot easily load fixture data into the database, we must use a different approach. The trick is to utilize all the resources we can find to make testing more stable.

One resource is a public-facing web API. If your website has a native mobile phone application or uses client-side API calls to load content, our tests can have the same data. All we must do is interrogate the API to get an idea of the state of the application.

A common API endpoint for most e-commerce websites is a list of all the available products. This list is used by mobile phones to display what a user can purchase. Our website stores the product catalog at http://demos.bellatrix.solutions/

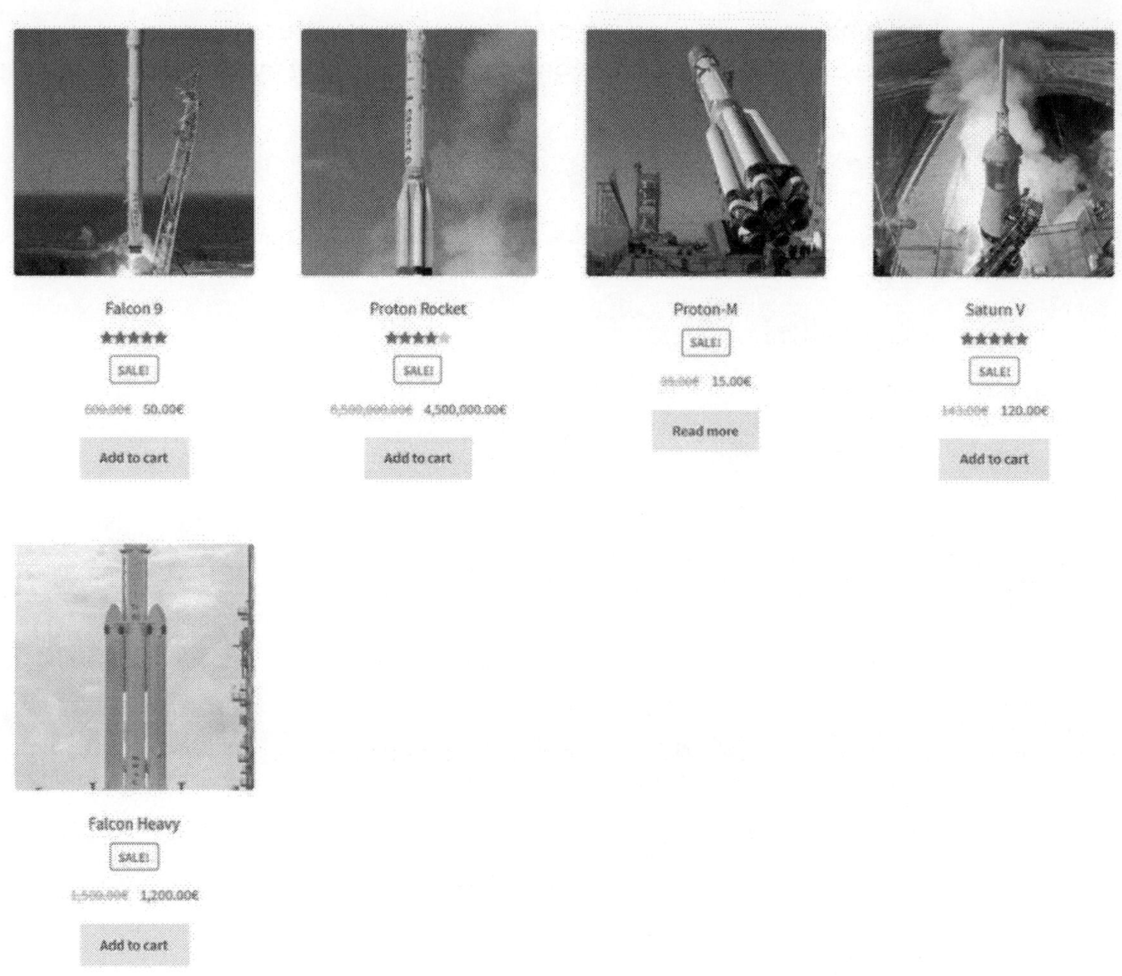

Using Data Stubs

Modern websites are complicated and combine many external services. Most ecommerce websites do not process the credit cards themselves. Instead, usually, a payment provider is used. It is a third-party application compliant with all requirements for secrets management, and it sends the data to the bank and parses the response.

Getting the external services running is a difficult task, especially if our website's service is also being developed with our project. We cannot afford to wait until the services are written and integrated to write our tests. So, we must stub some services until they are developed.

Stubs are premade responses to our application's requests. Stub responses are formatted and look like real responses, but they don't do any work. For example, the API endpoint we used to write our test does not communicate with the database. Instead, it responds with a premade JSON file. Stubbing the application is a great way to set up a test environment for automated tests and should be used as much as possible when running automated tests in the CI system.

There are generally two approaches. It is a lot better to instrument your DEV environment to use the mock API, but on PROD to use the real one. However, sometimes, this is impossible. Then you can use the **Black Hole Proxy pattern** we reviewed earlier to interrupt the call to API if the requests are made on the client.

Why not review a sample implementation?

```
public class UsingDataStubsTests {
    private WebDriver driver;
    private BrowserMobProxyServer proxyServer;

    @BeforeMethod
    public void testInit() {
        WebDriverManager.chromedriver().setup();
        proxyServer = new BrowserMobProxyServer();
        proxyServer.start();

        proxyServer.enableHarCaptureTypes(CaptureType.REQUEST_CONTENT,
CaptureType.RESPONSE_CONTENT);
        proxyServer.newHar();
        String proxyDetails = "127.0.0.1:" + proxyServer.getPort();
        final Proxy proxyConfig = new Proxy().
                setHttpProxy(proxyDetails).
                setSslProxy(proxyDetails);

        final ChromeOptions options = new ChromeOptions();
        options.setProxy(proxyConfig);
        options.setAcceptInsecureCerts(true);
        driver = new ChromeDriver(options);
        driver.manage().timeouts().implicitlyWait(10, TimeUnit.SECONDS);
    }

    @AfterMethod
    public void testCleanup() {
        driver.quit();
        proxyServer.abort();
    }

    @Test
    public void requestRedirected_when_usingProxyRedirect() {
        proxyServer.rewriteUrl("https://secure.gravatar.com/js/gprofiles.js?ver=2021Junaa",
"https://stub.gravatar.com/js/gprofiles.js?ver=2021Junaa");

        driver.navigate().to("http://demos.bellatrix.solutions/");
    }
}
```

Again, we use **BrowserMob** web proxy. We set the URLs to be redirected before the tests. We do that through the `rewriteUrl` method. In the example, when the page is loaded, the gravatar service requests are redirected to our local stub implementation of the service. When a request against the original URL is made, **BrowserMob** redirects it to the stub version.

Using an API or DB for Verification

Modern web automated tests are doing much more than just testing the UI. As you saw in the previous section, we go more and more into using DB or APIs for test data generation. The same is valid for assertion mechanisms. You can verify only a few things directly through the UI. There are many things usually that happen underneath - hidden from users' eyes. This is why we can leverage the existing test data generation infrastructure to verify those aspects too. This is why I like to call these tests - **system tests** or **system of system tests** instead of the generic term UI test. Any test that uses API or DB to set up or verify data is a system test.

Here is an example of how we can use the `UsersRepository` to verify whether a user was created successfully from the website's registration form.

```
@Test
public void newUserCreatedSuccessfully_whenUsedNewRegistrationForm() {
    // create a new user through the UI form.
    // ...
    // verify the new user in DB.
    var actuallyCreatedUser = usersRepository.getUserByEmail("newUniqueEmail@bella.com");
    Assert.assertEquals(actuallyCreatedUser.getFirstName(), "Anton");
    Assert.assertEquals(actuallyCreatedUser.getLastName(), "Angelov");
    Assert.assertEquals(actuallyCreatedUser.getPassword(), "superSecret");
}
```

Summary

This last chapter investigated ways to make our tests much more stable across test environments' executions. Instead of hard-coding the test data, we used JSON configuration files for each environment. We saw examples of configuring the websites' URLs, WebDriver timeouts, and billing default values. Also, we talked about using data stubs in the application under test.

There are three appendix chapters. The first one is discussing the problems that automated testing solutions must solve. It summarizes several topics we discussed across the book. The last two chapters contain a comprehensive list of the CSS and XPath selectors. The reason for including them here is that knowing all of them and using them in your tests will significantly improve the stability and readability of your automated tests.

Questions

1. Which dependencies do you need to use the JSON utilities?
2. How do you generate new values using the Faker library?
3. Why the hard-coding of test data leads to flaky tests?

Thank you for reaching the end of the book!

As a bonus, you can find video recordings with explanations for each chapter. To get them, you can join for free the book's LinkedIn group. There you can find even more info about design patterns in automated testing and best practices or use it as an easy way to reach me. Before joining, you need to provide proof that you purchased the book. Just go to https://bit.ly/3eGTAUl

To discuss something from the book or have a short question, I am always glad to connect on LinkedIn and chat. If you need more in-depth assistance or desire even more in-depth knowledge, I lead C# and Java training series regarding automated testing (web, desktop, mobile, or API). Additionally, we offer consulting, mentoring, and professional services. You can always find me in the LinkedIn group or connect directly. https://bit.ly/2NjWJ19

Now the bonus three Appendix chapters!

Appendix 1. Defining the Primary Problems that Test Automation Frameworks Solve

To list the benefits of test automation frameworks I must say that they naturally derive and extend the multiple benefits that come from test automation. Before talking about their advantages, we need to define what are the problems they try to solve. Like most business and software development things, there is a constant battle for resources- money and time. People often ignore these costs because they are not paying the bills and receive their checks every month no matter what. To define what is needed to deliver high-quality software, we have to understand what the problems are in the first place.

Sub Problem 1 - Repetition and People Boredom, Less Reliable

If you have to manually execute the same test case once per month- it is okay. But if you have to do it 3 times per day, we as humans get bored fast. Another natural thing that happens is that we begin to ignore the little details, and this is where thugs like to hide and lay eggs. Even the most conscientious tester will make mistakes during monotonous manual testing.

Automation Solution Hypothesis

ASH-1: Execute Same Tests Over and Over Again

When you can execute all tests the same way repeatedly, you have more time to concentrate on writing new tests. Also, you can have more time to learn new tools, programming languages, and test techniques.

Subsequent Problems

SP-1: Automated Tests Are Not Stable

Many teams face this issue. Their tests are not correctly written, and because of that, they fail randomly. Or even worse- providing **false-positive** or **false-negative** results.

> **NOTE**
>
> False-positive - a test result in which a defect is reported, although no such defect exists in the test object. False-negative - a test result that fails to identify a defect actually present in the test object.

SP-2: Initial Investment Developing These Tests

The process of creating stable automated tests that verify the right things is an expensive undertaking. You need to invest in tools, frameworks, training the staff, test data preparation, creation of test environments, test execution integration in CI/CD, test results visualization.

Sub-Problem 2 - Engineers Are Not So Good with Numbers, Accuracy

If you have to test a user interface, usually, it is a relatively doable job. Comparing labels, messages, clicking buttons, filling up forms, eventually check if something is populated in the DB. However, with time the systems got much more complicated. How do you compare without tools- huge XML/JSON messages or files? It is hard to manually check if 100000 orders are upgraded successfully with all calculations. There are many cases where automated scripts can do a job much better than us.

Automation Solution Hypothesis

ASH-2: Reuse Automatic Coded Checks

Once you write the logic for verifying that a single order is well migrated, you can create data-driven tests and execute the tests an unlimited number of times. The test result for run 15670 will be with the same precision and accuracy as the 1400 one.

Subsequent Problems

SP-3: Initial Investment Creating Shared Test Libraries

Sometimes, creating a generic solution that can be generalized for testing many scenarios and many test cases takes lots of effort. Sometimes you may not have the right people to create the library since significant coding and design skills may be required. Or even if you have these engineers, they may need to work on something else. It may be a significant time and money investment to code it right.

SP-4: Are Automated Tests Trustworthy? Test the Tests?

Even if you have the time to create these libraries. How do you make sure that they work correctly? It is code, meaning it may contain bugs. Do you spare time to develop tests for the tests or accept the risk- the checks not working correctly? Do you go to the next test once you see that your assertion has passed? Did you check it can actually fail?

SP-5: Library Modifications

Creating the initial version of the library may be easy. But it is a different thing whether it is designed in a way to support future modifications. Changes in the requirements and applications are something natural, and with them, our tests should evolve. Many IT professionals forget that it is often easier for them to rewrite the tests instead of making a little tuning because the code may not support that.

SP-6: Library Customization- Another Team's Context?

The whole point of creating a shared library is to be used by multiple teams across the company. However, the different teams work in different contexts. They may have to test a little bit different thing. So, the library code may not be working out of the box for them. How easy will it be for them to extend or customise it? Is it even possible to do it? Will they need to invest time to create the same test feature again with the required modifications?

SP-7: Knowledge Transfer

Shared libraries are great, but do the engineers across all teams know whether or not they have a particular feature of your framework? Do they know that you already created automated checks?

If they don't know that something exists, they will create it again. This is especially true for new team members. If you were a part of the team building the test features, then you know most. However, when you have just joined the team, if you don't have a way to find this information, someone has to teach you. Otherwise, you will face the problems we mentioned.

SP-8: Test API Usability

Is it easy for the users to understand how to use the library? Even if people know that something is there but don't know how to use or make it work, this will cause creating the same thing again.

If the API is not concise and confusing, you will need to invest time to teach the new team members how to utilize it.

Sub-Problem 3 - Time for Feedback- Release

When you need to release a security hotfix immediately, you don't want to release the new version untested. However, if you have 5000 test cases and your 10 QAs need 5 days to execute them by hand- this is not so fast, right?

Automation Solution Hypothesis

ASH-1: Execute Same Tests Over and Over Again

ASH-3: Utilize the Speed of Automated Tests

Let's face it- computers are much faster than us. Even if you drink 5 coffees and click fast, you will be much slower than a well-written automated test. Even if you can match its speed, you will eventually get tired or will miss some crucial details. Instead of waiting for 1 week for all 5000 test cases to be executed by 5 QAs, you can run all of your automated tests distributed on multiple machines for a couple of hours.

Subsequent Problems

SP-9: Test Speed

The automated tests are fast. However, this is not always the case. If the tests are not written properly, they can get slow. Some engineers use big pauses in their automation to handle various challenges in automating web or mobile apps. Another possible scenario where tests can get slow is when you put retry logic for various failing statements till the test succeeds. Or just retry all failing tests multiple times.

Sub-Problem 4 - Regression Issues Prevention

Regression Testing: "Testing of a previously tested program following modification to ensure that defects have not been introduced or uncovered in unchanged areas of the software, as a result of the changes made."

Often because of the time pressure, "less important" tests are not executed manually. This happens not only because of tight deadlines, but when some of your people are not available- holidays, sickness, or just your team is short-staffed.

Automation Solution Hypothesis

ASH-4: Execute All Tests before Deploying App

You can execute all of your tests before deploying. Only if all tests pass then the app is deployed. Since the automated tests are fast, you can deploy the tested version after 30-60 minutes.

Also, since the setup of tests is easy, the developers can execute some of the most important tests on their machines and fix the regression problems even before submitting the new code.

Subsequent Problems

SP-9: Test Speed

SP-10: CI and CD Readiness

Some older automation solutions are tough to be executed from the command line interface- meaning it is hard to integrate them into your continuous integration or continuous deployment tools. Whatever tool or framework you use, it now should allow being integrated relatively easily in CI systems. The same is valid for produced test results by the tool or framework. Usually, after CI execution, you want to publish them somewhere.

Sub-Problem 5 - Skipping Part of the Scope

After you test something, you need to show your managers what you have tested. If you don't have a test case management system, this can be hard. Some people cannot be trusted. They can lie they executed something or just forgot to do it. This is not the case with automated solutions.

Automation Solution Hypothesis

ASH-4: Execute All Tests before Deploying App

Subsequent Problems

SP-9: Test Speed

SP-10: CI and CD Readiness

Sub-Problem 6 - Ping-pong

With a dedicated QA team, there was the so-called ping-pong game of throwing bugs. How does this happen?

1. The developer produces a new version of the app and deploys it with no testing.

2. The QA starts testing when he gets free (this may not happen immediately). Testing begins 4 hours after the new version.

3. The QA logs a bug 2 hours later. However, the developer may head home.

4. The developer fixes the bug early in the morning and deploys a new version without testing it. This takes 1 hour.

5. The QA starts testing 3 hours later and finds that the first bug is fixed, but another regression appears.

6. The QA logs the regression bug 30 minutes later.

7. The developer is still there but started to work on a new feature, so promises to fix the new bug tomorrow.

Automation Solution Hypothesis

ASH-4: Execute All Tests before Deploying App

ASH-5: Developers Execute Automated Tests Locally

So, for a single feature to be tested and released, you needed from 2-3 days. If you have automated tests, the developer could execute them on his/her machine or at least the most important ones. Even if this is impossible, nowadays, most critical tests are performed right after the code is deployed, even if we are talking about UI/System tests. So, if any regression bugs appear, you will catch them within 1 hour after the code's submission.

Subsequent Problems

SP-9: Test Speed

SP-10: CI and CD Readiness

SP-11: Easiness of Local Test Solution Setup

How easy is it for a new colleague to set up everything needed to run the automated tests locally? Do you have instructions? How much time will he/she need? There are cases where a man needs half a day to install and configure everything required. This is a bummer since we programmers are lazy most of the time or have so many other things to code. So, many people will prefer to skip the process and just not follow it because there are too many steps.

SP-12: Easiness of Local Test Execution

If you have lots of tests most probably the developer won't be able to execute the tests before check-in his/her code.

How easy is it to locate which tests he/she needs to execute?

When the tests are executed, is it possible to continue working, or should I go drink a coffee? Some automation frameworks make it impossible to work during the test run. Browsers appear on top of all other programs; tests get the mouse focus, move your mouse or do real typing with your keyboard.

Is it possible for the tests to be executed locally but in an isolated environment like Docker?

Can the tests be executed smoothly against the developer's local environment instead of against the shared test environment?

Sub-Problem 7 - Money, Time, Effort for Maintaining Test Artifacts

What are the test artifacts? For example, these are all manual test cases you have. When a specific part of the application changes, you need to analyse and update your test cases. Otherwise, you have to rewrite them each time, even with the usage of a more sophisticated test case management system. This may be a task. More "agile" companies decide that the QAs won't use detailed test cases, which leads to untested or not-well tested areas of the app. This is especially true if you have to test part of the application developed and tested by people not part of the company anymore.

Automation Solution Hypothesis

ASH-6: Easier Tests Refactoring and Modification

Automated tests are testing artifacts too. But if you have a proper test automation framework and test structure, a single change can update multiple test cases at once, instead of editing each one by itself. Most modern IDEs provide tons of refactoring support features.

Usually, once a manual test case is automated, you don't need it anymore, so you can archive it.

Subsequent Problems

SP-5: Library Modifications

Sub-Problem 8 - Various App Configurations

If you have to test a modern website- you need to make sure it works on Edge, Firefox, Chrome, Opera, Internet Explorer, and Safari. If your software is related to banking or a similar service- you need to check if the app works the same way on the latest 5-10 versions of these browsers. But wait, you have to check the website's responsiveness on various screen sizes and mobile resolutions. It is doable to make all these tests manually, but they require lots of effort and sometimes money to buy and configure all these devices. The layout testing is hard for humans. It is a considerable challenge to verify "pixel perfect" designs without tools or code.

Automation Solution Hypothesis

AHS-7: Reuse Tests for Different Platform Setups

You can easily reuse the same tests for different browsers or mobile devices with various resolutions through code. Also, the code can enable you to perform pixel perfect layout testing if needed.

Subsequent Problems

SP-13: Cross-technology and Cross-platform Readiness

Is it possible to execute the tests with no code modifications on various browsers? Are the tests behaving the same way in different browsers? For example, if you use a pure WebDriver code, it will be almost impossible. How much code do you have to write to change the size of the browser or change the mobile device on which the tests will be executed? In most cases, it is better to skip the large configuration boilerplate code.

SP-14: Cloud Readiness

Some companies have their own farms of devices and computers with various browser configurations. However, nowadays, cloud providers such as SauceLabs, BrowserStack or CrossBrowserTesting are a reasonable solution. Is it possible for your tests to be executed there? How much code is needed to switch from cloud to local test execution?

SP-15: Docker Support

Another alternative of the cloud providers is to run your tests in Docker containers. However, the setup can be hard. Is it possible for your automation solution to be integrated easily with Docker (Selenoid, Selenium Docker)? Does it provide pre-created configured images with all browser versions or mobile emulators?

SP-16: Complex Code Configuration

Your tool or framework is one thing to support various browsers, devices, cloud or Docker integrations. But it is another how much code you need to write to make it happen. It is not only about the initial creation but also if the requirements change, how easy is it to reconfigure the tests to use another configuration?

Sub-Problem 9 - Low QA Team Morale

When you manually execute the same tests over and over again, testers get bored as mentioned. Most of us want to have fun and do something new occasionally. So, we usually get demotivated doing the same things and not improving ourselves. This is one of the primary reasons people want to change their teams or quit their jobs.

Automation Solution Hypothesis

ASH-8: Test Automation Novelty

Thinking about how to automate a particular app's functionality, prepare the test data or integrate your tests in CI is an exciting and challenging job. Most testers feel challenged working on test automation and must continuously learn new things, motivating them even more.

Subsequent Problems

SP-1: Automated Tests Are Not Stable

SP-4: Are Automated Tests Trustworthy? Test the Tests?

SP-17: Test Speed Creation

Time spent on maintaining the existing tests is essential. It can take significant time from the capacity of the QA team. However, for people to be motivated, it should be relatively easy to create new tests. For sure, QA engineers will be frustrated if, for the whole sprint, they can produce only a few tests. It shouldn't be rocket science to create a simple test. Or even if the scenario is more complicated, it shouldn't be hard to understand what needs to be done to automate it.

SP-18: Troubleshooting, Debuggability, Fixing Failing Tests Easiness

As we mentioned, a big part of maintainability is troubleshooting existing tests. Most in-house solutions or open-source ones don't provide lots of features to make your life easier. This can be one of the most time-consuming tasks. Having 100 failing tests and discovering whether there is a problem with the test or a bug in the application. If you use plugins or complicated design patterns, the debugging of the tests will be much harder, requiring lots of resources and expertise. Even if you spot the problem, how easy is it to fix it? Do you fix the code only in one place to fix multiple tests? If the library didn't reuse most of the logic but, for example, copy-paste it, then the fixing will take much more time. If you use a 3rd party framework (open-source or commercial one), is its support fast and helpful?

Sub-Problem 10 - Questioned Professionalism

Every QA wants to be a professional and be recognized for the job done well. However, as mentioned, if you have tight deadlines, management pressure to test and release the app as soon as possible, you cut out of the scope of your testing by executing only the most important test cases. Anyhow, most of the time, when a new bug is found on Production, QAs feel responsible that they didn't catch it. Sometimes, developers are not aware this is not our fault, and we had to cut out of the scope. So, they question how good we are. Even in some edge cases, people get fired or don't get their bonuses.

Automation Solution Hypothesis

ASH-4: Execute All Tests before Deploying App

ASH-5: Developers Execute Automated Tests Locally

ASH-8: Test Automation Novelty

ASH-9: More Time Writing New Tests- Exploratory Testing

With time you will have more automated tests, each checking for regression bugs. This will reduce the time for performing the same tests repeatedly. Also, the locating-fixing bug cycle will be drastically shortened, since the developers can execute the tests locally or all tests will run before deploying the app. The QA team will be more motivated since it will execute more exciting tasks, thinking about automating more complicated and challenging scenarios. We can spend more time experimenting- using manual testing techniques such as exploratory testing to locate new bugs.

Subsequent Problems

SP-1: Automated Tests Are Not Stable

SP-4: Are Automated Tests Trustworthy? Test the Tests?

SP-17: Test Speed Creation

SP-19: Upgradability

Fixing unstable tests is not the only time-consuming task of having an in-house automation framework. Every two weeks, new browser versions are released. With each, a new version of the low-level automation libraries is released- WebDriver, Appium, WinAppDriver. However, since these libraries and tools are open-source, nobody can guarantee they will be bug-free or backward compatible with everything you have. From my own experience, this task takes at least 3-4 hours per week if no significant problems appear. If a problem occurs, it can take much more time. This is especially true if you need to support all browsers and a couple of their versions (not only the last one). The same is even more valid for mobile automation low-level libraries since there is an unlimited number of devices and configurations.

Because of these problems, many teams don't upgrade so often to spare some time. However, not testing the latest versions of the browsers hides many risks of not locating regression bugs.

Sub-Problem 11 - Provide Evidence What You Did

When you manually test something, it is hard to prove what you did. Sometimes it may go by unnoticed by developers and other colleagues, because it is something "invisible". In more mature test processes, you have detailed manual test cases, test reports, etc. but in general- why not be honest? When you write code, it is much more noticeable and measurable what you did. Because of this issue, I have heard many IT professionals complaining that they cannot get a promotion or a bonus. For me, this is one reason why QAs should want better reporting tools- to show developers and management what they did. (Software won't get any better because you have a fancy dashboard showing how many test cases you have executed.)

Automation Solution Hypothesis

ASH-10: More Visible Results

Since most of the test cases will be translated into coded tests- it will be more visible what the tests are. The code can be measured and seen. If needed, the test results can be displayed in beautiful dashboards or sent via emails.

Subsequent Problems

SP-20: Test Code Readability

Sometimes, your developer fellows or your managers may want to check what you did. If you name your tests and methods right, you use page objects and other design patterns, and it will be much easier for other engineers to understand what your tests do. If this is true, it will be questionable whether you need more detailed reports.

SP-21: Test Results, Reports, Logs, Portal Integrations

If you use an in-house framework, does it produce well-looking test result files? Are these files compatible with the most popular extensions for CI tools? How much effort is required to visualize them with these tools? Is it even possible? There are at least 2 popular open-source solutions for visualizing test results (ReportPortal, Allure). Is it possible to integrate your test results with these tools?

Sub-Problem 12 - Holidays and Sickness, 24 Hours

If you have 1 QA per app area and he/she goes on holiday or gets sick. How do you release your application? Do developers start testing or what? Most people can work up to 8 hours. There are situations where your managers tell you need to come on Saturday to test the new version because you need to release it on Monday. But you won't often hear- "Let's stay up 2 nights in a row to finish everything". Engineers need to sleep and rest. (Automated tests don't care whether it is 3 in the morning, Sunday, or New Year's Eve)

There is another aspect of this problem. When someone leaves your team or the company, all of his/her knowledge is lost. Regularly automating new functionalities leaves valuable knowledge within the team.

Automation Solution Hypothesis

ASH-1: Execute Same Tests Over and Over Again

ASH-4: Execute All Tests before Deploying App

ASH-5: Developers Execute Automated Tests Locally

ASH-11: Tests as Documentation

If the automated tests are readable enough and the test scenario is visible through reading the code, your colleagues will know what the test does even if you are missing. If they can quickly orient themselves to what is automated and what is not, they will know what they need to check manually till your return.

Subsequent Problems

SP-7: Knowledge Transfer

SP-8: Test API Usability

SP-20: Test Code Readability

SP-21: Test Results, Report, Logs

Sub-Problem 13 - Some Things Cannot be Tested Manually

How do you perform a load or performance test manually? The same about testing "pixel perfect" designs. Probably you can use some non-automated way using tools, but it is hard.

Automation Solution Hypothesis

ASH-12: Reuse Automated Tests for Complex Test Scenarios

You can reuse some of your existing automated tests and reconfigure them to perform performance and load tests. Also, you can use different APIs from the framework to test pixel-perfect layout testing.

Subsequent Problems

SP-5: Library Modifications

SP-17: Test Speed Creation

SP-18: Troubleshooting, Debuggability, Easiness Fixing Failing Tests

SP-22: Learning Curve

Is it easy to figure out how to create these complex performance or load tests? Should you read huge documentations (if they even exist), or can you figure out everything from the demo example or the public API comments while typing in the IDE? How much time should a new team member learn to write and maintain these tests?

Should you spend countless hours passing your knowledge to him/her, or the authors of the framework give you better alternatives?

Sub-Problem 14 – Consistency

If there is no documentation on writing automated tests, different people might write them in different ways. For example, one may use page object models. Another may use vanilla WebDriver directly, and so on. The same is valid for the naming of methods, elements, and tests. These inconsistencies lead to hard-to-understand/read/maintain test code.

Automation Solution Hypothesis

ASH-13: Unified Coding Standards

A significant part of what the test automation frameworks are is that they give all people involved unified ways of writing tests. Unified team standards make the tests look identical and much easier to write. The shared libraries part of the framework provides an API that clarifies it for the user which scenario will be executed if the particular method is called.

Subsequent Problems

SP-7: Knowledge Transfer

SP-8: Test API Usability

SP-20: Test Code Readability

SP-22: Learning Curve

SP-23: Unified Coding Standards

Coding standards are good. However, you need an automated way to enforce them. Does the framework you use give you a default set of coding standards? Does it give you an automated way to apply and follow them? Is it easy for people to see what they did wrong? Is it easy to customise the default set of rules? (Some popular solutions for Java are EditorConfig and CheckStyle-IDEA)

Sub-Problem 15 - Faster Scale-up and Scale-down

Let's say you have lots of things to be tested for the new release. You have 2 QAs in the team, but to finish on time, the manager has to bring in one more. These transitions don't happen for a day. With longer release cycles, this is doable and maybe the right decision, but when you release each week and need more workforce, this approach cannot scale. Imagine that you scale-up for the next release after two months, now you have 4 QAs, but after that, the summer comes, and the releases will stop for a while (in an imaginary scenario where all developers go on vacation). Two QAs will be enough to test all new features. What happens with the 2 additional QAs you brought to the project? Do you move them again? It is not only a problem how you scale-up but also how you scale-down.

Automation Solution Hypothesis

ASH-14: Cloud Test Agents and Docker

Living in the era of public clouds, you can have additional test agent machines for a couple of minutes. The same is valid if you use Docker to execute your automated tests. If you use the appropriate runner, the tests can be distributed across remote machines and executed in parallel.

Subsequent Problems

SP-14: Cloud Readiness

SP-15: Docker Support

SP-24: Parallel and Distributed Test Execution

Does your framework support your automated tests to be executed in parallel? Is there a runner for your tests to run them in parallel or distribute them across multiple machines?

Summary

As you can see, there are lots of reasons test automation is necessary. However, like all things that evolve, the first generations of test automation tools were not as good as promised. This is why test automation frameworks started to be a much more popular solution. However, creating stable, fast, and easily maintained tests with them requires lots of upfront planning and thought. Many more subsequent problems occur that tool and framework vendors don't mention on their marketing pages. If you know all these problems, you can make much more educated choices about where to invest or not.

Appendix 2. Most Exhaustive CSS Selectors Cheat Sheet

A big part of the job of writing maintainable and stable web automation is related to finding the proper element's selectors. Here will look into a comprehensive list of CSS selectors.

Element Selectors

Selector	Explanation
ul#myId	<ul> element with @id= 'myId'
#myUniqueId	any element with @id='myId'
ul.myForm	<ul> element with @class = 'myForm'
.myForm.front	any element with @classes = 'myfor' and 'front'

Contextual Selectors

Selector	Explanation
ul#myUniqueId > li	direct child element
ul#myUniqueId li	sub child element
div > p - all <p>	elements that are a direct descendant of a <div> element
div + p - all <p>	elements that are the next sibling of a <div> element (i.e. placed directly after)
div ~p - all <p>	elements that follow, and are siblings of <div> elements
form myForm.front + ul	next sibling
div.row *	selects all elements that are descendant (or child) of the elements with div tag and 'row' class

Attribute Selectors

Selector	Explanation
ul[name = "automateName"][style = "style_name"]	<ul> element with attributes @name ='automateName' and @style= 'style name'
ul[@id]	elements with @id attribute
ul[id = "myId"]	<ul> element with @id='myId'
*[name='N'][value='v']	elements with name N and specified value 'v'
ul[id ^= "my"]	all elements with an attribute beginning with 'my'
ul[id$= "Id"]	all elements with an attribute ending with 'Id'
ul[id *= "unique"]	all elements with an attribute containing the substring 'unique'
ul[id ~= "unique"]	all elements with an attribute containing the word 'unique'
a[href='url']	anchor with target link 'url'

Useful n Values

- **odd or 2n+1** - every odd child or element
- **even or 2n** - every even child or element
- **n** - every nth child or element
- **3n** - every third child or element (3, 6, 9, ...)
- **3n+1** - every third child or element starting with 1 (1, 4, 7, ...)
- **n+6** - all but first five children or elements (6, 7, 8, ...)
- **-n+5** - only first five children or elements (1, 2, ..., 5)

Pseudo-class Selectors that Apply to Siblings

Selector	Explanation
ul#myUniqueId li:first-child	first child element
ul#myUniqueId li:nth-of-type(1)	first child element
ul#myUniqueId li:last-child	last child element
ul#myUniqueId li:nth-of-type(3)	last child element
#TestTable tr:nth-child(3) td:nth-child(2)	cell by row and column (e.g. 3rd row, 2nd column)
p::first-letter	selects the first letter of the specified 'p'
p::first-line	selects the first line of the specified 'p'
p:first-of-type	selects any <p> that is the first element of its type among its siblings
p:last-of-type	selects any <p> that is the last element of its type among its siblings

Pseudo-class Selectors for Link and User States

Selector	Explanation
input:focus	the <input> element which has focus
input:read-only	<input> elements with the 'readonly' attribute specified
input:required	<input> elements with the 'required' attribute specified
input:checked	checkbox (or radio button) that is checked
a:contains('Log Out')	anchor with inner text containing 'Log Out'
td:contains('t') ~td	cell immediately following cell containing 't'
p:lang(language)	all <p> elements with a @lang attribute equal to 'language'

:not(p)	selects any element that is NOT a paragraph
p:not(.fancy)	<p> elements that are not in the class '.fancy'
p:not(.crazy, .fancy)	<p> elements that are not '.crazy' or '.fancy'
div:empty	returns all <div> elements that have no children
:root	selects the root element of the document
input:in-range	selects all elements with a value that is within a specified range
input:out-of-range	select all elements with a value that is outside a specified range
a:visited	all visited links
a:link	all unvisited links
a:hover	all links on mouse hover
input:active	every active <input> element
input:disabled	every disabled <input> element
input:enabled	every enabled <input> element

Further Reading

Download CSS Selectors Cheat Sheet PDF - https://bit.ly/3rUFJxM

Appendix 3. Most Exhaustive XPath Selectors Cheat Sheet

The other types of very useful selectors are the XPath ones. Knowing them, in detail, can help you significantly improve the stability and the readability of your tests.

Contextual Selectors

Selector	Explanation
//img	image element
//img/*[1]	first child of element img
//ul/child::li	first child 'li' of 'ul'
//img[1]	first img child
//img/*[last()]	last child of element img
//img[last()]	last img child
//img[last()-1]	second last img child
//ul[*]	'ul' that has children

Attribute Selectors

Selector	Explanation
//img[@id='myId']	image element with @id= 'myId'
//img[@id!='myId']	image elements with @id not equal to 'myId'
//img[@name]	image elements that have name attribute
//*[contains(@id, 'Id')]	element with @id containing
//*[starts-with(@id, 'Id')]	element with @id starting with

//*[ends-with(@id, 'Id')]	element with @id ending with
//*[matches(@id, 'r')]	element with @id matching regex 'r'
//*[@name='myName']	image element with @name= 'myName'
//*[@id='X' or @name='X']	element with @id X or a name X
//*[@name="N"][@value="v"]	element with @name N & specified @value 'v'
//*[@name="N" and @value="v"]	element with @name N & specified @value 'v'
//*[@name="N" and not(@value="v")]	element with @name N & not specified @value 'v'
//input[@type="submit"]	input of type submit
//a[@href="url"]	anchor with target link 'url'
//section[//h1[@id='hi']]	returns <section> if it has an <h1> descendant with @id= 'hi'
//*[@id="TestTable"]//tr[3]//td[2]	cell by row and column
//input[@checked]	checkbox (or radio button) that is checked
//a[@disabled]	all 'a' elements that are disabled
//a[@price > 2.50]	'a' with price > 2.5

XPath Methods

Selector	**Explanation**
//table[count(tr) > 1]	return table with more than 1 row
//*[.="t"]	element containing text 't' exactly
//a[contains(text(), "Log Out")]	anchor with inner text containing 'Log Out'
//a[not(contains(text(), "Log Out"))]	anchor with inner text not containing 'Log Out'
//a[not(@disabled)]	all 'a' elements that are not disabled

Axis Navigation

Selector	Explanation
//td[preceding-sibling::td="t"]	cell immediately following cell containing 't' exactly
//td[preceding-sibling::td[contains(.,"t")]]	cell immediately following cell containing 't'
//input/following-sibling::a	'a' following some sibling 'input'
//a/following-sibling::*	sibling element immediately following 'a'
//input/preceding-sibling::a	'a' preceding some sibling 'input'
//input/preceding-sibling::*[1]	sibling element immediately preceding 'input'
//img[@id='MyId']::parent/*	the parent of image with id

Math Methods

Selector	Explanation
ceiling(number)	evaluates a decimal number and returns the smallest integer greater than or equal to the decimal number
floor(number)	evaluates a decimal number and returns the largest integer less than or equal to the decimal number
round(decimal)	returns a number that is the nearest integer to the given number
sum(node-set)	returns a number that is the sum of the numeric values of each node in a given node-set

String Methods

Selector	Explanation
contains(space-string, planet-string)	determines whether the first argument string contains the second argument string and returns boolean true or

	false
concat(string1, string2 [string]*)	concatenates two or more strings and returns the resulting string
normalize-space(string)	strips leading and trailing white-space from a string, replaces sequences of whitespace characters by a single space, and returns the resulting string
starts-with(spacetrack, space)	checks whether the first string starts with the second string and returns true or false
string-length([string])	returns a number equal to the number of characters in a given string
substring(string, start [length])	returns a part of a given string
substring-after(spacetrack, track)	returns a string that is the rest of a given string after a given substring
substring-before(spacetrack, tra)	returns a string that is the rest of a given string before a given substring
translate(string, ghj, GHJ)	evaluates a string and a set of characters to translate and returns the translated string

Further Reading

Download XPath Selectors Cheat Sheet PDF - https://bit.ly/3rSlzEi

Bibliography

[Sgt 18] “Standard Glossary of Terms used in Software Testing Version 3.2”, ISTQB, Feb 2018

[Sdp 14] “Selenium Design Patterns and Best Practices”, Dima Kovalenko, Sep 2014

[Isg 19] “ISTQB Glossary”, International Software Testing Qualification Board, Dec 2019

[Rid 18] “Refactoring: Improving the Design of Existing Code”, Martin Fowler, Nov 2018

[Caa 17] “Clean Architecture: A Craftsman's Guide to Software Structure and Design”, Robert C. Martin, Sep 2017

[Cgt 18] “Complete Guide to Test Automation: Techniques, Practices, and Patterns for Building and Maintaining Effective Software Projects”, Arnon Axelrod, Sep 2018

[Hfd 04] “Head First Design Patterns: A Brain-Friendly Guide”, Eric Freeman, Elisabeth Freeman, Kathy Sierra, Bert Bates, Oct 2004

[Sfd 18] “Selenium Framework Design in Data-Driven Testing: Build data-driven test frameworks using Selenium WebDriver, AppiumDriver, Java, and TestNG”, Carl Cocchiaro, Jan 2018

[Fdg 08] “Framework Design Guidelines: Conventions, Idioms, and Patterns for Reusable .NET Libraries (Microsoft Windows Development Series), 2nd Edition”, Krzysztof Cwalina, Oct 2008

[Dpe 94] “Design Patterns: Elements of Reusable Object-Oriented Software”, John Vlissides, Richard Helm, Ralph Johnson, Erich Gamma, Nov 1994

[Kia 18] “Kotlin in Action”, Dmitry Jemerov, Svetlana Isakova, Feb 2017

[Mja 18] “Modern Java in Action”, Raoul-Gabriel Urma, Mario Fusco, Alan Mycroft, Sep 2018

[Jms 13] “The Java Module System”, Nicolai Parlog, Jun 2019

[Wcc 14] “What Is Clean Code and Why Should You Care?”, Carl Vuorinen, Apr 2014

Made in United States
Orlando, FL
10 August 2022